"Until Our Hearts Are On the Ground"

Aboriginal Mothering, Oppression, Resistance and Rebirth

D. Memee Lavell-Harvard and
Jeannette Corbiere Lavell, Editors

For my dear friend Kate,
You are always in my heart.
In unity
D Memee Lavell Harvard.

DEMETER PRESS
TORONTO, ONTARIO

lished by:
neter Press
Association for Research on Mothering
Atkinson College, York University
0 Keele Street
onto, Ontario M3J 1P3
phone: (416) 736-2100 x 60366
il: arm@yorku.ca Web site: www.yorku.ca/crm

es Editor: Andrea O'Reilly
tant Series Editor: Rénee Knapp

ted and Bound in Canada

er/Interior Design: Luciana Ricciutelli
t Cover: Jeannette Corbiere Lavell and son, Nimkii (one week old), 1970.
o: David Mills Lavell

ry and Archives Canada Cataloguing in Publication

our hearts are on the ground : aboriginal mothering, oppression, resist-
and rebirth / D. Memee Lavell-Harvard and Jeannette Corbiere Lavell,
rs.

1-55014-461-8

tive women – Canada. 2. Mothers – Canada. 3. Motherhood – Canada.
ell-Harvard, D. Memee (Dawn Memee), 1974– II. Lavell, Jeannette
ere

V8U58 2006   305.897'3071082
6-905761-3

"Until Our Hearts
On the Ground

Aboriginal Mothering, Op
Resistance and Reb

C

A
an

Pu
D
c/
72
47
T
Te
En

Se
As

Pri

Co
Fr
Ph

Lib

Un
anc
edi

ISB

1. N
I. L
Co

E98
C20

Dedicated to Rita L. Corbiere, in her 91st year,
our mother, grandmother, and great grandmother. You are our inspiration.
For Autumn Sky, Eva Lillie, Kyanna and Neegonii,
the youngest members of our clan.
It is for you that we work to make the world a better place.

And for Indigenous mothers everywhere. You hold the future in your arms!

A nation is not conquered until the hearts of its women are on the ground. Then it is done, no matter how brave its warriors nor how strong their weapons.

—Cheyenne Proverb

Contents

Acknowledgements

We would like to begin by expressing our gratitude to Kiche Manitou, Great Spirit of our people, for providing us with the opportunity and the strength to continue our work here, and for providing us with the great number of days in which to do it. We would like to thank the many Aboriginal women and mothers who have walked this path before us, for they are our inspiration and our source of wisdom.

We must acknowledge the hard work of all who have contributed to the production of this volume—The Association for Research on Mothering for allowing us the opportunity; the contributors for sharing their stories and their wisdom; David Lavell for his many years of listening to our ideas and many hours of editing *our* work; John Harvard for his continued support and encouragement; and to our little ones, for allowing us "just five more minutes to finish this." We hope that the multitude of voices that have contributed to this volume come across loud and clear with their messages of strength and transformation.

Finally we would like to recognize the late Harry Daniels, Métis leader, a rare voice of support from the official Aboriginal leadership, for Aboriginal women generally and Jeannette specifically, during the many years of fighting for our right to remain "Indians."

Thunder Spirits

Reclaiming the Power of Our Grandmothers

D. MEMEE LAVELL-HARVARD AND JEANNETTE CORBIERE LAVELL

"This is the oppressor's language yet I need it to talk to you."
—Adrienne Rich

These often-quoted words illustrate a fundamental dilemma for Aboriginal peoples generally, and Aboriginal women specifically. In order to share our stories and our knowledge we must articulate our experiences through a foreign and arguably fundamentally incompatible language. The language of the oppressor is inherently deficient when it comes to adequately describing our worldviews and our values, much less the complexity of our experiences as Aboriginal mothers. A fact that became painfully obvious as we set about editing this volume. Despite our collective decades of experience as Aboriginal mothers, we still had difficulty articulating an adequate definition of "Aboriginal Mothering," which one might assume ought to be the starting point of such an endeavour. The ongoing debates surrounding politically correct terminology when referring to the original inhabitants of this land, or their descendants, have only added to our dilemma.[1]

While some claim the initial label of "Indian" came as the result of misidentification on the part of Columbus, who believed himself to be in India, and is therefore not only misleading and inappropriate, but downright offensive, the fact that we (Aboriginal women specifically) have fought, and won, the right to be deemed an "Indian" under the meaning of the *Indian Act*, leads to substantial disagreement regarding the usage of this term. As a result of amendments to the *Indian Act* in Bill C-31, which came about as a result of the court action begun in 1971 by Jeannette Corbiere Lavell, thousands of people proudly reapplied for their status as "Indian people" in this country. However, legally the category of "Indian" as defined by the Indian Act includes only status Indians, thereby excluding the Métis, Inuit, and those who, for a variety of historical reasons, were deemed non-status. Thus, despite our long struggle to regain the right to call ourselves Indian people, in order to be as inclusive as possible, for our purposes herein we have agreed upon the use of the term Aboriginal.[2]

1

However, this solves only a portion of our dilemma since, as Devon Mihesuah points out, within this group that we have now identified as *Aboriginal* there are "many, many different worldviews, values, and traditions" (29). Indeed, as it has been argued elsewhere, and we fully acknowledge, the term "Aboriginal" is misleading as it implies a "degree of homogeneity" that "undermines" the reality of diversity both between and among various tribal populations (Schissel and Wotherspoon 7). We must openly acknowledge that Aboriginal people generally, and Aboriginal mothers specifically, are distinguished from other Canadians by particular legal statuses and historical, social, and cultural experiences. However, as Wotherspoon claims, like any social group, "their circumstances are also marked by internal differences and inequalities" (Schissel and Wotherspoon 7). Indeed, there is no universal, or essential experience of Aboriginality, much less Aboriginal motherhood. Mihesuah clarifies,

> Because of vast differences in tribal cultures and personalities, in addition to identity issues … no one Indigenous woman can speak for all of us, and it is not possible for any one feminist theory or thought to summarize Native women. Native women do share historic oppression, but the cultural, racial, and economic variations among Native women render any sort of national coalition virtually impossible…. Our needs and wants may be similar, but they are not the same. (xix-xx)

Thus, we come to the central paradox of this project: having identified this apparently endless diversity of experience among Aboriginal mothers, how do we present a coherent perspective on Aboriginal mothering? Or indeed, is such a thing even possible?

There is such a range of Aboriginal women's experiences existing somewhere between "traditional" and "modernized" that perhaps the only thing we do share is what Mihesuah calls a "commonality of difference" (31). Indeed, if we have nothing else in common, we share the experience of being different from (and often fundamentally opposed to) the dominant culture, which has a significant impact on our ability to mother as we see fit, according to our own values, and traditions. The Aboriginal mother who adheres too closely to her traditions has historically found it difficult if not impossible to meet the standards of the "good mother" as set out by the dominant patriarchal culture. While it may be hard to adequately categorize what "Aboriginal Mothering" actually is, even the smallest child among us quickly comes to realize what it is not:

> According to my father, as a young child I once claimed that I did not have "the kind of mother that I would prefer." She regularly sent me to school with sandwiches of moose meat or venison, or partridge, on fried

bread. I longed for the normalcy of peanut butter and jam on white bread. At the time I could not understand why she didn't seem to even know how to make a "proper" grilled cheese sandwich. Hers were always too thick as they started with homemade bread which didn't come precut into perfect thin slices from the Wonderbread company; they were dotted with little chunks of fresh butter which never spread nicely the way that the margarine did at my friend's house, and worst of all our cheese never came in little cellophane envelopes. I was firmly convinced that I had a bad mother (and I am sure all the "experts" would have agreed as they were the ones who had convinced me). My mother's food choices, and preparation methods, were out of sync with those promoted by Betty Crocker and Uncle Ben—two guests who never seemed to find their way to our dinner table. Not only did my mother grow all our own vegetables, raising our own pork, poultry, and on occasion a side of beef or two (while the other families bought theirs at the store in colorful plastic-wrapped packages), but she and my father also insisted on doing so organically. While the indignity of eating homegrown organic foods was enormous, worse still was the fact that in an era when babies were being fed scientifically-fortified infant formula in sterilized bottles, my mother went about breastfeeding. We did not even have a "pen" for the baby to "play" in, and I am quite sure none of us were "Ferberized." People were amazed we survived at all. (D. Memee Lavell-Harvard)

Clearly we were different. We were "not white" and it showed. However, the historical persistence of our cultural difference generation after generation (despite the best assimilative efforts of both Church and State) is a sign of our strength and our resistance. That we have historically, and continually, mothered in a way that is "different" from the dominant culture, is not only empowering for our women, but is potentially empowering for all women. To that end we have brought together in this volume, a multiplicity of Aboriginal voices, each bringing a unique and valuable contribution to the dialogue. Each contributing author, in her own way, brings light to a particular aspect of Aboriginal mothering. The process of becoming a mother, various conceptions and practices of mothering, and the role of the state in the performance of mothering, as well as literary depictions of mothering, are all examined in our effort to give a sense of the Aboriginal mothering experience.

This expression of our experiences as Aboriginal mothers is of great importance not only because it provides alternatives to the oppressive model of motherhood provided, and promoted by the dominant patriarchal culture, but also because it provides a position outside of the dominant culture from which to critique. Citing the 1972 work of Freire, feminist scholar Magda Lewis suggests that the sharing of "memories of violation and exploitation are pedagogically powerful" because they have the potential to expose the oppressive ways in which our society is organized (9). Apparently the "personal" is not only "political', it is also powerful. Arguing that "reality" is itself subjective, empirical sociologists Marcia Millman and Rosabeth Moss Kanter agree the "collective delusions" that support the inequity of society can be "undone by introducing fresh perspectives" (qtd. in Harding 62).

Furthermore, citing Sylvia Wynter, Gloria Ladson-Billings contends, those who exist on the margins, having been constructed as "Other," possess an advantage as a result of the "way that not being positioned in the center allows for 'wide angle' vision" (262). It is possible then, as Robert W. Connell asserts, that the point of view of "those who carry the burdens of social inequality," (i.e., women, ethnic minorities, or Aboriginal people) is in fact a much "better starting point for understanding the totality of the social world" than is the position of privilege held by those who enjoy the luxuries of societal advantage (39). Indeed, as Sandra Harding explains, the "view from the perspective of the powerful is far more partial and distorted than that available from the perspective of the dominated" because the dominant have "far more interests in obscuring the unjust conditions" than the do the oppressed, who would in fact only stand to benefit from exposing and critiquing the conditions that produce their misery (59). Clearly therefore, Aboriginal women, who are marginalized on the basis of race, gender, and social class (and are unquestionably the most oppressed members of our society) would seem to be in the best position to provide a critique of patriarchal society. Unfortunately, it was the potential for opening the dominant patriarchal society to critique that has lead to the fear, persecution, and oppression of Aboriginal women in our nation.

According to Andrea Smith, in her analysis of the roots of systemic violence against Aboriginal women, in comparison to the fundamentally oppressive and sexist nature of the European societies,

> prior to colonization, Indian societies for the most part were not male dominated. Women served as spiritual, political, and military leaders, and many societies were matrilineal [and not as has been suggested because our women were whores]. Although there existed a division of labor between women and men, women's labor and men's labor were accorded similar status. As women and men lived in balance, native societies were consequently much less authoritarian than their European counterparts. (18)

Mihesuah concurs, claiming that prior to colonization, most Aboriginal groups were egalitarian, and "women's and men's roles may have been different, but neither was less important than the other … none were inferior" (42). Having carefully constructed patriarchy in general, and patriarchal conceptions of motherhood in particular, as not only natural but also as divinely ordained, the existence of alternative social structures created a significant threat to the overall social order. A society that maintains its gendered hierarchical social structure through violence and the domination of women, cannot bear such egalitarian beliefs, much less the existence of actual matriarchies. As the following description indicates, the opportunity to use violence is lessened, if not outright eliminated by such social structures.

> In traditional matrilineal societies, the husband left his home to live with his wife close to her extended family. Children belonged to their mother's clan and traced their lineage through their mother's line. Girls received education from their mother and aunts. Boys learned to hunt from their mother's brothers. After divorce, the children could stay with their mother, and women retained family property. Females held responsibility for agricultural activities, while men either hunted or also worked the fields. (Mihesuah 44)

In such a structure women were "secure knowing they would always have food, shelter and support from their extended families and clans" (Mihesuah 42). Since these women were not dependant solely upon their spouses they were not vulnerable to violence, abuse, and domination. However, lest we fall prey to romantic tendencies to portray pre-contact Aboriginal communities as utopian societies, it is important to point out that both women and men toiled hard to ensure their collective survival. In traditional cultures the "stay-at-home mom" would have been a very cold and hungry woman.

Thus, we see, as Ella Shohat and Robert Stam argue, the real purpose behind the colonial persecution of Aboriginal women, was not so much to force the "Indigenes to become Europeans," (especially since it was generally accepted at the time that their demise was imminent) but rather to "keep Europeans from becoming Indigenes" (qtd. in Smith, 18). Apparently, the foundations of patriarchy are not as secure as they are portrayed to be if the mere presence of empowered Aboriginal women has the power to throw the legitimacy of patriarchy into question. Clearly, as Smith concludes, the "demonization" of our Aboriginal mothers can be understood as a strategy in the struggle of "white men to maintain control over white women" (21).

Andrea O'Reilly's contention that "patriarchy resists empowered mothering precisely because it understands its real power to bring about a true and enduring cultural revolution" (50) illustrates the need for a book such as this. The voices of our sisters, and their accounts of our longstanding resistance to the imposition of patriarchal motherhood and all it entails, can be a source of empowerment in the struggle for revolution. We, as Aboriginals, have always been different, we have always existed on the margins of the dominant patriarchal culture, and as mothers we have operated outside of, if not in actual opposition to, their definition of acceptability. We are, to use the words of Adrienne Rich, the original "mother outlaws" (qtd. in O'Reilly 35).[3]

Dawn Memee Lavell-Harvard, Wikwemikong First Nation, Manitoulin Island, Ontario, is currently President of the Ontario Native Women's Association, a full-time student currently completing her Ph.D. in Education at University of Western Ontario, and is the first Aboriginal person ever to receive a Trudeau Scholarship. Perhaps more importantly, she is also a full-time mother of two little girls, Autumn Sky (eight years) and Eva Lillie (two years). Her research addresses the epidemic of low academic achievement and high drop-out rates among Aboriginal populations in Canada. In examining the experiences of those few Aboriginal people who have successfully completed post-secondary education, she seeks to help define appropriate directions for educational restructuring. She is inspired by her mother, Jeannette Corbiere Lavell, who in 1971 became the first woman to challenge the notion (found in the Indian Act *of 1876) that a woman who marries a "non-Indian" "shall cease to be an Indian," and loses all associated rights, privileges or identity therein. Active in the Aboriginal community, she is also the President of the Southern Ontario Aboriginal Diabetes Initiative; Vice-President of the Ontario Aboriginal HIV/AIDS Strategy; and on the Board of Directors of the Native Women's Association of Canada.*

Jeannette Corbiere Lavell, is Ojibway First Nation, and member of the Wikwemikong Unceded Indian Reserve on Manitoulin Island, Northern Ontario. Educated on the Reserve and fluent in her own language, Ojibway, she left her community at twelve years of age to complete high school at St. Joseph's Convent, North Bay, Ontario. She received her Ontario Teacher's Certificate from McMaster University, Hamilton, Ontario in 1976 after spending many years in the social services field working with her own people in the city of Toronto. On April 11, 1970 she married David Lavell from Woodstock, Ontario resulting in the loss of her rights to membership to her Reserve under the Indian Act, *a piece of Federal legislation governing the affairs of Status Indians in Canada. This initiated the start of three years of pursuit to ensure that the rights of Indian women were equal to the rights of Indian men in the* Indian Act. *This also precipitated the creation of several Aboriginal Women's Organizations, with Jeannette as one of the primary and founding Board members of the Ontario Native Women's Organization (ONWA); Indian Rights for Indian Women; and the Native Women's Organization of Canada. In August 1973, Jeannette's case, now known as the Lavell case was lost at the Supreme Court of Canada, by one vote. In April 1985, after the Canadian Charter of Human Rights and Equality was enacted in the new*

Canadian Constitution, Jeannette regained her Indian Status and was re-instated to the Band List of the Wikwemikong Unceded Indian Reserve along with her three children. Jeannette has been teaching Fine Arts, and Parenting to Secondary Students at Wasse-Abin Wikwemikong High School. She and her 91- year-ld mother, Rita L. Corbiere, are still active in community, band council and Aboriginal Women's Organizations.

[1]Consider the confusion as we left our Indian Reserve to go to the Indian Friendship Center, on behalf of Native Women's Association of Ontario, to celebrate National Aboriginal Day on June 21. To borrow the words of Mihesuah in her work on Indigenous American Women, we are all "well aware of the debates over these terms and [are] cognizant that many find 'Indian' offensive; however, my family and most friends and 'Indians' I know say 'Indians.' 'First Nations,' 'Indigenous peoples,' and other terms are fine for scholars, but most Indians, especially older ones, are puzzled at hearing them" (Miheusah xxii).

[2]Due to the ongoing attempts by government to define and categorize the original inhabitants of this continent, as well as the peoples" resistance to this imposed definition, not to mention the current concerns with politically correct terminology, any discussions regarding the original populations of our nation are fraught with confusion. While some prefer to be called Native (or Native American as is popular south of the arbitrary border that divides our nations), this term also lends itself to confusion as it can simply be an indication of one's birth in the specific geographic area and may therefore be used just as legitimately by second generation immigrants, although the use of capitalization generally indicates Aboriginal reference. Thus, in the interests of clarity the term Native will also be avoided, again unless used in the words of another writer. While most prefer to refer to themselves by their own individual tribal affiliations in their own languages, such as the Anishnawbe people, these terms are not functional when context demands reference to the entire Indigenous population.

In order to prevent confusion, for the purposes of this research, we have used the term Aboriginal whenever possible, which quite simply means from the original people. In doing so, we are referring to all those who are the direct descendants of the original inhabitants of this continent. Indeed, we as Aboriginal people do not recognize the arbitrary borders that divide the nations on this continent, that were imposed within our traditional territories, and upon our then sovereign nations, without consent or even consultation. According to our own oral traditions, we have been here since time immemorial, and are clearly the original people. The category of Aboriginal encompasses the multiplicity of distinct tribal cultures, as well as legal entities, including Status, non-Status, Métis, and Inuit.

[3]Given Andrea O'Reilly's observation, in her work on feminist mothering, that

according to the dominant ideology "good mothers as portrayed in the media or popular culture more generally, are white, heterosexual, able-bodied, married, and in a nuclear family with usually one or two children" (36), it should come as no surprise that we have failed to measure up. Aboriginal mothers are not, nor will they ever be, white (despite more than a decade of legal protestations to the contrary in the Lavell case). While homosexuality is not notably more prevalent in the Aboriginal culture, many have argued that it is more accepted. For a variety of reasons Aboriginal mothers (at least in Canada) are more likely than non-Aboriginal women to be disabled, unmarried, and living in an extended family with more than three children. Apparently, we as Aboriginal mothers are too brown, too independent, and too fertile to be "good mothers."

Furthermore, according to O'Reilly's description of the patriarchal institution of motherhood, "Good mothers are the primary caregivers of their children" and "care other than that provided by the mother (i.e., daycare) is viewed as inferior and deficient" (36). In many Aboriginal cultures generally (especially those that were matriarchal, or matrilineal) and in the Anishnawbe tradition specifically, mothers are not necessarily the primary caregivers, and certainly not the sole caregivers, for their children. Indeed, mothering is not an activity reserved for the biological mothers, it is practiced by the grandmothers, aunties, older siblings, cousins, etc. As the following words illustrate,

> The tendency for everyone in the family, indeed anyone in the household, to be responsible for the care of small children is so great that my father, a non-Aboriginal, often joked that if he sat still too long in an Indian woman's house he would end up holding someone's baby. (Dawn Harvard)

While many espouse the notion that it "takes a village to raise a child," the Anishnawbe people actually practice it, much to our chagrin during the adolescent years when we found it impossible to do anything without someone noticing us.

The dominant culture's conception of the good mother, to which we, as Aboriginal women, have apparently failed to adhere, also "requires mothers to be well-versed in theories of childrearing" (O'Reilly 37). In contemporary society women are bombarded with a plethora of, often contradictory, opinions from a variety of (likely male) "experts" on how to properly feed, care for, and stimulate the development of the child right from the moment of conception. It is no coincidence that the "proper" method tends to involve the purchase of numerous costly "scientifically developed" products. When research indicated that infants preferred to look at human faces, they developed mobiles with black and white photos of faces to hang over the crib, when they found that infants were soothed by the sound of the mothers heart beat, they made tape recordings and stuffed them along with battery packs in teddy bears to be put in the crib next to baby, they have products that simulate the warmth of the mother, that vibrate to simulate the motions of the mother. While the dominant patriarchal culture promotes the belief that only biological mothers provide the necessary care, clearly she can be easily replaced (or perhaps improved upon) by a plastic product.

While a quick perusal of any parenting magazine is sufficient to confirm this assertion, it also reveals another interesting point. In the average 200-page magazine we are lucky to find one or two "Tips for Daddies" pages. Articles on the "Secrets of Happy Moms" (which tend to focus on hair and makeup tips for the time challenged) abound, and even gender neutral topics tend to have titles like "Mom's guide to medicines" or most recently "Discipline Tips From Mom's Who Don't Yell." The advertisements show mom diapering, changing, feeding and bathing children, while the rare sighting of a man typically finds him driving the car, or fishing boat, or in the farm field. Whether it is called Parents, or Today's Parent, or Canadian Parent, what these publications all reveal is that in the discourse of the dominant patriarchal culture "parenting" is really just a synonym for mothering, and clearly not a job for men. We have often wondered where are the articles on how to make Halloween costumes with staple guns and duct tape, or how to balance the conflicting demands of school projects and Superbowl weekends. Perhaps they do not exist because these things are not an issue, because men don't parent. Further, we wonder where are the articles on what to pack when taking your children on the all important first protest or demonstration (sunscreen, hats and water in summer or snow pants, hats, and gloves in winter—we are still waiting for Jeannette to find the time to author that one) or, better yet, how to avoid being thrown in jail during these events (not to mention what to tell the in-laws in the event that it can't be avoided). These are the things we need to know—not how to cut your kids veggies into appealing shapes to get him or her to eat more (my apologies to those who rely on this method).

References

Connell, R. W. *Schools and Social Justice*. Philadelphia, PA: Temple University Press, 1993.

Harding, S. *Whose Science? Whose Knowledge? Thinking from Women's Lives*. Ithaca: Cornell University Press, 1991.

hooks, b. *Teaching to Transgress: Education as the Practice of Freedom*. New York: Routledge, 1994.

Ladson-Billings, G. *Crossing Over to Canaan: The Journey of New Teachers in Diverse Classrooms*. San Francisco: Jossey-Bass, 2001.

Lewis, M. *Without a Word: Teaching Beyond Women's Silence*. New York: Routledge, 1993.

Mihesuah, D. A. *Indigenous American Women: Decolonization, Empowerment, Activism.* Lincoln: University of Nebraska Press, 2003.

O'Reilly, A. *Rocking the Cradle: Thoughts on Motherhood, Feminism, and the Possibility of Empowered Mothering.* Toronto: Demeter Press, 2006.

Rich, A. "The Burning of Paper Instead of Children." *The Will to Change: Poems 1968-1970.* New York: Norton, 1971.

Schissel, B. and T. Wotherspoon. *The Legacy of School for Aboriginal People: Education, Oppression, and Emancipation.* Toronto: Oxford University Press, 2003.

Smith, A. *Conquest: Sexual Violence and American Indian Genocide.* Cambridge: South End Press, 2006.

Wynter, S. "We Know Where We Are From: The Politics of Black Culture from Myal to Marley." Unpublished manuscript, 1973.

FROM THE WOMB

BECOMING AN ABORIGINAL MOTHER

New Life Stirring

Mothering, Transformation and Aboriginal Womanhood

KIM ANDERSON

Prelude – Awakening

> there is a story
> it begins with darkness, it begins in a beautiful place, and there is a
> woman, and somehow it comes to be that this woman falls through a
> dark hole to another world, and this other world is begun in a beautiful
> way.
>
> —Laura Schwager (Mohawk) (9)

The Iroquois story about Sky Woman, like so many Indigenous stories, teaches about the power of creation and about how blessed we are as women to be so closely connected with that power. There are many versions and interpretations of the Sky Woman story,[1] but they commonly tell of a pregnant woman who falls from another world into the waters below. With the help of birds, she settles on Turtle's back, setting in motion a creative process that results in the completion of our first mother, the earth.

I begin with this story because for me, getting pregnant was like falling through a hole in the sky to discover a new world. At 29, it had never occurred to me in any real way that every human life is connected to the hard work and sacrifice of a woman. Sitting on a crowded bus or jostling through subway commuters, I wondered about the thousands of women who had produced the lives around me. I marveled at all those women who must have done what I was now doing: worrying, loving, waiting. Some had surely been fearful or sad, others elated, but each woman had gone through a series of awakenings: the discovery of her pregnancy, feelings of being hungry or sick or emotionally fragile or vigorously spiritual. I discovered that every human life is connected to a woman's story of new life stirring, because every human life begins inside a woman.

The physical experience of being pregnant thus represented a profound mental, emotional and spiritual transformation for me. It was the start of both a personal

13

journey and a scholarly career of exploring what it means to be an Aboriginal
woman and a mother.

∞

My first pregnancy was unplanned, but I suppose it was time. I was in a secure,
happy relationship and I was turning 30 that year. I hadn't really thought about
being a mother, and certainly had no desire to care for children. I'd never been
particularly interested in kids and had no skills, having never babysat or spent any
concentrated time in the company of children. Children were foreign to me, and
although Aboriginal communities tend to be child-friendly or child-centered, I
had not paid much attention to the children that crossed my path.

Both my partner and I had spent most of our twenties traveling and living
without any responsibilities or commitments. We knew there would be change,
but had no idea how profound it would be.

∞

I am on the cusp of being visibly pregnant when we take off on a credit card for a last
fling trip to Portugal. Wandering along a dusty golden cliff in the Algarve, we get lost
trying to find Europe's most southwesterly tip. I want to explore where Prince Henry
the Navigator first schooled Vasco de Gama and Columbus, the point where Europe
launched herself towards other worlds. This is a cliff where time stretches out in all
directions and different domains overlap through complex histories and uncertain
futures. We stumble along, lost but happy as faint glimpses of our own evolving universe
begin to filter in. This is our time.

Suddenly, he stops to tell me how moved he is to be partner and witness to all the
changes I am experiencing as a woman. I realize that women are made of cycles and
seasons, and that I've entered a new life stage.

∞

That first pregnancy ended at 21 weeks. David and I were working at a retreat
centre several hours north of the city, and he had just given me my first mother's
day present. A friend with four children had laughed at the gift: "You're not a
mother *yet*," she said, but I knew differently.

The midwives had detected something wrong with my triple-screen blood test.
They called to tell us to go into the closest hospital for an ultrasound.

I feel delicate and vulnerable, watching the technician's expressionless face to see if
I can detect any signs of danger. Later, we wait in a quiet, comfortable room at the local

midwifery office. When the midwife comes in, we know that our baby is gone.

I am in day surgery at Toronto General Hospital. There are about a dozen of us, perched in blue gowns on top of beds, waiting our turns for abortion. I'm here because I won't let him go. I am sure he was a beautiful boy. The woman next to me tells me about how she has cancer, about her decision to abort. There is so much grieving.

I was lucky when I lost my first baby to have access to a thriving Aboriginal health centre. After the abortion, I called one of the workers at Anishnawbe Health Toronto, and she made arrangements to have the fetus returned to us. Hospital policy won't permit the removal of "human remains," but she made it work, calling on sovereignty rights and enlisting the help of a Chief who wrote a letter to assure the hospital that the fetus would be properly buried on his reserve. As a third-generation urban Cree-Métis, I gained a greater appreciation for what it means to have land and homeland.

The hospital technician hands us a shoe-sized box, which we wrap in deer hide. We drive several hours north, into the country of rocks and lakes and birch trees. Our friends are waiting for us. The child will be buried in the abandoned gravesite, high on a hill and sheltered by dense bush.

The ceremony lasts all day, and there are many teachings about the doorways, lives, and connections between different worlds. These teachings help David to find relief from nightmares in which he helplessly tries to save our baby from falling into the darkness, first grievings of a father in his failure to protect.

That baby's short visit taught us many lessons about the sacredness of life. We left the experience with a tremendous longing, determined to welcome the one who was ready.

Opening – Full Pregnancy

> When you are pregnant, it's like the wind blows through you. I was
> rootless in a world where time stretched in both directions. That is part
> of women's ways of knowing. Pregnancy allows you to be immediately
> connected to the time before, to where you are now and to where you are
> going in the future.
>
> —Joan Glode (Mik'maw)[2]

I had a successful full-term second pregnancy, and this one brought many more teachings. I was so fearful of losing another baby that I spent much of the pregnancy tiptoeing around my body, trying not to disturb the delicate growth process inside. I was worried I would fall in love again, and initially hesitant in my communication with the new little spirit. But after passing the milestones of the first trimester, and then the dreaded 21 weeks, I fully opened myself to the feelings of love, beauty, joy, and strength. Throughout the pregnancy, David treated me like a goddess, and by the end I felt like one.

Looking back, I can draw parallels between the elevated status that I was given in our household and the care that many Indigenous cultures advocate for their pregnant women. I am most familiar with Haudenosaunee and Algonquian cultural practices, which have numerous taboos and instructions about care during pregnancy. These traditions essentially teach that a woman must be careful about not only her physical state, but also about her mental, emotional and spiritual states as well.

The care of a pregnant woman is not her sole responsibility; the community must be active in creating an environment that will foster an optimal state of health for the mother and child. Situations of violence or conflict, for example, are to be avoided, as this will have an impact on the unborn. For this reason, both the Haudenosaunee and the Anishnaabe have teachings about the need for men to refrain from hunting while their partner is pregnant. Tom Porter has written about the role of the Mohawk father during pregnancy, stating:

> It must be understood that when a woman is pregnant, her husband is also pregnant. Whatever health and mental precautions are observed by pregnant women, the father is also obligated to observe as well. This is the traditional Mohawk or Iroquois understanding. (115)

According to Porter, men should also not consume anything that changes the "natural state of mind" while their partner is pregnant. He teaches that it is the man's s duty to *en ha te nikon riioste* (be very kind and patient during this nine-month period)" (115).

We live in a volatile world and too many mothers and children suffer from direct violence on a daily basis. I was fortunate to pass through my pregnancies in a peaceful home, but I instinctively took precautions to shelter myself as much as possible from the violence of the outside world. This included doing simple things, such as turning off the news, or avoiding busy streets, where I felt highly sensitive to the energies swirling around me. I felt like I was wide open, and had to be very careful about the types of situations and environments I found myself in.

I sit at my computer, wearing my bathing suit top and a pair of low riding shorts. The apartment must be about 30 degrees, but I have no desire to go out. We pass these last languid days of pregnancy together and alone. I imagine her curled up like a cat inside me, napping as I write. I leave my belly exposed so I can watch her roll over, running my fingers along delicate limbs as they make ripples across my taut skin. Most people say they are anxious to birth by this time, but I don't want to part with her.

My partner observed the same health practices and precautions as me during pregnancy, which included abstinence from alcohol. He did his own preparations by having evening chats through my bulging abdomen, telling jokes, and imparting life lessons. He built a crib, reasoning that the baby would rest better in a something that carried the energy of his own dad, as opposed to that of an assembly line. Our children ended up being "family bed" babies in the end, and I took solace in realizing that sleeping with your children is common among many Indigenous peoples. But I thought back to the crib-building episode recently, when I learned that Haudenosaunee men are deemed responsible for building their baby's cradle-board, right from the picking of the tree and the respectful communications that must be made at that time. We weren't aware of the rich and multiple Aboriginal traditions of pregnancy during that first full pregnancy. These were just things that we did to create our gentle nest.

Birth – The Ceremony

> They say that medicine people have certain requirements, near-death experience. Some even have out-of-body experiences. Go into the spirit world and they have the constant communication with the spirits. But the woman does this each time she gives birth. It's a near-death experience.
>
> —Betty Laverdure (Ojibway) (qtd. in Wall 109-110)

We had planned a home birth, not really knowing what to expect. Reflecting on a comment I had once heard about how modern people are born in hospitals and then die in hospitals, I decided to try to avoid this with our baby. I wanted him to arrive in an environment we had created. I wanted to surround him with comfort and tranquility, because I knew it would be scary. The home birth was for him; only later would I understand how much I benefited from the privacy, comfort, and security of my own home. Ultimately, I think a woman needs to plan a birth in the way that makes her most comfortable, and that's what we did.

The pains have started, but are faint yet, and I am full of nervous energy. We've had a good dinner and have stocked the kitchen with food and snacks for the midwives, and with plenty of hydrating drinks for me. We've got light and funny movies to keep my mind off the pain. I pace around, half- watching the TV while chatting distractedly with Dave.

As the evening progresses, I can feel myself receding from the material environment of our bedroom. I go to the altar and light some sweetgrass, and this is when I feel the floor begin to shift beneath me. I have a sense that several people have just entered the room. I am surrounded and no longer in contact with the floor. I pray to the grandmothers to help me with this work.

I felt really strong going into the birth, and was naively unaware about what was in store for me. This is a good thing, as the birth was long and complicated. At a few points, the midwives raised the possibility of transferring to the hospital, but I was not in any position to consider such earthly details. I was halfway between this world and the next, dancing, as David later reported, straddling spirit and material realms. I was both living every pain in my body and walking outside of it, rootless in that place where the wind blows through you.[3]

By the time Rajan was born, I fully occupied two spaces. That final pushing burned to the core, but I also found myself hovering above, bearing witness as my son broke his way into the gray light of that afternoon.

There are many Aboriginal ceremonies that simulate the birth experience, and Rajan's birth gave me insights about how extreme pain and/or physical exertion can stimulate spiritual epiphany. I don't believe we need to suffer to achieve transformation, but I now understand why many spiritual practices include physical challenge or deprivation. People fast, sweat and dance in most Aboriginal traditions, and many of our ceremonies simulate birth. The sweat lodge is a womb-like place where we go to find birth and renewal. It can be mild or it can be difficult, but it always involves physical challenge for spiritual gain. The Sun Dance is a ceremony in which dancers labour for days, without sleep, without shelter, eventually tearing their flesh. Dancers thus make sacrifices for the community through total physical exertion.[4]

In the past, women did not dance or tear at the Sun Dance, and women did not always go into the sweat lodge. It was understood that women achieve cleansing and transformation through their own bodily cycles and experiences. Women's bodies allow for a coming together of the physical and the meta-physical. Birth is the most powerful teacher of this sacred ability.

∞

There are teachings in that birthing experience that can tell you about the purpose of that child's life. One of my roles as a midwife is to notice, from all the different signs in the birth, what this baby's here to do, and what ceremonies the mother and father have to do to make sure that baby grows a certain way, what attentions need to be paid to this child, any particular weaknesses or strengths.

—Katsi Cook (Mohawk) (qtd. in Harvey and Wessman n.p.)

After the spiritual experience of my son's birth, and in spite of the intense pain, I was greatly looking forward to the birth of my second child. I expected that all births were spiritually transformative, given the "right" conditions. I had not yet learned that births are as unique as the individuals they produce.

My daughter arrived on her due date to teach me that not every birth experience is so highly spiritual. Denia's arrival was quite simply all about the pain. When it was over, the same midwives who had attended my son's birth remarked on how it had been a very "straightforward" birth; how it had been lovely to watch; how "triumphant" I must have felt. But for me, it was a very humbling experience. I didn't know what everyone was so happy about. Instead of feeling "triumphant" I felt that I had not risen to my sacred duty; I had only felt what I considered to be base and desperate thoughts of wanting to escape. I had none of the quiet stoicism of my first birth, choosing, rather, to yell and cry out and fully engage in the drama and noise of the event. I knew if I'd had the opportunity, I would have taken every medication possible to make it stop. I was no spiritual hotshot after all, no superwoman.

Post-partum, I continued to feel depressed about how I had "managed" this birth, but today I am utterly grateful for the lessons it provided. Denia saved me from being prescriptive or judgemental about a woman's experience of childbirth. Her birth taught me to respect difference, as she and her brother have continued to teach. Through birth and the lives they lead, they have given me the physical and the metaphysical, the silent and the noisy, the cerebral and the dramatic.

Sometime after Denia's birth, I heard Sylvia Maracle talking about how the old ladies always recognized both the singers and the dancers in the world. The distinct birth experiences of my two children gave me this recognition, and the understanding I gained in birthing them has helped me to parent them ever since.

∞

That first one is the one that cracks
you open, where you break through, sound
barriers, enter the thunder
of relations, carry the future, become
creator.

In a wordless trance,
I floated on the ceiling one moment
struggled for grounding the next,
stretched thin and wide
he, stubbornly holding back
methodically placing his arrival in the world.

I woke, silent
hearing that first breath, a little squawk
eyes clenched tight
rounded face like a monk, quietly greeting, breathing
small, rapid bits of heaven into
our new universe.

I have been twice blessed,

my little joker, making sure I paid full attention
made me wait,
knowing all about timing, delivery, performance
wrapping anticipation with humour, layer upon layer in that dance
screaming, both, a duet of an announcement,
she halfway out, her tiny head twisting and turning to take us all in
me, enjoying the singular chance for explosion,

so generously spilling out imaginings
she arrived.

There are dancers
and there are singers
in this world.
We need them both.

I have been twice blessed.

New Life – The Early Years

> Hormones, milk, heaviness, no sleep, internal joy, all jam the first few months after a baby is born, so that I experience a state of tragic confusion. Most days, I can't get enough distance on myself to define what I am feeling.
>
> —Louise Erdrich (Ojibway) (113)

New motherhood brought new feelings that I had not anticipated. My pregnancy had been so blissful and fulfilling that I was not prepared for the loneliness and fear that I suffered during Rajan's first few months of life. The changes in my body chemistry were undoubtedly at the root of my depression, but social factors were also at play. I had always been confident in my abilities, but here I felt incompetent and unprepared to take on the biggest and most important responsibility of my life. In a strange way, I was scared of the baby. He seemed so unpredictable.

I place Rajan on a flannel receiving blanket, a small square of pastel patterns stretched out on the white expanse of our bed. I carefully tuck him in between the foam triangles that are supposed to prop his body at just the right angle. Not on his back, but not on his front. During the night, I frequently open one eye to peek at him, to assure myself that he is still breathing. Every time he gasps or mutters, my heart skips a beat and I go into a panic. I want him to stay. Please let him stay.

Many Aboriginal cultures teach that infancy is a precarious time, as the spirit can easily slip back into the other world. Some Anishnaabe people advise keeping the baby in the home environment for the first forty days. It is deemed particularly dangerous to take the newborn into environments where she or he might come into contact with negative energy, or where there may be spirits waiting to take baby back. This is why babies do not attend wakes.

Some Aboriginal peoples put holes in a newborn's moccasins as a protective measure. Western Cree say that this gives the baby an excuse not to go if a spirit should come to take them. Some Cree tie a black string around the infant's wrist to ward off malevolent spirits, or set a small stick beside the sleeping infant so they can defend themselves. The soft spot is also a significant reminder of the baby's borderline status. Algonquian and Haudenosaunee peoples say that this opening on the baby's head represents openness to the spirit world. The baby is still connected to that world until that soft spot closes.

∞

Every morning, Rajan and I walk with David to the park, his final point of departure for work. We watch him ride away on his bike, getting smaller and smaller until turns the corner. I try to plot out each hour of the day to ensure my survival. I measure the time, hour by hour.

There is only one other mother in the park at this early hour. She has a toddler slightly older than Rajan. She only speaks Arabic, but she and I find each other—smiling and trying our best to laugh together at the play of our children. I wonder if she is as lonely as me.

Although I loved my son passionately, day-time care giving in those early years continued to be clouded by feelings of loneliness and boredom. This caused me to reflect on the shortcomings of the nuclear family, the separation of public and private, and the absence of community. It wasn't that I didn't want to be with my baby; I just didn't want to be with him alone. I thought about traditional societies where there might have been older women around who could teach me something about babies, or younger women to share my experiences and my workload. I craved work that would make me feel fulfilled, and I particularly longed for adult company to stimulate my mind. I did my best to seek out company by meeting other parents in parks or in playgroups. But these were not people from my own longstanding community. I felt like my people were all out there carrying on with their interesting lives while I was losing myself in an endless series of diaper changes, feedings, and baby jiggling. I couldn't wait to go back to full-time work, but thoughts of separating from my boy also made me anxious.

I was better prepared for my second baby. If I couldn't change my body chemistry, at least I could change my social environment. I started by asking my parents to look after Rajan during the day temporarily while I adjusted to the newborn. Mothering infant Denia was, as a result, much easier. My body adjusted quickly to post-partum and I was much more confident in my abilities. Without my toddler in tow, I also had a chance to re-enter the adult world of my previous life. I took Denia to meetings, sat in coffee shops, attended to my volunteer and community work, and even went for a job interview. This was my way of being me while being a mother. Sensing that this would be the last time I would mother an infant, I also fully indulged in the intimacy of our physical bond.

I breathe in every day of her babyhood, the rapture of her newborn smell, the rise and fall of her belly, so tightly bound to me. My heartbeat. The nursing. Her grip on my finger. Her dainty eyes, blinking open.

Post-Script – Moving Forward

Women are powerful because they birth the whole world.
—Shirley Bear (Mingwon/Maliseet) (133)

Since the time of my earliest pregnancy, I have been like Sky Woman, dancing and creating and laying tracks for a new world. I've made a career out of researching and writing about Aboriginal women and children because I believe the health of a society is deeply connected to the health of its women.

My work is grounded in an understanding that, in spite of shifting gender roles, women retain a primary relationship to the children of the world, and the children are the future. This is not to say that men are insignificant or that roles are inflexible. I had a partner who walked beside me through every step of the pregnancy, who worked through the birth, woke up to keep me company during night feedings, changed diapers, cooked and cleaned and sang to the babies. He took parental leaves to look after our children while I went back to school. As such, he was a vital helper, protecting and providing so we could all grow. But I experienced parenting as only a woman can: through the physical, mental, emotional and spiritual transitions of pregnancy, birth, post-partum, breastfeeding, and primary caregiving during the early months and years. Through it all, my body taught me about cycles and seasons, about intergenerational and metaphysical connections, about honouring life.

Motherhood also moved me to reflect on how poorly we treat the women and children in our societies. I have been humbled by my privilege, as a woman so loved, supported, and honoured. But I have also been demoralized to think about all the women and children who pass their early years together in situations of abuse or neglect. The implications are immeasurable. Motherhood gave me a new starting place for making social change.

∞

> The situation that we are in today is such that our women and children aren't respected as they used to be. It is not the fault of the men. It is because of the layers and layers of influence we have had from another culture. We are in a state of confusion and we are trying to work our way out of it. People are calling it healing. Well, whatever it is, we are trying to find our balance, and when we find the balance, we will know it because the women won't be lost. They will be respected and taken care of and so will the children.
> —Catherine Martin (Mi'kmaw) (qtd. in Anderson 13)

As Aboriginal peoples, we can move forward by building on traditions that kept our people healthy in the past. We come from many different nations and cultures, but I have discovered that we are linked by cosmologies and systems that once ensured gender equity, recognized the sanctity of women and children and protected against abuse. Our women were traditionally granted significant authority in recognition of their power as creators and nurturers. These core values and principles are built into our various and multiple creation stories, our traditional political and economic structures, our extended family structures, and our spiritual practices.[5] It is up to us to retrieve these concepts and to plant them like seeds in our new world. This is what I take forward as my children grow up and I continue my lifelong work as a student and a teacher.

I would like to thank the teachers who have directly contributed to the culture-based knowledge I have shared in this piece: Jaynane Burning-Fields (Onondaga), Maani Elliot (Anishnaabe), Joan Glode (Mi'kmaw), Sylvia Maracle (Mohawk), Violet M. Meguinis (Tsuu T'ina), and the people listed in the footnotes. Many thanks to Karen Houle, Sandra Sabatini and Laura Schwager who also reviewed this work.

Kim Anderson (Cree/Métis) is the author of A Recognition of Being: Reconstructing Native Womanhood *(Sumach Press, 2000) and co-editor, with Bonita Lawrence, of* Strong Women Stories: Native Vision and Community Survival *(Sumach Press, 2003). She is currently a Ph.D. student in the Department of History at the University of Guelph. Kim is the mother of eleven-year-old Rajan and nine-year-old Denia.*

[1]One story involving Sky Woman, as told to me by Sylvia Maracle, is published in Kim Anderson, "Honouring the Blood of the People: Berry Fasting in the Twenty-First Century," in Ron. F Laliberte, Priscilla Setee, James B. Waldrum, Rob Innes, Brenda McDougall, Lesley McBain and F. Laurie Barron, Eds. *Expressions in Canadian Native Studies*, Saskatoon: University of Saskatchewan Extension Press, 2000, p. 374-394.
[2]From a personal interview with the author, May 4, 2006.
[3]As described by Joan Glode in the opening quote of this section.
[4]As discussed by Anishnaabe midwife Carol Couchie in *A Recognition of Being: Reconstructing Native Womanhood*, pgs. 164-165.
[5]This is what I documented in my first book, *A Recognition of Being: Reconstructing Native Womanhood* .

References

Anderson, Kim. *A Recognition of Being: Reconstructing Native Womanhood.* Toronto: Sumach Press, 2000.

Bear, Shirley. "Equality Among Women." *Canadian Literature* (Spring/Summer 1990): 133-137.

Erdrich, Louise. *The Blue Jay's Dance: A Birth Year*. New York: Harper Collins, 1995.

Harvey, Neil and Jeff Wessman. "An Interview With Katsi Cook." *Talking Leaves: A Journal of Our Evolving Ecological Culture* 10 (1) (Spring/Summer 2000). Online: http://www.talking leaves.org/s00cook.htm. Accessed: September 25, 2006.

Porter, Tom "Pregnancies and Mohawk Tradition." *Canadian Woman Studies/les cahiers de la femme* 10 (2/3) (1989): 115-116.

Schwager, Laura . "Inside Us." *Atlantis: A Woman's Studies Journal/Revue d'etudes sur les femmes* 29 (2) (Spring/Summer, 2005): 9-12.

Wall, Steve. *Wisdom's Daughters: Conversations with Women Elders of Native America*. New York: Harper Collins Publishers, 1993.

Birthing an Indigenous Resurgence

Decolonizing Our Pregnancy and Birthing Ceremonies

LEANNE SIMPSON

> Our grandmas tell us we're the first environment, that our babies inside of our bodies see through the mother's eyes and hear through the mother's ears. Our bodies as women are the first environment of the baby coming, and the responsibility of that is such that we need to reawaken our women to the power that is inherent in that transformative process that birth should be. (Cook 2000)

Bringing my two children through the doorway into this world, with the help of midwives, in my home and surrounded by my culture were the two most transformation experiences of my life. Up until that time, I had spent a number of years on the edges of the academy, working with Elders and traditional knowledge holders, researching, writing, and teaching. The transformative power of the Anishinaabeg birth ceremony, and the responsibilities of mothering grounded in Anishinaabeg values, caused a radical shift in both my spiritual and political consciousness, eventually causing me to leave the academy to focus on mothering and Indigenous nation-building.

I spent much of my academic career influenced by Indigenous thinkers such as Kiera Ladner and Patricia Monture-Angus who have been writing for a number of years now that in order for Indigenous Nations to liberate ourselves from the violence of colonialism and to achieve a peaceful self-determining nationhood based on our own culturally grounded visions, we must be prepared to liberate ourselves from the ideological constraints of the colonial mentality that plagues present day Indigenous political and governing structures and Indigenous thought. They have also both written that this liberation is not enough, that Indigenous Peoples must also undergo a re-traditionalization of thinking and of *living* based on our individual Indigenous cultural and intellectual traditions.

Similarly, I have spent much time considering and reflecting on Mohawk scholar Alfred Taiaiake's work and what his ideas mean to me as an Anishinaabekwe (an Anishinaabeg women). In his new book, *Wasáse: Indigenous Pathways of Action and Freedom,* he points out that true decolonization, living authentically as Onkwehonwe, the original people, requires our people to be culturally rooted, physically and spiritually strong, capable of living independently in natural environments, and capable of maintaining and nurturing the relationships that support Indigenous kinds of governance (31-32). He also maintains that in order to achieve this kind of spiritual and political Indigenous resurgence, we need a spiritual revolution to awaken our minds and our hearts, to rebel against colonialism by living our traditions and honouring our cultures, and in doing so, liberation from fear, domination and the "cage of colonialism" will follow (282).

Indeed, many Indigenous people of my generation are speaking and writing similar things, and although their statements ring true in both my heart and my mind, I have struggled to figure out what this means to me and my family both on a personal level in terms of our own Anishinaabeg Giikendam (Anishinaabe Knowledge), mino-bimaadiziwin ("the good life"), and to our collective Anishinaabeg nationhood. Becoming a mother I have realized that it is critical that we work to prepare and equip the next generation to bring about an indigenous resurgence based on indigenous interpretations of our traditions. This resurgence is a necessary prerequisite to bring about the kind of radical transformation that will allow us to emerge from being occupied nations into being free. But I am also left wondering, how do we equip ourselves, and our children, for the revolutionary nature of our traditional teachings? How can we nurture our children in our Indigenous ways of being so that they can carry on our liberation work with authenticity and integrity? How can we ensure that our children are knowledgeable enough about our cultures to appropriately interpret our ancient teachings?

Our grandmothers tell us that the answers lie within our own cultures, ways of knowing and being, and in our languages. When I listen to them talk about pregnancy, childbirth, and mothering, I hear revolutionary teachings with the potential to bring about radical changes in our families, communities, and nations. For Anishinaabeg people, the first seven years of a child's life are very important. Children come from the spirit world, and they have a close and vital relationship with that realm. Children are respected as spiritual beings, and are looked up to, because they have knowledge their parents, who live largely in the physical world, do not. That is a very different way of positioning children in comparison to settler society. Children are not viewed as helpless babies who need to be controlled, they are viewed as independent spiritual beings, who have many things to teach their parents. Children are gifts. They are leaders. They are gifts that require respect, patience, love, attachment, listening; gifts that require us to face our own conflicts, faults, and misgivings. In our culture, children have a lot of freedom to experience the world for themselves, they have few boundaries, and they learn the natural consequences of their actions under the careful watch of their mothers, fathers, aunties, uncles, and grandparents. This is often mis-interpreted to mean that Anishinaabeg parents do not parent, but this kind of approach requires a very strong attachment to children, nurtured in those first seven years, and including things like long-term breastfeeding, on cue feeding rather than on schedule feeding, co-sleeping, baby-wearing, and gentle, positive, non-violent guidance, discussion, and empathy. The *way* we mother is incredibly important, because the way we conduct ourselves as mothers, models for our children how to live as Anishinaabeg people. I believe the way we mother is the way we inoculate our children against consumeristic throw-away culture, the fear and self-doubt of colonialism, and provide them with the skills, knowledge, and courage to bring about this transformation. Mothering is the way we nurture our children with Indigenous interpretations of our teachings, and this transformation begins with birth.

When I became pregnant with my first child, my dreams of liberation, of freedom, of self-determination and of nationhood, became stronger and more urgent. My pregnancies and the subsequent births of my children were opportunities to put the politics of liberation into practice by challenging the contemporary western medicalization of pregnancy and birth and by grounding my process in the knowledge of Anishinaabegweg (Anishinaabe women). Pregnancy became a way of linking personal self-determination with the self-determination of the Anishinaabeg Nation and the responsibilities of women in re-building Indigenous nations. As I began to understand the power of the physical process of birth and re-birthing, it became clear to me that the responsibilities of Indigenous women as life-givers, as transformers, and as vitalizers are responsibilities Anishinaabewekeg have to our nation whether or not we physically give birth. The reclamation of this responsibility has a tremendous impact for other occupied Indigenous nations and our collective Indigenous visions of sovereignty, freedom, and justice.

Colonized Wombs, Imprisoned Nations

In the times prior to contact, we lived in extremely healthy communities. Indigenous societies valued women and their responsibilities as life-givers. Birthing was viewed in both its physical and non-physical forms as transformative, and the power to transform, to create, and to *re-create* lies within Indigenous women. Women had the power to infuse vitality into thoughts, beings, and other entities, thereby assisting them in realizing their potential (Gunn Allen 27-28). Creation stories in several different cultures speak to the ability of Indigenous women to give new life to beings, to transform, and to vitalize. Women had important responsibilities in traditional governance based on their knowledge of birthing and mothering. Women were honoured and respected by our nations for our contributions, for our power and for our responsibilities as nourishers. And unlike today, committed, full-time mothering was recognized for its importance in growing and maintaining healthy nations, and the social structure of our nations was set up to support mothers and children. Mothering was respected, and it "did not imply slaves, drudges, drones who are required to live only for others rather than for themselves as it does so tragically for many modern women" (Gunn Allen 27-28).

Calculated colonialism changed birthing. Okanagan writer Jeanette Armstrong, writes that by specifically targeting the power of Indigenous women as life-givers, colonizers we able to disintegrate our communities and move our peoples towards genocide (ix). The western medicalization of birth replaced our ceremony. Bottles and substandard formula took the place of nursing, detachment supplanted attachment, and mothering was replaced by the physical, psychological, sexual, and spiritual abuse of the residential school system. By undermining our most sacred and powerful ceremony and our most sacred responsibilities as mothers, our colonizers thought they could achieve the destruction of our nations.

The birth of a child became something our women had to endure alone, rather than celebrated with the support of her extended family and community. Women were medicated and hospitalized, told that we could not give birth without the assistance of western medicine. White doctors, who were "experts" on birth, replaced our midwives and displaced our confidence in our bodies, our reliance on our traditional knowledge, and our trust in our clans, our spirit-helpers, and our ancestors. Our midwives, aunties, and grandmothers were not allowed in delivery rooms, and neither were our medicines, our singing, our drumming, and our birthing knowledge. We were strapped flat on our backs on hospital beds, not allowed to use our knowledge of birthing which told us which positions to use, ways of minimizing pain, and ways of birthing naturally and safely. Our male partners were stripped of their traditional responsibilities around birth and were relegated to waiting rooms. We were told that for the safety of our babies we needed medical intervention and to rely on the western medical system; to do anything else, we were told, would be irresponsible.

When colonialism hijacked our pregnancies and births, it also stole our power and our sovereignty as Indigenous women. And when colonialism stole that power from us, it undermined our sacred responsibilities as life-givers (Couchie and Nabigon 41-43; Patel and Al-Jazairi 55). It made us feel powerless and afraid of our most important and powerful ceremony —the one where we have the honour of carrying another spirit-being inside the water in our bodies. It made us afraid of ourselves. It made us question our body's knowledge and our Grandmothers' and aunties' knowledge, and our ability to bring forth new life.

In order to heal our Nations, our communities, and our families we need to reclaim this ceremony. By reclaiming pregnancy and birth, we are not only physically decolonizing ourselves but we are also providing a decolonized pathway into this world. It is our responsibility to the next generation. In my role as an academic, I often speak about sovereignty and self-determination, re-building our Nations, and re-gaining jurisdiction over our lands because colonialism is the root cause of all of the major environmental problems we face. Patricia Monture-Angus writes that that self-determination begins at home. I like to take that one step further—that self-determination begins in the womb. If more of our babies were born into the hands of Indigenous midwives using Indigenous birthing knowledge, on our own land, surrounded by our support systems, and following our traditions and traditional teachings, more of our women would be empowered by the birth process and better able to assume their responsibilities as mothers and as nation-builders. More of our children would be able to gain guidance from the story of their emergence from the spirit world through the doorway to this world. More of our men would be connected to their traditional responsibilities in pregnancy, birth, and fathering. The foundation of our nations would be strengthened. Katsi Cook (1989), a Mohawk traditional midwife, writes that the production and reproduction of human beings is integral to sovereignty and that this sovereignty falls in the domain of the female universe. She writes that women are the base of the generations, the carriers of the culture. So when we find ourselves in a crisis, like the one colonialism has created, it is our responsibility as the base of the generations to lead the resurgence by bringing forth a generation of children that are strong, healthy and properly prepared to live their traditions.

Reclaiming our responsibility as the carriers of the cultures, whether we have children or not, means reclaiming our responsibilities as aunties, grandmothers, teachers, and visionaries. Without the voices of women at the table when our leaders talk about governance, we are missing the ones responsible for carrying and protecting our culture, our language, our knowledge, and our philosophies. We are missing the ones with the connection to life-giving waters. By nurturing these connections, we will bring back the respect and honour that our nations once had for mothers and mothering.

When I first left my academic position to focus on mothering my children and my work in Indigenous communities, I found little support from anyone. Some people even felt that I was avoiding my responsibilities to my nation by focusing on my children. For me, my choice (and I had a choice, unlike many women), was based on my politics and my Anishinaabeg interpretation of our traditions. It may not be the right choice for other Indigenous women equally committed to breaking the destructive cycle of colonialism, but it was the right choice for my family and me. It is not easy to break the cycle of colonialism, that cycle of violence, and I find it takes nearly all of my energy and focus to break those cycles. Mothering from an Anishinaabeg place requires time, commitment, and support. It requires us to do our own healing work and confront the colonialism within us as we model relationships and ways of being for our children. Mothering provides the very first instruments of Indigenous governance and law (Armstrong ix), and

29

it is critical for an Indigenous resurgence that those instruments come from a peaceful, loving, and nurturing atmosphere. We cannot expect our children to carry on our liberation work if we do not take the time and effort to equip them with the attachment, the love, and the endless nurturing they require in the first years of life. We cannot expect our children to carry on our liberation work if they do not know their culture, their language, and our collective values. We cannot expect our children to carry on our liberation work if they grow up surrounded by violence, by crushing poverty, or by hopelessness. By reclaiming our responsibilities as carriers of our cultures, we resist, we revitalize, and we teach another way is possible.

I chose to dedicate the vast majority of my time to mothering, in order to give my children the knowledge and values they would need to carry on along this pathway. I hope my children will be able to live in contemporary times with an Anishinaabeg consciousness, with authenticity and integrity, with the courage to stand up to the violence of the conquest and to do their part to help grow an Indigenous resurgence.

Rebelling Against Colonialism

Colonialism has had tremendous impacts on the women of my family, like all Indigenous families. My Grandma was one of the few in her generation of Indigenous women that did not attend residential school. She spent the first part of her life in Peterborough on Wolf Street, a few blocks from our house now, and my Great Grandfather was a canoe builder. When tuberculosis went through the reserve and both of her parents were placed in a sanitarium, she entered the child welfare system. Her life in "care" was full of abuse. She gave birth to four daughters, all in hospitals, all medicated and medicalized.

My mother laboured alone in a sterile hospital environment with no food and no water for nearly 40 hours to bring me into the world. I was delivered with forceps; my mother eventually drugged and utterly exhausted. When I thought of having children, I knew I wanted to do as much as possible to avoid this kind of birth experience. I wanted to reject and resist the western medicalization of pregnancy and birth. Like other Indigenous families of my generation, we wanted to reclaim Anishinaabeg knowledge around pregnancy and birth, and I wanted to ground our birth experience in my culture.

I saw this as part of my responsibility as the seventh generation, a prophecy in our traditions that predicted the arrival of white people to our lands and the devastation that would follow. The seventh generation refers to the seventh fire, a time where young Anishinaabeg people would turn back to traditional teachings, reclaim our culture, and move toward building strong people, communities, and nations. Our elders tell us that we are in the seventh fire now and, as such, I knew that for the first time in four generations in my family I had the potential to birth at home and with the support of my cultural traditions.

When my partner and I first became open to having children pass through our lives, we knew that we had some work to do to become good parents. We believed that children choose parents who will guide them in the beginning stages of their lives when they are still spirit beings. I knew that the act of carrying a child for nine months was a very powerful women's ceremony, and I felt that for one of the first times in a long time I had the power, support, and resources to decolonize and reclaim my body, my womb, and this powerful, beautiful ceremony.

It was an honour to be pregnant. I felt powerful. I felt like I was doing important work. I had no fear of labour or birth. I knew that my body, the Ancestors, and my Spirit Helpers knew how to birth. I longed to have a community of Indigenous women, of aunties, and Elders, and midwives that could teach me and support me through this process. But of course, colonialism has still for the most part stolen the pregnancy and birth ceremony from our women, undermining our sovereignty and our knowledge and our power as women. I could not look to the women in my own family for knowledge. I did not have the option of finding an Anishinaabekwe midwife or birthing center like my Haudenosaunee sisters in Six Nations or Akwesasne. Our culture is a "listening culture," and I needed to find a women Elder who was knowledgeable in these traditions and these ways to guide me through this process. Edna Manitowabi, who is a very prominent Grandmother and Elder in the Anishinaabeg Nation, was able to assist me.

Edna taught me the things I needed to do to prepare for the birth of our first baby and our re-birth as parents, and later for the birth of our second child. Both Nishna and Minowewebeneshiinh were born at home, facing the east. The first words they heard were mine, greeting them in Anishinaabe. The first teachings our Spirit-babies brought to us was Love—a love that we had not felt or even imagined existed. I nursed both children right away, and the first teaching I gave them was therefore about Sharing, the basis of our treatied relationships with other nations. Nishna was able to be present at the birth of his sister Minowewebeneshiinh, and that experience has helped him to be a gentle, nurturing, caring, older brother. My pregnancy and birth ceremonies led to placenta-burying ceremonies, naming ceremonies, and feasts. Home birth, long term nursing, co-sleeping, and teaching our children the political reality they face has led to spiritual and political revolution within our own extended family and community.

Now that I am a mother, I feel like I know what it is to be woman in a way that I didn't before I had someone depending on me for virtually everything. When I think about our first mother, the earth, as a mother, I am seeing and feeling things differently. Our earth mother gives and gives and gives, and I am not sure about how much we are giving back. My Ancestors knew how to give back. They knew how to build communities and Nations that gave back, and because they knew how to give back, their families, their communities were healthy and well. That's my vision for the future—to revitalize and reclaim and decolonize and re-build our Nations. It takes a lot of courage, a lot of conviction, and it takes a lot of strong voices standing up for themselves and their people and the land. We also have to look to our Elders to relearn how to interact with the land and how to live in a way that honours our first mother. We must say thanks a lot more—by praying, singing, dancing, speaking our languages, eating our traditional foods, and learning to live our cultures in everything we do. It also means that we have to re-examine our reliance on aspects of western culture— like our cars whose exhaust is slowly giving mother earth a fever, like our over-reliance on electricity which is causing our sisters and brothers in Anishinaabeg and Cree lands to the north to be flooded, like our over-consumption of wood and paper that is causing our sisters and brothers in the boreal forest regions of Ontario to lose their traplines and hunting grounds and sacred areas to defor-estation, and I could go on and on. By living our teachings and living our sovereignty we will ensure a healthy first environment for our babies inside of our women and a healthy second environment when our spirit-babies emerge through the doorway to this world. By living our self-determination as vital women, we become powerful catalysts allowing our nations to rise through state-prescribed agendas and to carry pre-conquest visions of self-determination into reality. We are our children's first environment. We are responsible for bringing these new spirits through the doorway into this world. Reclaiming Indigenous traditions of pregnancy, birth, and mothering will enable our children to lead our resurgence as Indigenous Peoples, to rise up and rebel against colonialism in all its forms, to dream independence, to dance to nationhood.

Leanne Simpson is of Mississauga ancestry. She holds a Ph.D. from the University of Manitoba and is past Director of Indigenous Environmental Studies at Trent University. She is currently on extended leave from academia to focus mothering her two young children, Nishna and Minowewebeneshiinh, and she continues to work with a number of Indigenous communities and organizations on issues regarding Indigenous Knowledge, the environment, and traditional governance, both nationally and internationally.

References

Armstrong, Jeanette (Okanagan). "Invocation: The Real Power of Aboriginal Women." *Women of the First Nations. Power; Wisdom, and Strength.* Eds. Christine Miller and Patricia Chuchryk. Winnipeg, MB: University of Manitoba Press, 1996. ix-xii.

Cook, Katsi. (Mohawk) "The Women's Dance Reclaiming Our Powers [Creation Story]." *New Voices of the Longhouse.* Ed. Joseph Bruchach. Greenfield Center, NY: Greenfield Press, 1989. 79-81.

Cook, Katsi (Mohawk). "An Interview with Katsi Cook." *Talking Leaves* 10 (1) (Spring/Summer 2000). Online: <15 May 2006. http://www.talkingleaves.org/s00cook.htm> Date accessed: May 15, 2006.

Couchie, Carol (Anishinaabe) and Herb Nabigon (Anishinaabe). "A Path Towards Reclaiming Nishnawbe Birth Culture: Can the Midwifery Exemption Clause for Aboriginal Midwives Make a Difference?" *The New Midwifery: Reflections on Renaissance and Regulation.* Ed. Farah M. Shroff. Toronto: Women's Press, 1996. 41-51.

Deloria, Vine (Lakota). "Intellectual Self-Determination and Sovereignty: Looking at the Windmills in Our Minds." *Wicazo Sa* (Spring 1998): 25-31.

Gunn Allen, Paula (Laguan Pueblo/Lakota). *The Sacred Hoop: Recovering the Feminine in American Indian Traditions.* Boston: Beacon Press, 1992.

Ladner, Kiera. *When the Buffalo Speaks: Creating an AlterNative Understanding of Traditional Blackfoot Governance.* Unpublished Ph.D. Dissertation, Department of Political Science, Carleton University, Ottawa, 2000.

Monture-Angus, Patricia (Mohawk). *Journeying Forward: Dreaming First Nations' Independence.* Halifax: Fernwood, 1999.

Patel, Sapna and Iman Al-Jazairi. "Colonized Wombs." *The New Midwifery: Reflections on Renaissance and Regulation.* Ed. Farah M. Shroff. Toronto: Women's Press, 1996. 51-83.

Taiaiake, Alfred. *Wasáse: Indigenous Pathways of Action and Freedom.* Toronto: Broadview Press, 2005.

Becoming an Aboriginal Mother

Childbirth Experiences of Women from One Mi'kmaq Community in Nova Scotia

JOANNE WHITTY-ROGERS, JOSEPHINE ETOWA AND JOAN EVANS

According to Karen Michaelson, "in every culture, the birth of a baby—the coming into being of a new member of society—is greeted with wonder, and usually joy" (1). Pregnancy is an emotional time when women need to feel valued and able to safely disclose their feelings, without being judged. Validation and emotional support from family, friends, and health care providers are essential to attaining and maintaining a healthy mental health state during childbirth (Driscoll). Anxiety, a common phenomenon during childbirth, is often due to women feeling uncertain about having the capacity to cope with labour (Creehan). Knowledge, realistic expectations, and maintaining control in labour account for positive outcomes (Mercer 1995). Feeling afraid and vulnerable is not exclusive to any one culture; women from a variety of cultures experience similar feelings. Since every childbirth experience is unique, nursing care must be individualized to meet each woman's needs.

P. L. Rice asserts that different cultures in the world communicate the meaning of childbirth through their traditions, values, and practices. Being culturally sensitive to the needs of people, means that health care providers are more aware of not saying anything that may be offensive to clients (Purnell). Josephine Enang maintains that the link between culture and health is apparent with marginalized groups, in reference to racially visible individuals experiencing social and economic hardships as a result of unemployment. According to Willis "models of care that are patient-driven and that respect cultural preferences and motivations are most likely to promote the desired health behaviors and positive health status" (58).

This chapter will provide an analysis of the childbirth experiences of Mi'kmaq women living in a First Nations community in Nova Scotia, based on the findings of a recent qualitative study on this phenomenon. This research study specifically focused on the intrapartum period of the childbearing process. The intrapartum period is defined as the "time from the onset of true labour until the birth of the infant and placenta" (Ladewig, London, Moberly and Olds 173). The aim of this qualitative study was to generate new knowledge about Mi'kmaq women's childbirth experiences, which occurred in a tertiary health care center outside their First Nations community in Nova Scotia. The study explored Mi'kmaq women's perceptions of the provision of care during childbirth using the following research questions: 1) What is the experience of Mi'kmaq women giving birth outside their cultural community? 2) What do Mi'kmaq women perceive to be an optimal birth experience from their own cultural perspective?

Significance of the Study

The childbirth experiences of women provide valuable nursing knowledge (Callister, Seminic, and Foster). Therefore, understanding the childbirth experience from a holistic prospective means that the cultural, spiritual, physiological, psychological, and social dimensions of the birth are taken into consideration at this time. In Canada, cultural minority groups often find themselves receiving health care from people who have beliefs, values, and attitudes different than their own (Baker and Daigle; Sokoloski). Although most women require minimal interventions during labour and delivery, childbirth is associated with perinatal risks and challenges for women, babies, families, and health care providers (Kendrick and Simpson). Aboriginal women experience significant health problems such as hypertension and diabetes (Health Canada 1999), which affect childbirth outcomes despite overall improvement in perinatal morbidity and mortality rates in Canada (Chalmers and Wen). In fact, some Aboriginal women have more serious health problems than the general population, which place them at higher risk for maternal and infant complications (Smylie, Lesser, Bailey, Couchie, Driedger, and Eason). Mi'kmaq women living in a First Nations community in Nova Scotia receive the majority of their prenatal care and postnatal follow-up care at the Health Center in the community, primarily by First Nations care providers. However, their actual childbirth experiences are primarily managed by non-Aboriginal health care professionals and occur in a tertiary care center approximately 45 minutes from their community. In a society dominated by non-Aboriginal culture, women from a minority group such as Mi'kmaq may experience childbirth in an arena that is not culturally sensitive to their needs. Prior to the establishment of an Aboriginal Health Center in the First Nations community four years ago, women received health services at neighboring facilities. Since the First Nations Health Center does not provide intrapartum and immediate postpartum care, women continue to receive these services away from their community. This scenario is similar to other Aboriginal and non-Aboriginal communities in Canada where women often find themselves being cared for at a distance from their home communities and often by non-Aboriginal healthcare professionals (Baker and Daigle).

During the literature review, it became evident that minimal research had been undertaken on childbirth experiences of Mi'kmaq women. Although considerable research has been written on culture and transcultural nursing, little attention has been directed toward childbirth experiences (Willis). Culturally competent care allows women choice and support during childbirth. Respect for cultural strengths is a key factor in helping mothers and families feel empowered, and enables them to maintain their cultural beliefs, values, and health practices throughout the childbirth experiences.

Method and Methodology

Women's health needs include many dimensions of their lives, such as pursuing a career, being a caregiver for others, and dealing with chronic health problems. Phyllis Stern suggests women's beliefs about their social status, and meanings relevant to health and to society, leave endless variables to investigate. Qualitative research helps to provide answers to questions that may not be quantifiable and to reveal similarities and differences among individuals, as well as the meaning of particular experiences for them. It is recognized as a meaningful and important methodological approach to developing a concrete body of nursing knowledge (Streubert-Speziale and Carpenter). The childbirth experiences of Mi'kmaq women were explored using a qualitative inquiry process.

Heather Clarke emphasizes that research approaches, in addition to being culturally appropriate, need to be culturally suitable to the population being studied in order "to generate valid knowledge about culture, to develop theory, and to translate this into culturally suitable nursing and health care" (12). Since feminism has historically focused on valuing women and challenging injustices based on gender (Du Gas, Esson, and Ronaldson), feminist research methodology guided the study. According to Beverly Du Gas, Lynne Esson, and Sharon Ronaldson, "feminism has historically focused on valuing women and confronting systemic injustices based on gender" (315). From a feminist perspective, caring requires that nurses use a feminist critique, and to advocate for gender equality and promote equal rights (Du Gas, Esson, and Ronaldson). Enang asserts, "as nurses become more involved with feminism, we must not ignore the feminist perspective that is relevant to the experiences of women of colour and other marginalized groups" (47). Joan Evans adds that feminist research can in fact act as a healer regarding issues related to equality and social justice for women.

An indigenous framework was also used to provide a deeper understanding of First Nations people, including the importance of oral tradition and respecting indigenous ways of knowing. Recognizing the significance of traditional knowledge is based on lived experiences of Aboriginal peoples and also on information passed down from their ancestors (Cardinal, Schopflocher, and Svenson *et al.*). Indigenous knowledge is obtained from a variety of sources such as the talking circle, ceremonies, dreams, and visions specific to Aboriginal peoples. Thus, this qualitative research method provided an optimal forum for Mi'kmaq women to tell their birth stories.

This research was conducted in a First Nations community in Nova Scotia where approximately 60 to 100 Mi'kmaq women give birth each year. This community has a Health Centre that provides prenatal and postnatal care services to Mi'kmaq women. A community health nurse of Mi'kmaq ancestry employed at this First Nations community health center provides prenatal and postnatal health care for Mi'kmaq women within their community. The community health nurse is recognized as a knowledgeable and valuable health care professional in the community. Her credibility and the rapport she had with the community facilitated the process of participant recruitment for the research. The nurse made the initial contact with women who met the study criteria to inform them of the study and to invite them to participate in the study.

Purposive sampling selection was used as outlined by Michael Patton on the basis of the following criteria: Mi'kmaq women, 19 years or older living in this Nova Scotia First Nations' Community, first time mothers, having given birth within the past two years at a hospital in a city geographically located outside this First Nations community. Approval to engage in this study was obtained from the Human Ethics Review Committee, Dalhousie University. Also, additional approval was obtained from the Mi'kmaq Ethics Watch Committee in Nova Scotia, prior to commencing the study.

All participants signed the participant consent forms prior to commencing the study. Participants were informed that they could withdraw from the study at any time without influencing the health care they receive. They were assured that confidentiality would be maintained throughout the research process and in the dissemination of information by the researcher.

Data were collected by means of a one-on-one in-depth interview and a follow-up discussion with each participant. Interviews were conducted in a private area in the Mi'kmaq women's home, or at the Health Center located in their First Nations community. The aim of the interview was to allow the participants an opportunity to express their feelings and beliefs. Therefore, establishing a permissive atmosphere for the participants helped to achieve this result (Oakley).

Interviews were audio-taped and transcribed verbatim to ensure accuracy of data. Data was examined using thematic-analysis. Janice Morse and Peggy-Anne Field describe thematic analysis as "the search for and identification of common threads that extend throughout an interview or set of interviews" (139). The researcher was looking for commonalties among the participants' childbirth experiences and watching for emerging themes (Polit, Beck, and Hungler). Participants were assured that confidentiality was maintained throughout this research process and in the dissemination of information.

Research Findings

In collaboration with the Mi'kmaq women in the study, four key themes were identified from the research with the purpose of revealing a true picture of the women's childbirth experiences in a non-Aboriginal setting. The four major themes that emerged from the interviews with the Mi'kmaq women included: Theme I-Unpreparedness for Childbirth; Theme II- Professional Relations as Sites of Invalidation; Theme III-Access to Health Care; and Theme IV-Support During Birthing. Although their birth stories varied, as one would expect, there were frequent commonalties found among the women's experiences.

Three sub-themes associated with unpreparedness for childbirth were found. They included: lack of knowledge, fear related to safety, and feeling prepared.

Unpreparedness for Childbirth

Unpreparedness for childbirth referred to lack of knowledge and fear about what to expect when having a baby for the first time. Prenatal education is a fundamental component of prenatal care for women and their families (Health Canada 2000). Prenatal health care provides a means to appropriately assess and diagnose prenatal complications that may occur during a woman's pregnancy (Wong, Perry, and Hockenberry). Women who do not receive adequate prenatal care may not be promptly diagnosed when prenatal complication(s) arise. As a result, the medical condition may advance to a point where women become critically ill.

Lack of Knowledge

The participants described a lack of information on pre-existing and pregnancy-induced diseases, normal changes in pregnancy and the labour process, parenting and mothering. They also described the impact of this lack of information as including stress, isolation, uncertainty, and anxiety. The women also offered good examples of the benefit of getting timely information. Lack of knowledge relating to the participants' prenatal health during pregnancy was also a common finding during this research. Many participants discussed the need for more education about their pregnancy and resulting changes in their bodies. Margaret recalled her lack of knowledge about gestational diabetes as:

> *I had lack of knowledge of diabetes. No one told me that the baby could die. You could be fine but your baby could die because your sugars are high....*
> *I was concerned because they won't tell me much.*

She described how distressed she felt after being informed by her doctor that her baby could have died as a result of her high sugars. Her distress also stemmed from a lack of knowledge regarding her high blood pressure and blood sugar, in addition to having poor eating habits, all of which could have harmed her baby.

It is important for women to be assessed as early as possible during pregnancy in order to receive information about pregnancy complications. A common prenatal complication found in this research and also known to be higher in the Aboriginal population than in the general population is gestational diabetes. Five of the eleven women interviewed had gestational diabetes. Gestational diabetes (GDM) is defined as "any degree of glucose intolerance that has its onset or is first diagnosed during pregnancy" (Ladewig *et al.* 267). One participant, Angela was unaware of the signs of preeclampsia and was angry with the physician for failing to promptly diagnose her. She recalled:

> *When I was about five months I was at the beach at my grandparents and I was just walking around ... and all of a sudden I noticed my feet were swollen and I couldn't even put my shoes on and I said oh my God ... they tested me for a diabetic pregnancy but my cousin ... she said you don't have a diabetic constitution you have preeclampsia toxemia.... Like, eat right then she said, keep your feet up and so I had to stay in bed and my diabetic test results came back negative and I told the doctor and the community health nurse what if I have toxemia and they said no and they said you're just going to have a large baby and that scared me ... but when I was in the hospital they told me I had very bad toxemia ... I was scared. I wasn't really aware of my condition.*

Women may require hospitalization for preeclampsia, in which case, mothers will require bedrest, a quiet dark room and restriction on visitors among other standard protocol. Being informed helps to minimize stress, a key factor in lowering blood pressure (Pillitteri).

Wendy stated that she "would like to attend prenatal classes if they fit in" her high school class schedule. Contrary to western prenatal care practices, First Nations women do not regularly receive prenatal care (Sokoloski). This study found that some women viewed prenatal care as important while others viewed pregnancy as a natural experience and relied on cultural traditions and practices to maintain a healthy pregnancy (Sokoloski). Shirley Hiebert debates whether antenatal care is culturally appropriate for Aboriginal women in western society. She suggests that further research is required to determine what Aboriginal women perceive to be culturally competent antenatal care. However, participants in this study reported they all received prenatal care including prenatal education from the community health nurse at the health center. From their responses, it was evident that this care was viewed as important for healthy birth outcomes. Their views are consistent with those of the dominant society and surprisingly different from the traditional practices of most First Nations people.

Adele Pillitteri claims "fear of the unknown is one of the hardest fears to conquer" (545). Childbirth fear is common and generally women are able to overcome their fears (Bewley and Cockburn). Women are primarily concerned about the safety of their baby and their own health outcomes during this time (Rubin). In a study of women in high-risk perinatal situations, Colleen Stainton, Sheila Harvey, and Deborah McNeil found that fear was generated from uncertainty as women waited during the pregnancy. Many Mi'kmaq women in this research voiced being afraid during labour and delivery, and they were also concerned about health outcomes for themselves and their babies.

Jo M. Kendrick asserts that women are generally anxious regarding their ability to accurately draw up the insulin and self-administer it. One participant described her lack of knowledge and fear of self-administering insulin in the following manner: Margaret remarked "the first week I had that insulin I was shaking and crying giving myself the insulin. I was terrified of it." Since childbirth outcomes are innately unpredictable, with some risk to the mother and baby, it is not unusual for women to be fearful of this experience (Bewley and Cockburn). Several participants expressed fear about their own and their babies' health. For example, Angela remarked:

> *I wasn't really aware of my condition ... I was concerned about my freedom. I have fear of being a first time mother. At four months, I didn't feel the baby move. I rushed to the hospital. I was scared of losing the baby at three months. My baby was cleared of being a Downs Syndrome.*

Joan remarked "I had most fear about my baby. He was okay, healthy though." Elizabeth's fear points to the need for greater knowledge of gestational diabetes. She stated "I was frightened my baby might have caught diabetes. She may have symptoms." Cathy recalled :"I had fear about labour, my own health."

Feeling Prepared for Childbirth

Although the majority of women in the research voiced concerns about not being prepared for childbirth, there were two Mi'kmaq women who felt they had enough knowledge from various sources to prepare them for the birth. For example, one participant who had a prenatal tour of the labour/delivery unit in her last trimester described feeling more prepared for what to expect when she was admitted to the birthing room. Angela stated "so I was able to familiarize myself with what's going to happen and who's going to be there and like that.... " Angela further explained how beneficial she found the resources at the Health Center. Her comments included:

*The pamphlets that I got from here from the community health nurse and any
questions or concerns that I had about having like the ways of having a baby
I was young, I turned to [community health nurse] a lot—like I did and I
would call her during her office hours and ask her questions....*

Similarly, Marie remarked "I had enough knowledge, did a lot of research, read
what they gave me, watched *Birth Stories*, used internet, and talked to people who
already have babies."

Being informed about the process of childbirth can enable women to feel more
confident and help them prepare for it. Joanne Solchany adds that first time
mothers need to accept themselves as mothers and have the confidence that they
will be able to carry out this role. Women and families need to be knowledgeable
about issues around childbirth so that they can make informed decisions (Health
Canada 2000).

Professional Relations as Sites of Invalidation

According to Health Canada, "giving birth represents a major transition in a
woman's life" (2003: 5.5) and memories of the birth experience remain with a
woman throughout her life. Communication and collaboration between health
care providers and mothers and families are most important at this time. Health
care professionals providing prenatal care must uphold the principles of providing
family-centered maternity and newborn care, which includes informed choice,
continuity of care, respect and evidenced-based care (Health Canada 2000).
Providing perinatal care in an environment that recognizes cultural differences
and provides culturally sensitive care is paramount (McNaughton Dunn). Nursing interventions will be more effective if culturally competent care is provided
(Willis). Research by Baker and Daigle describes hospital experiences of Mi'kmaq
people. These researchers found recurring themes in the narratives of participants
revolving around misunderstanding and feeling misunderstood, similar to the
findings in this research. The following sub-themes associated with Mi'kmaq
women's encounters in the health care system include: relationship with health
care professionals, medicalized care failed women, and communication barriers
and miscommunications.

Relationship with Health Care Professionals

The relationship between Mi'kmaq women and non-Aboriginal health care
professionals in this research was sometimes unprofessional. When the needs and
the expectations of clients are not explored, dissatisfaction, non-compliance and
poor health outcomes may prevail (Salimbene). Ramona Thieme Mercer (1989)
reports that hospitalized pregnant women experience increased stress for several

reasons such as separation from family and their home, emotional issues, family changes, health concerns and self-image problems. Often they describe feeling lonely, bored and powerless, in addition to feeling physical discomforts and loss of control. Women's concern for their pregnancy and the safety of their baby makes them feel vulnerable at this time (Mercer 1989).

During hospitalization for hypertension and diabetes in pregnancy, one participant gave an account of her experience with a doctor on call, while her own doctor was away on the weekend. This encounter with the physician was experienced as bullying and disrespectful of her. Margaret consequently felt angry and powerless:

> *The doctor told me off, not even a hello or nothing ... started telling me off. I said I don't know who you are, you were my [doctor] when I was a teenager and I didn't like you then and I still don't like you. I apologize but I'm sorry.... [The doctor] told me that my sugars got to come down. I said, I'm eating properly ... you know it doesn't do it within five minutes of me eating and my blood pressure, I gotta quit smoking. [The doctor said] you got total bed rest, you don't even get any more for a cigarette ... you'll get up maybe nine o'clock, one o'clock, and five or six o'clock three times a day.... That's when I almost lost it. I wanted my doctor back, I didn't want this one telling me off. My doctor don't even talk to me like that....*

In another incident during the same admission, this participant communicated that the doctor said to her "I hear you are giving the nurses a hard time." Margaret was offended in response to this remark. Another participant conveyed how angry she felt about being told by a physician that she was the "worst" patient. The mother was fuming with this remark. She was also angry at the reaction of the nurse when she was not sure that her membranes had ruptured. Her experience of receiving unprofessional care was demonstrated in the following example:

> *Yes, so I was like I'm not sure if my water broke, and she was like—you're not sure, and she kind of laughs and I said yes, and she says hold on, I'll get the doctor. So they send me to labour and delivery—and he said you didn't know your water broke? Yes, he even told me I'm the worst patient here (laughs), I said I can't believe you said that to me. Yes—he said you're the worst patient I've ever had.*

Penny Simpkin found in her study of first time mothers giving birth, that the manner in which health care professionals treat women during childbirth could have a lasting effect on how they feel for the rest of their life. Women are most vulnerable during this experience, with their private body parts exposed to the world and crying in pain to strangers (Simpkin). When women are not treated with dignity and respect or they are taken advantage of, the outcome is a negative permanent experience (Simpkin). On the other hand, if women are nurtured and treated with respect, and made to feel like an active participant, then a positive experience will result (Simpkin). The participants in this research did not feel respected, nor did they feel they were consistently part of an autonomous process.

In another situation a participant described the traumatic experience of having a caesarean section without adequate anesthetic, despite telling the physicians that she was feeling pain. Wendy described:

> *They gave me the epidural and it didn't work—because I felt the tugging— I felt them cut and I felt them tugging. I told them—I was crying and I was telling my boyfriend I can feel them and they weren't listening.... They came to check on me a few days later and one of the doctor's says like she's doing pretty good considering she felt most of her—what happened to her in the OR.*

Labouring women rely upon healthcare providers to ensure they have a safe outcome for their babies and themselves (Mozingo, Davis, Thomas and Droppleman). Often their initial reaction is fear and even terror at the possibility of complications occurring during birth. When women receive insensitive childbirth care or when there are poor interpersonal interactions between the client and the health care provider, feelings of anger arise (Mozingo *et al.*). The results of research revealed that women felt angry when their expectations of trust, power, control and being informed were not met (Mozingo *et al.*). Their experiences of anger echo similar responses of Mi'kmaq women.

In this research, some participants' fear of labour and delivery was decreased by a number of strategies. Prayer helped one mother manage her fear in labour. Lisa remembered "I had fear in labour. What you pray for is a healthy baby and healthy delivery." Another participant described one of the nurses as "a God" whom she admired, and was grateful for the supportive care she received. Jenny stated "I wrote her a thank you card and told her that—you were an angel sent by God and there should be more people like you."

Medicalized Care Failed Women

Although childbearing is an exciting milestone in the lives of many women, it is a frightening and potentially terrifying experience for some (Maestas). For many women, the only way to ensure a healthy outcome for themselves and their babies is to rely on health care providers to make decisions regarding their care. With the physician being the gatekeeper, women may become passive in their role and thus feel helpless and frightened of their childbirth experience (Maestas). Consequently, some women view the use of medical interventions as a means of ensuring a safe birth.

First Nations women believe pregnancy to be a natural and normal process with no interference (Sokoloski). However, non-medicalized care is not the standard perinatal care practice in most healthcare facilities. Elizabeth Sokoloski reports that technological interventions in pregnancy are considered by many First Nations women to be harmful, and they are afraid of them. They believe that procedures such as ultrasound may create problems in the baby's development and therefore should be avoided. Similarly, during labour and delivery, First Nations women believed that medical induction of labour, fetal monitoring, pelvic examinations, the use of forceps and other procedures may cause harmful results to their baby (Sokoloski). However the participants in the study did not outwardly object to any medical interventions. They were of the understanding that the medical procedures used were necessary to ensure healthy outcomes for their babies and themselves. Savage adds that the standard for medical care in today's society isolates the family, by placing them in "austere rooms of porcelain-coated furniture" where women are restricted to bed, and subjected to intravenous therapy, forcep deliveries and other hospital routine procedures (8).

The experience of epidural anesthesia however did not live up to one participant's expectations. Jenny said:

> *I was really exhausted. The epidural didn't work ... they put the needle in again the second time; the freezing whatever the numbness went to my leg, my thigh it didn't numb me here at all.... It didn't do anything, I felt everything.*

Having to wait two hours for an epidural was upsetting to one of the participants. Margaret described her labour pain:

> *[The anesthetist] did one patient and left ... I was ripping from ten o'clock, he came back at a quarter after twelve. I was just ripping because at the time he was putting the epidural in me he had to put it in three times before he found the right spot and I got three contractions within the half an hour that he was trying to put it in and I was screaming and I was crunched up in a ball.... He finally got the epidural inserted but he was in too much of a joking mood. I didn't find it funny.*

Communication Barriers and Miscommunications

Communication challenges are one of the many barriers to providing culturally competent nursing care. Effective communication requires a sincere commitment of health care providers to understand what the client is saying (Callister).

Some of the women described situations in which interactions with health care professionals were characterized by misunderstanding and miscommunication.

Cathy described how she misunderstood her doctor's request to be admitted to the hospital in the following manner:

> *Yes, so I really listened to [the doctor]. I thought I'd go home—like he says your water broke, oh, okay. Well I'm not in labour so I started putting my clothes on and he was like where do you think your going? I said I'm going out for breakfast. I'm going out and I'm going to go back home; and he said no you're not. I said I'm not in labour and he goes, you can't go home your water broke, and I said oh, well I'll be back then. I said, I wasn't actually ready to come in.*

Access to Health Care

Access to care is an important consideration for pregnant women. Janice Morse states: "as communities demand services so women may give birth in their own communities, nurses recognize, in normal circumstances, that normal birth is a not a medical risk, and should not be considered as such" (Morse 88). Having a baby is a family event and removing the mother from her community poses increased hardship on mothers and families. These hardships include lack of social support, vulnerability to the language barrier, and separation from family resulting in ineffective family coping. Physical location of the health services, birthplace preferences, cultural competence and cultural attitudes of providers were among the main sub-themes associated with access to health care.

Physical Location of the Health Services

Deborah Blackwell found that access to prenatal care services, particularly for nutritional services, childbirth education, social services and prenatal assessment located within the same area is important to women. Women value their time and want to use it efficiently. Prenatal care services scheduled over several days with long waiting times and in different locations are frustrating and do not meet the client's needs (Blackwell).

Despite diabetic care being available in the participants' home community, one participant was referred to the Diabetic Clinic a 45-minute drive away. This caused undue hardship and stress as reflected in this narrative by Cathy:

> *So I'd have to get up at 6:30, take a shower, drive … go there and wait and my pressure would always go up and my sugar and they're like, what's … what's stressing you and everything. I told them—coming here … then the fasting because I'm hungry and I said I don't like coming here so it took them a while to refer me to the [local] Diabetic Clinic and the doctor…. I had to ask—I asked like three times … it's bad enough I'm going to the doctor every*

week, I'm going to blood work every week, and it would always be on different days, it wouldn't be one day.

Kathleen Bloom, Michelle Bednarzyk, Deanna Devitt, Rebecca Renault, Veronica Teaman and Donna Van Loock found that there is minimal data available on what women perceive to be barriers to receiving adequate prenatal care. Studies have shown that low-income women find transportation, long waiting times and family and social issues to be a factor influencing prenatal care (Bloom *et al.*). Many of the Mi'kmaq women in this research identified lack of transportation as a major obstacle to obtaining prenatal and intrapartum care in the tertiary health care setting, located 45 minutes from their First Nations community. For example, Angela indicated that her friend delivered at home because "they [didn't make it, the reserve] being secluded is really dangerous. If the phone is out ... Women could see a wet nurse-midwife, someone to contact"]. Joan said, "my friend lost a baby. The cord was around the neck." Lack of transportation was a concern for Marie, another participant. Marie recalled that "accessibility is a problem. Hospital taxi is not reliable.... Not everyone has transportation."

A lack of transportation for participants and families was voiced as a concern because many people living in the First Nations community do not have cars. In addition to women having to travel away from their community to give birth, Mi'kmaq women have also had to travel a long distance to the hospital to access prenatal care. This care is now available in their First Nations community and a physician comes to the reserve once a week. The positive impact of accessing respectful medical care on the reserve was voiced by Jenny, who noted that:

> *We don't have a full time doctor, a prenatal doctor and the thing was I started seeing a prenatal doctor [off the reserve] ... so I started seeing her, everybody ... was seeing her, she was taking us on as her patients ... and she's a caring doctor....*

Jenny also added that having prenatal care facilities in the First Nations community reduced travel time and gas costs.

Birth Place Preferences

When participants in this study were asked where they would prefer to deliver their babies, three responded that they would prefer to deliver at home or in their First Nations community and eight participants wanted to deliver in the hospital in the event of complications occurring. Lothian reports that many people tend to believe that birth can only occur in hospitals with routine standards of care to make birth safer for women and babies. However, Lothian acknowledges that evidence does not necessarily support this viewpoint. Linda Maestas found that women who choose home-births had less fear of childbirth, were less dependent on others and wanted to be actively involved in the childbirth experience. Alternate birthing centers or individual rooms in the hospital setting provide women and families a homelike environment that allows an unlimited number of persons present, and the possibility of different options for positions and procedures for labour and delivery. Free-standing centers outside of a hospital are even less formal, giving women more options for their birth experience (Michaelson).

Participants who preferred to give birth in their local community affirmed the freedom it would provide in relation to having their family members present. For instance, Cathy said:

> *Well for me personally I hate being in the hospital ... Yes but I would have been nervous something would happen if she delivered at home or in a birth center but she said that if everything was set up I would be happy to deliver at home with my family present.*

Margaret commented that she would want to deliver at home. She was concerned about the possibility of acquiring infections in the hospital. She would prefer a home birth but wants medical technology and care that is available in the hospital.

> *I figure if I had it at home I know what's been washed.... Well probably because there's no difference having a baby at home or at the hospital, no difference other than having the technology, but we have that portable fetal heart monitor, you have portable stuff that can come with them [healthcare providers] when they come.... I prefer at home ... but if I end up at the hospital, I end up in the hospital.*

Cultural Competence

Patricia Ottani states that communication may be the greatest barrier to health care professionals providing culturally competent care. Josepha Campinha-Bacote describes five constructs, which she believes must be addressed by health care providers. Cultural awareness, cultural knowledge, cultural skill, cultural encounters, and cultural desire all play an important role in providing culturally competent care. Suzanne Salimbene asserts that heath care providers must discard the assumption that all clients will evaluate the care provided to them by the same criteria that was developed for basically mainstream society. Instead health care providers need to change the way health care is delivered by increasing cultural awareness (Salimbene).

Participants described several instances where the nurse lacked knowledge of

47

Mi'kmaq culture. For one participant, the expression "feeling sick" was not understood by her nurse in the assessment and in the meaning of the word "feeling sick" in the Mi'kmaq culture. This participant could not understand why a nurse would not believe she was in labour and sent her home. Wendy recalled:

> *I went in and the nurse that was there to help me did not believe me I was having contractions because the machine that she put on me wasn't picking them up and she was going to send me home and I said well I don't want to go home because I'm really sick—and I said well I'm getting one right now and she pushed on my stomach and she noticed and she looked at my mom right scared and she goes OK let me try this again and as soon as she tried it out that's when she found my contractions—and they kept me for a little bit and they told me you can go home but come back if they get closer, so I went home that night and went back the next morning.*

Annette Browne noted similar findings in her research with Cree-Ojibway participants in a northern First Nations community. Her study reported that nurses overlooked their perception of the problem, which made participants feel not respected. This negative clinical experience led to feelings of misunderstanding (Browne).

Cultural Attitudes of Providers

Ellen Hodnett states that "culture and ethnicity appear to play a role only insofar as they affect caregivers' attitudes and behaviors toward women, in particular their ability to communicate with women and involve women in decisions about their care" (166). Cynthia Baker and Monique Cormier Daigle suggest that "members of cultural minority groups may find themselves surrounded by people whose values, beliefs and interpretations differ significantly from their own during hospitalization" (8). Participants in this study received childbirth care in the hospital setting from non-Aboriginal professionals. Although they were accustomed to caring for Mi'kmaq women, the nurses did not always reflect a sense of caring and sensitivity characteristic of cultural competence but rather a cold, detached feeling was perceived by many of the participants.

Cynthia Baker emphasizes that nurses need to realize the importance of the extended family and how they may want to be involved in health decisions about their loved ones. Some participants in this study felt that they had little or no choice regarding visitors and they were unhappy with the limited number of support persons allowed in the labour/delivery room. For example, Joan recalled: "I felt I had no choice. The rules for the family limited two people throughout the labour. This really bothered me." In addition, Wendy noted:

Family, that's a really big thing because they limit the people in the delivery room. If it were our—like my way—all my aunts would have been there and it would have been like crowded. Yes it's hard like having a limit of two because there's so much people that show up …

However, she also described some flexibility in the number of visitors when her plan of care changed from vaginal to caesarean birth. Wendy remembered:

Well there was two at a time…. But after they told me I had to go to a c-section they were all allowed in, they were trying to calm me down and tell me it's best for the baby that you go so that he's all right and so I finally you know—I had no choice.

Cultural Attitudes of Providers

Patricia Benner emphasizes the importance of establishing caring nurse-client relationships so clients feel at ease disclosing their fears and discomforts. When clients feel rushed or when care is focused on nurses completing tasks, they may be reluctant to share their true feelings. Kristen Swanson shares similar views on caring. She believes that nurses need to understand what client's value as important caring behaviors, which in turn will help them become more competent in care giving. In contrast, nurses caring for participants in this research did not recognize issues of significance. For example, a nurse failed to recognize the importance of allowing a mother to touch the baby's head at delivery. Margaret remembered:

She [nurse] said she's had this contraction for seven minutes and then they checked me and oh my God there's the baby's head. I was trying to touch it and she was like what are you doing and she moved my hand away….

Discrimination is a form of treating people unfairly because they represent a minority group (Boyle; Potter, Perry, Ross-Kerr, and Wood 2006). Although people may not be conscious of this stereotypical behavior (Potter *et al.* 2006), this behavior means that clients receive inequitable care. Jenny stated:

Just with the one nurse because she—I don't know she was like she really didn't care like she made me feel uncomfortable, she made me feel I don't know stupid or weird—she made me feel really low, that one nurse.

Evidence of marginalization and discrimination were evident in the following remarks by Marie:

There are nurses that won't even say hi. Is it because I am native? She [the nurse] is teaching like she is judging you without any interaction. You want

49

> *that care, know you are safe, protected and supported. They need to make an effort to get to know you, who you are, and make you feel comfortable. You need to feel that you can depend upon her to be more understanding of what you're going through instead of just thinking of what it is just another woman having a baby. Some nurses won't talk to you.*

This was consistent with the findings of Annette Browne and Jo-Anne Fiske who reported that First Nations women living in their community in northwestern Canada experienced discrimination during similar clinical encounters. This mistreatment resulted in women feeling socially marginalized from the health care system.

Providing culturally competent care includes being aware of changing trends in language and making an effort to include them in everyday language in health care (Callister). Lynn Callister suggests avoiding medical terms and jargon that are difficult for clients to comprehend or explaining them. Although English language was not an issue for one mother, she could understand why other Mi'kmaq women may have difficulty understanding the medical jargon. Jenny explained:

> *Some people ... can't speak English very well but what I'm thinking you know probably scared and the doctors and nurses were talking the medical. Yes, and they're like freaking out probably ... and I said oh my God what are they saying you know—oh they are just saying you know they have to take this out just in case and when the baby is born they have to use this and that ... I think that it would be really scary....*

Another participant remarked that it would have been helpful to have a Native nurse for a birth coach during labour/delivery. In addition to understanding Mi'kmaq language, she would also have the benefit of understanding the Mi'kmaq culture in relation to birth. Lisa noted:

> *It would have been nice to have a Native nurse there or you know just to help me deal with all this what we were going through.... Just support ... understand you and you know what you're going through you know....*

Support During Birthing

Women need to be reassured that they can have trust in the birth process (Lothian). Therefore the role of the perinatal nurse must be to provide nursing care that "promotes, protects and supports women's efforts to give birth normally and naturally" (Lothian 18). Increasing women's confidence in the childbirth experience and helping them to feel they are supported emotionally and physically during this time is an important responsibility for nurses (Lothian). Sub-themes associated with support identified in this research included: support by family and friends, and health care professionals' support.

Support by Family and Friends

In this research, Mi'kmaq participants were highly receptive to sharing their birth stories. Mi'kmaq women value prenatal and birth advice passed on to them from their mothers, sisters, grandmothers and friends. According to Anderson, storytelling has always been a forum for Native people and therefore processes need to be created to facilitate storytelling. Passing down stories is critical to development as Native people (Anderson). Sharing birth stories with others gives meaning to the experience and helps to explore and manage emotional reactions (Farley and Widmann). Offering to share birth stories helps to positions oneself relative to the culture of motherhood (Nelson). Since there was a lack of childbirth research in the Mi'kmaq population, participants were asked if their mothers and other family members passed on birth stories. They all responded that their family provided valuable childbirth information. Angela, one of the participants noted:

> *During my pregnancy, if I didn't have my mother, I would have been in trouble.... My mother passed down birth stories but she couldn't tell me about pushing but my aunts told me. My mom had caesarean sections. I would trust her [my mother] point of view.*

Nelson reports that when many first-time mothers become pregnant, they search for birth stories from family and friends in order to be more prepared for the birth. Some women feel that birth stories are beneficial, even if it is an account of an unpleasant experience (Nelson). This is consistent with the experiences of some participants in this study. A number of participants said they learned about childbirth from their mothers, sisters, grandmothers, and friends. She was seventeen when she had her baby.... " Wendy described her mother's birth experience at the age of 17 years in the following manner:

> *Her experiences, she had seven.... She was telling me stories how it was to have me and my other brothers and sisters.... She didn't want me to take an epidural or no medication. She didn't take nothing but I took something. Yes and she would love to have more but she can't.*

Sololoski describes the advice a First Nations pregnant woman received from an elder "take care of yourself as the way that the creator would want you in order for your child to be healthy ... You don't drink, you don't smoke, you eat properly..." (95). First Nations women's philosophy on promoting a healthy pregnancy is to take care of themselves (Sololoski).

Family, friends and the community health nurse were all great resources for another participant. Joan remarked:

> *Well mostly my family, my friends, and the ... [community health nurse], she gave me like a folder ... and usually my friends that have babies they used to talk about it like what happened to me and I was like, oh my God, and usually it doesn't exactly happen, what happened to them doesn't happen to me ...*

While lack of support during childbirth was disappointing for some Mi'kmaq mothers, others reported satisfying birth experiences in which they felt cared for and supported. Social support is considered a prime factor in women adapting to their pregnancy, which leads to healthier maternal and infant outcomes (Michaelson). According to Stainton , Harvey and McNeil, "caring for the woman with a high-risk pregnancy often includes caring for an apparently well-person with a serious potential for loss of an expected full-term healthy infant" (1). Providing continuous support during labour and delivery can actually reduce the need for interventions and complications requiring epidural anesthesia and caesarean section birth (Lothian).

Judith Lothian affirms that perinatal nurses play a pivotal role in assisting women through the obstetrical maze to make birth feel like a normal experience. Some mothers felt supported. These feelings are demonstrated by one of the participants. Jenny stated that "yes ... this younger nurse—she helped me all the way through it—she made me feel so comfortable and so welcome and I was happy and relaxed and calm." She further described the nurse's caring and supportive manner and what it meant to her:

> *I wrote her a thank you card and told her that "you were an angel sent by God and there should be more people like you." I told her how she made me feel ... because she was really special to me.... Because all the nurses—the other nurses didn't do anything for me. They were freaking me out instead and ... I was really scared. But this certain nurse made me feel really special and really calm. ...I said, "if there were more nurses like [you] were here, this place would be beautiful, you're a beautiful person...." She [the nurse] really made me feel comfortable and she explained everything to me—"do you know what an epidural is ... do you know what's happening to your body?"*

Browne and Fiske report instances where First Nations women share stories of exceptional care and describe the caring attitude demonstrated by mainstream health care providers during clinical encounters. A feeling of trust is created when the participants feel health care providers sincerely care. As Jenny describes:

She sat there with me and she held my hand and she was rubbing my back and she would talk to me. She talked to me and she asked me questions or she'd tell me about her story, her childbirth or her children.... She told me it's going to be a beautiful experience after I have my child and I'll look back on it someday.... She really made me feel comfortable, I felt welcomed and I'm sure she was an angel.

Interestingly, Baker and Daigle also cite an instance where a Mi'kmaq woman (like Jenny) nicknamed her nurse "the angel" because of the kindness and general concern she bestowed on the woman (19).

Discussion

The Mi'kmaq women in this research described childbirth in varying ways such as a beautiful experience, a miracle, a painful experience, and one of fear of labour and delivery. Prenatal health conditions during pregnancy and/or potential complications contributed to Mi'kmaq women feeling uncertain, fearful, and vulnerable during the childbirth process. Some women expressed concern about the possibility of dying—themselves or their baby. Rubin describes the fear as a dread of delivery, but delivery is also associated with relief through contractions from the burdensome pregnancy, hope for the child, and fear the baby would not exist if there were no bonds of physical and fantasized experience. Mi'kmaq women felt connected to their babies and wanted to ensure healthy outcomes. Many of these first time mothers were apprehensive because of past stories they heard about birthing, combined with a lack of knowledge about what to expect.

While some women felt empowered by the support they received from family, friends and health care professionals, others were afraid and anxious about the birthing process. Modern medicine and technology have replaced women's ways of knowing about childbirth and substituted it with fear (Savage). This goes against the beliefs of Canadian First Nations women who view childbirth as a natural process requiring no interventions (Sokoloski).

In the analysis, the Aboriginal Health Model described by Murdena Marshall, a Mi'kmaq educator, was used to gain a better understanding of the Mi'kmaq women's views on health and how their health is connected to their childbirth experiences. For example, in order to understand relationships with health care providers, Marshall's unpublished manuscript provided valuable information. She stated: "he baby feels everything the mother goes through. If the mom is angry or resentful, the baby will be born with an attitude since all emotions are passed down" (3). Marshall adds: "the elders believe that a baby shouldn't know or feel anything unpleasant but rather come into the world with feelings of peace and balance on humanity" (3). Similarly this dichotomy was evident in the experiences of the participants of this study as some experienced anger while others expressed joy and happiness during childbirth. Since there was limited research on Mi'kmaq women's childbirth experiences, Marshall's view on health provided valuable insights in this study.

It became evident during this research that the Mi'kmaq women's childbirth experiences are complex. Issues regarding accessibility to health care, one of the major themes identified in this research, may be due to many factors as outlined in this study. However, health care providers are well educated and appropriate individuals to assume a leadership position to effect change through healthy public policy. Mi'kmaq women like many minority women want the best possible health care for their families. Having said this, they face many barriers such as access to health care, language barriers, racism and discrimination, and therefore experience feelings of isolation.

This research revealed the importance of education about childbirth. Although a number of women would have preferred to attend formal prenatal classes, they appreciated the limited childbirth education they received from their health center. Mi'kmaq women, like other Canadian women, experience fear during labour and birth. Being prepared for childbirth through prenatal education decreases women's fear in childbirth, lowers their dependence on health care providers and enables women to be more active participants in care (Maestas). In this way transition to motherhood is more easily attained and women feel a sense of control.

In recent years, despite the belief of health care providers that the best place to give birth is the hospital, there has been no sound evidence to support that the hospital is the safer delivering site for women to deliver with uncomplicated pregnancies (Lothian). Although seven of the Mi'kmaq women in this study did not fit into the category of uncomplicated pregnancies, because of medical problems associated with pregnancy placing them at high-risk, four of these women had no complications during pregnancy or childbirth. Therefore, the Mi'kmaq women with no medical problems during pregnancy would be the same as other women advocating for a home birth in Canada. Women with uncomplicated pregnancies have begun advocating for the establishment of birthing centers and home births. Although this change is gradual in North America, women in general are beginning to make some significant strides toward natural childbirth. For example, the Reproductive Care Program in Nova Scotia reported that, although most women in Canada deliver in hospitals, there are some free-standing birth centers and a small but increasing number of Canadian women giving birth at home. According to Ivy Bourgeault, Cecilia Benoit, and Robbie Davis-Floyd, there has been a growing movement toward home births since the late 1960s and 1970s. Currently in Canada, midwifery has been adopted in Ontario, British

Columbia, Alberta, Saskatchewan, and Manitoba (Potter *et al.* 2001). Thus, unique forms of midwifery practice will emerge giving women an option of choosing home birth.

Social, political, and economic factors prevent Mi'kmaq women from receiving the same privilege as many other women in society. Aboriginal peoples have suffered extreme stress for generations as a result of the social, cultural, political and economic strain of colonization (Bartlett). In addition to the burden of colonization, Mi'kmaq women like all women and minority women in particular, experience marginalization in patriarchal society.

bell hooks, a well-known African American feminist author, educator, and scholar who has spent many years researching and educating people about racism, sexism and classism, contributes to our understanding of the meaning of marginalization. Although her work stems from her experiences of Black women, there are some similarities with some of the experiences of the Mi'kmaq women in this research. For example, one Mi'kmaq woman described the nurses as failing to believe that she was in labour and sent her home, leaving her feeling misunderstood. Another participant reported that the nurses would not say hi to her in the hospital, making her feel discriminated against. One participant recalled the doctor yelling at her, making her feel angry, powerless and disrespected. hooks (1984) refers to her personal experiences of being ignored, misunderstood, disrespected, silenced, dehumanized, and disempowered as feelings experienced by many who were affected by domination.

hooks (1989) describes how she values a Native American Indian poem because it expresses disapproval of betrayal, and exemplifies that what is most important is being truthful. hooks (1989) further notes that colonization and imperialism are evidence of lies and dishonesty experienced by Native American people. This parallels Aboriginal peoples' experiences in Canada as a result of colonization. Marie Battiste points out that isolation is a devastating outcome of colonization. Aboriginal people were isolated from outside information and barraged with misinformation such as how they were so backward, weak, and unimportant and lucky to be colonized (Battiste).

Denise Spitzer asserts that "marginalization, economic disadvantage and gender are closely related, and social exclusion engendered through low income, culture, gender, ability or geography can have deleterious health effects" (S85). In Canada, Aboriginal peoples among the members of the visible minority are marginalized (Spitzer). As a result, Aboriginal peoples have limited opportunities and varying experiences that may not contribute to good health. Marginalization as experienced by Mi'kmaq women in this research is associated with inequitable access to health care resources and culturally incompetent health care both of which are necessary to attain and preserve health. hooks (1994) claimed that she too felt like a marginalized person teaching in university where the majority of the students were white, similar feelings that she experienced when she was a Black university student. Being left out was just enough motivation to make her create a classroom environment that engages all students.

The lack of generalizability of these findings given that this data comes from only one First Nations community, and cannot be generalized outside that community may be identified as a limitation. However, like the findings of many qualitative studies, the findings from this study are not intended to be generalizable, instead they offer valuable insights into the childbirth experiences of Mi'kmaq women delivering in a non-Aboriginal setting. Future research is needed to explore the experience of other First Nations women. These experiences can be compared to the birth experience of women from other visible minorities and other Canadian women, to determine similarities and differences. Volunteer bias was a limitation of the study, as women who volunteered.

Conclusion

The findings in this research affirm that issues of gender, sexism, racism, and class affect the lives of Mi'kmaq women and their families during childbirth. To provide accessible and culturally competent health care to Mi'kmaq women and other minority populations during childbirth, health care professionals must understand the impact of these issues and the lived experiences of others. Although health care professionals strive to provide the best possible childbirth care, it is apparent in this study that many physicians and nurses lacked knowledge in cultural awareness and cultural sensitivity, key attributes necessary to providing culturally competent health care. Making education on culture and health mandatory in universities, nursing and medical schools would be a beginning. Continued collaboration and commitment from stakeholders including governments, health professionals and administrators, academics and communities are required to address and improve health inequalities for Mi'kmaq women and their families as well as other minority people.

Joanne Whitty-Rogers is an Assistant Nursing Professor at St. Francis Xavier University, Antigonish, N. S. She recently completed her MN degree from Dalhousie University, Halifax, Nova Scotia. Her research thesis is entitled "Childbirth Experiences of Women From One Mi'kmaq Community in Nova Scotia." In the fall of 2006, she plans to begin doctoral studies at the University of Alberta.

Josephine Etowa is a faculty member at Dalhousie University School of Nursing and co-supervisor of this Master's thesis. Her employment history spans across international, diversity and community development issues. Dr. Etowa has worked in a number of capacities including as a nurse, an educator, a lactation consultant, and academic researcher. She has been involved in a number of community development initiatives and research projects on African Canadians focusing on issues such as health, minority health, childbirth, and immigrant women's health.

Joan Evans is Associate Professor in the School of Nursing at Dalhousie University and also co-supervisor of this Master's thesis. Early in her nursing career, Joan Evans worked in First Nation communities in northern Ontario. Her subsequent appreciation for culture as a determinant of health has been evident in her teaching of maternal-child, family and community health nursing and in her research that explores the relationship between gender and health.

References

Anderson, Kim. "Speaking From The Heart: Everyday Storytelling And Adult Learning." *Canadian Journal of Native Education* 28 (2004): 123-129.

Baker, Cynthia. "The Mi'kmaq." *Canadian Transcultural Nursing: Assessment and Intervention.* Eds. Ruth E. Davidhizar and Joyce N. Giger. St. Louis, MO: Mosby, 1998. 313-327.

Baker, Cynthia and Monique Cormier Daigle. "Cross Cultural Hospital Care as Experienced by Mi'kmaq Clients." *Western Journal of Nursing Research* 22 (1) (2000): 8-28.

Bartlett, Judith. G. "Involuntary Cultural Change, Stress Phenomenon and Aboriginal Health Status." *Canadian Journal of Public Health* 94 (3) (2003): 165-166.

Battiste, Marie. *Reclaiming Indigenous Voice and Vision.* Vancouver: University of British Columbia Press, 2000.

Benner, Patricia. "Relational Ethics of Comfort, Touch, and Solace - Endangered Arts?" *American Journal of Critical Care* 13 (4) 2004: 346-349.

Bewley, Susan and Jayne Cockburn. "Responding to Fear of Childbirth." *The Lancet* 359 (2002): 2128-2129.

Blackwell, Deborah. "Prenatal Care Services in The Public And Private Arena." *Journal of the American Academy of Nurse Practitioners* 14 (12) (2002): 562-564.

Bloom, Kathleen C., Michelle S. Bednarzyk, Deanna L. Devitt, Rebecca A. Renault, Veronica Teaman and Donna M. Van Loock. "Barriers to Prenatal Care for Homeless Pregnant Women." *Journal of Obstetric, Gyneocological and Neonatal Nursing* 33 (4) (2004): 428-435.

Bourgeault, Ivy. L, Cecilia Benoit, and Robbie Davis-Floyd. *Reconceiving Midwifery in Canada.* Montreal: McGill-Queen's University Press, 2004.

Boyle, Joyceen. S. "Culture and The Community." *Transcultural Concepts in Nursing Care.* Eds. Margaret. M. Andrews and Joyceen S. Boyle. Philadelphia:

J. B. Lippincott, 1995. 323-351.

Browne, Annette J. and Jo-Anne Fiske. "First Nations Women's Encounters With Mainstream Healthcare Services." *Western Journal of Nursing Services* 23 (2) (2001): 126-147.

Browne, Annette J. "The Meaning of Respect: A First Nations Perspective." *Canadian Journal of Nursing Research* 27 (4) (1995): 95-109.

Callister, Lynn Clark. "Integrating Cultural Beliefs and Practices Into the Care of ChildbearingWomen. " *Perinatal Nursing.* 2nd ed. Eds. Kathleen R. Simpson and Patricia. A. Creehan. Philadelphia: Lippincott, 2001. 68-93.

Callister, Lynn Clark, Sonia Semenic and Joyce Cameron Foster. "Cultural and Spiritual Meanings of Childbirth." *Journal of Holistic Nursing* 17 (3) (1999): 280-295.

Campinha-Bacote, Josepha. "A Model And Instrument For Addressing Cultural Competence in Health Care." *Journal of Nursing Education* 38 (5) (1999): 203-207.

Cardinal, Josie C., Donald. P. Schopflocher, and Larry W. Svenson, Kenneth B. Morrison, and Lory Laing. *First Nations in Alberta: A Focus on Health Service Use.* Edmonton: Alberta Health and Wellness, 2004.

Chalmers, Beverly and Shi Wu Wen. "Women's Health Surveillance Report-Perinatal Care in Canada." Public Health Agency of Canada, 2003. Online: http://www.phac-aspc.gc.ca/publicat/whsr-rssf/chap_27_e.html. Retrieved May 22, 2006.

Clarke, Heather. F. "Research in Nursing And Cultural Diversity: Working With First Nations Peoples." *Canadian Journal of Nursing Research* 29 (2) (2004): 11-25.

Creehan, Patricia. "Pain Relief and Comfort Measures During Labour." *Perinatal Nursing.* 2nd ed. Eds. Kathleen R. Simpson and Patricia. A. Creehan. Philadelphia: J. B. Lippincott, 2001. 417-444.

Driscoll, Jeanne W. "Psychosocial Adaptation to Pregnancy and Postpartum." *Perinatal Nursing.* 2nd ed. Eds. Kathleen R. Simpson and Patricia. A. Creehan. Philadelphia: Lippincott, 2001. 115-124.

Du Gas, Beverly W. Lynne Esson, and Sharon E. Ronaldson. *Nursing Foundations: A Canadian Perspective.* Scarborough, ON: Prentice-Hall, 1999.

Enang, Josephine. "The Childbirth Experiences of African Nova Scotia Women." Unpublished MA thesis, Dalhousie University, 1999.

Evans, Joan. A. "Feminism And The Evolution of Nursing Knowledge, Theory And Research." *Nurse to Nurse* 2 (4) (1993): 28-30.

Farley, Cynthia and Sarah Widmann. "The Value of Birth Stories." *International Journal of Education* 16 (3) (2001): 22-25.

Health Canada. *The Health of Aboriginal Women.* Ottawa: Author, 1999.

Health Canada, trans. *Family-Centered Maternity And Newborn Care: National*

Guidelines. Ottawa: Author, 2000.

Health Canada, ed. *Family-Centered Maternity And Newborn Care: National Guidelines.* Ottawa: Author, 2003.

Hiebert, Shirley. "NCN Otinawasuwuk (Receivers of Children): Taking Control of Birth in Nisicawayasihk Cree Nation." Unpublished dissertation, University of Manitoba, 2003.

Hodnett, Ellen D. "Pain And Women's Satisfaction With The Experience of Childbirth: A Systematic Review." *American Journal of Obstetrics and Gynecology* 186 (5) (2002): S160-S172.

hooks, bell. *Talking Back: Thinking Feminist Thinking Black.* Toronto, ON: South End Press, 1989.

hooks, bell. *Teaching to Transgress: Education as The Practice of Freedom.* New York: Routledge, 1994.

hooks, bell. *Feminist Theory: From Margin to Centre.* Boston: South End Press, 1984.

Kendrick, Jo M. "Preconception Care of Women With Diabetes." *Journal of Perinatal Neonatal Nursing* 18 (1) (2004): 14-25.

Kendrick, Jo M. and Kathleen Rice Simpson. "Labour and Birth." *Perinatal Nursing.* 2nd Ed. Eds. K. R. Simpson and P. A. Creehan. Philadelphia: Lippincott, 2001. 298-377.

Ladewig, Patricia W., and Marcia L. London, Susan M. Moberly, and Salley B. Olds, *Contemporary-Maternal-Newborn Nursing Care.* Upper Saddle River, NJ: Pearson Education, 2002.

Lothian, Judith A. "Back to The Future: Trusting Birth." *Journal of Perinatal and Neonatal Nursing* 15 (3) (2001): 13-22.

Maestas, Linda M. "The Effect of Prenatal Education." *International Journal of Childbirth Education* 18 (1) (2003): 17-21.

Marshall, Murdena. "Parenting And Traditional Beliefs Are Essential." Unpublished manuscript, 1992.

McNaughton Dunn, Ardys. "Culture Competence And Primary Care Provider." *Journal of Pediatric Health Care* 16 (3) (2002): 105-111.

Mercer, Ramona Thieme. *Becoming a Mother.* New York: Springer Publishing, 1995.

Mercer, Ramona Thieme. *First-Time Motherhood: Experiences From Teens to Forties.* New York: Springer Publishing Company, 1989.

Michaelson, Karen. L. *Childbirth in America: Anthropological Perspectives.* Massachusetts: Bergin and Garvey Publishers, 1998.

Morse, Janice. "Last Words: A Summary of The Northern Childbirth Issue." *Childbirth in the Canadian North: Epidemiological, Clinical and Cultural Perspectives.* Eds. John D. O'Neil and Penny Gilbert. Winnipeg: University of Manitoba, Northern Health Research Unit, 1990: 87-89.

Morse, Janice. M. and Peggy-Anne Field. *Qualitative Research Methods For Health Professionals.* Thousand Oaks, CA: Sage, 1995.

Mozingo, Johnie N., Mitzie W. Davis, Sandra P. Thomas and Patricia G. Droppleman. "I Felt Violated." *Maternal Child Nursing* 27 (6) (2002): 342-348.

Nelson, Fiona. "Stories, Legends And Ordeals: The Discursive Journey Into The Culture of Motherhood." *Organization Development Journal* 2 (4) (2003): 15-32.

Oakley, Ann. "Interviewing Women: A Contradiction in Terms." *Doing Feminist Research.* Ed. Helen Roberts. Boston: Routledge and Regan Paul, 1981. 30-61.

Ottani, Patricia A. "Embracing Global Similarities: A Framework For Cross-Cultural Obstetrical Care." *Journal of Obstetric, Gynecological and Neonatal Nursing* 31(2002): 33-38.

Patton, Michael Q. *Qualitative Research and Evaluation Methods.* Thousand Oaks, CA: Sage, 2002.

Pillitteri, Adele. *Maternal and Child Health Nursing.* Philadelphia: Lippincott Williams and Wilkins, 2003.

Polit, Denise. F, Cheryl T. Beck, and Bernadette P. Hungler. *Essentials of Nursing Research: Methods, Appraisal, And Utilization.* (5th ed.). Philadelphia: Lippincott Williams and Wilkins, 2001.

Potter, Patricia, Anne Perry, Janet C. Ross-Kerr, and Marilyn J. Wood. *Canadian Fundamentals of Nursing.* (2nd ed.). Toronto: Mosby, 2001.

Potter, Patricia, Anne Perry, Janet C. Ross-Kerr and Marilyn J. Wood. *Canadian Fundamentals of Nursing.* (3rd ed.). Toronto: Mosby, 2006.

Purnell, Larry. "The Purnell Model For Cultural Competence." *Journal of Multicultural Nursing and Health* 11 (2) (2005): 7-15.

Reproductive Care Program. "Care of Healthy Women During Labour And Birth."A Nova Scotia Consensus Document. Halifax, NS: Author, (2003).

Rice, P. L. "What Women Say About Their Childbirth Experiences." *Journal of Reproductive and Infant Psychology* 17 (3) (1999): 237-253.

Rubin, R. *Maternal Identity And The Maternal Experience.* New York: Springer Publishing, 1984.

Salimbene, Suzanne. "Cultural competence: A Priority For Performance Improvement Action." *Journal of Nursing Care Quality* 13 (3) (1999): 23-35.

Savage, Jane. S. "Postmodern Implications of Modern Childbirth." *International Journal of Childbirth Education* 17 (4) (2002): 8-10.

Simpkin, Penny. "Just Another Day in a Woman's Life? Women's Long-Term Perceptions of Their First Birth Experience. Part 1." *Birth* 18 (4) (1991): 203-210.

Sokoloski, Elizabeth. H. "Canadian First Nations Women's Beliefs About Pregnancy and Prenatal Care." *Canadian Journal of Nursing Research* 27 (1) (1995):

89-100.

Solchany, Joanne. E. *Promoting Maternal Mental Health During Pregnancy: Theory Practice and Intervention.* Seattle, WA: NCAST Publications, 2001.

Smylie, Janet, Pierre Lesser, Karen Bailey, Carole Couchie, Mary Driedger, and Erica Lise Eason. "SOCG Policy Statement. A Guide for Health Professionals Working with Aboriginal Peoples. Health Issues Affecting Aboriginal Peoples." *Journal of Society of Obstetricians and Gynaecologists of Canada* 23 (1) (2001): 54-68.

Spitzer, Denise L. "Engendering Health Disparities." *Canadian Journal of Public Health* 96 (2) (2005): S78-S96.

Stainton, M. Colleen, Sheila Harvey, and Deborah McNeil. *Understanding Uncertain Motherhood: A Phenomenological Study of Women in High-Risk Perinatal Situations.* Calgary, Alberta: University of Calgary, 1995.

Stern, Phyllis. N. "Conceptualizing Women's Health: Discovering The Dimensions." *Qualitative Health Research* 6 (2) (1996): 152-162.

Streubert-Speziale, Helen. J., and Dona. R. Carpenter. *Qualitative Research in Nursing: Advancing The Humanistic Imperative.* 3rded. Philadelphia: J. B. Lippincott Williams and Wilkins, 2003.

Swanson, Kristen M. "Empirical Development of a Middle Range Theory of Caring." *Nursing Research* 40 (3) (1991): 161-166.

Willis, Winnie O. "Culturally Competent Nursing Care During The Perinatal Period." *Journal of Perinatal and Neonatal Nurses* 13 (3) (1999): 45-59.

Wong, Donna. L., Shannon E. Perry, and Marilyn J. Hockenberry. *Maternal Child Nursing Care.* St Louis: Mosby, 2002.

CONCEPTIONS AND PRACTICES OF ABORIGINAL MOTHERING

An Anishinaabe-kwe Ideology on Mothering and Motherhood

RENÉE ELIZABETH MZINEGIIZHIGO-KWE BÉDARD

Aanii (Anishinaabe greeting). *Mzinegiizhigo-kwe ndizhinikaaz. Dokis First Nation ndoonjibaa. Waazheshii ndoondem.* My Anishinaabe name is Mzinegiizhigo-kwe. My French Catholic name is Renée Elizabeth Bédard. I am Marten Clan, from Dokis First Nation. My mother is Anishinaabe-kwe and my father is French Canadian. Anishinaabe-kwe means *woman* in Anishinaabemowin (Ojibwe). I was surrounded by the women on my mother's side of the family all my life. These women nurtured, fostered, and taught me my identity as an Anishinaabe-kwe. Now, as a scholar, painter, and craftswoman, I try to honour them in my writings, paintings, and craftwork. When I think back on the women who raised and shaped my identity as an Anishinaabe-kwe, I realize I had many mothers. What I give you here is my knowledge, research, and opinions of the nature of Anishinaabe motherhood and mothering.

The purpose of this discussion is to explore the nature of motherhood and mothering from my Anishinaabe-kwe perspective as a daughter, sister, niece, and cousin of strong Anishinaabe women. I feel that it is important to discuss and celebrate the gift of motherhood and mothering as Anishinaabe women. If we as Aboriginal women do not acknowledge the importance of such roles and respon-sibilities who will? In writing about motherhood and mothering, I seek to share with those young Anishinaabe girls and women who might read this contribution, some of the teachings and knowledge that have been passed down to me from the Anishinaabe women who have raised me up to be a strong Anishinaabe-kwe.

The Anishinaabe people talk about the *Seven Stages of Life* and one of those stages includes being a parent, the "planting stage" of life. As Anishinaabe women we have the ability to bring children into the world, and for this gift we were traditionally held in high respect. From a young age, Anishinaabe girls are taught through teachings and ceremony about that gift the Creator gave them to create life with their bodies and be "life-givers" in this world to the next generation. Our Elders talk about our roles and responsibilities as women, and their teachings form the basis of an Anishinaabe ideology on mothering and motherhood, which is grounded in spiritual and cultural rights. In Anishinaabe beliefs of motherhood, all Anishinaabe women have responsibilities to raise-up and nurture the next generation. The Anishinaabe ideology of mothering and motherhood is not dependent on whether, as individuals, we produce children biologically. Women can be mothers in different ways, such as aunties, grannies or even through adoption. In Anishinaabe culture, mother, auntie, and grannie are fluid and interchangeable roles, not biologically-defined identities. Further, producing life and raising children is understood as the creation of a people, a nation, and a future.

As Anishinaabe women, we are given the gift of bringing the children into the world, and for this women have been seen as sacred. The act of being a mother is recognized as sacred work in our communities. As Ojibwe Elder Art Solomon puts it:

> In each family the woman
> was "the centre of the wheel of life."
> The women "were of the earth"
> they were connected to the earth mother
> and to the grandmother moon
> whose work was to govern when all things
> were to be born
> plants, animals, humans,
> fertility was her working element.
> Hence "the woman's cycle" or her "moon."
>
> The power of birth was given to the woman.
> It was given by the Creator
> and it is an immutable law.
> It was given as a sacred work
> and because it is a sacred work
> then a sacred way was given to the women.
> The woman stands between man and God.
> She takes from both and she gives to both.
> That is the place made for her
> by the Creator.
> It is a place of highest honour
> And the reasons why men should honour
> Women. (iii)

Anishinaabe women have passed down knowledge and traditions that celebrate our ability to not just bring forth life, but to mother. Mothering and motherhood extends far beyond the act of giving life to another human being. Anishinaabe mothering and motherhood includes the concepts and ideas of lifegiving, fostering, adoption, raising-up, aunties, and grannies.

My people come from Dokis First Nation, which is located on the French River in northern Ontario, Canada. While my mother was alive, she was a strong Anishinaabe-kwe who raised four children, while her husband, my father, worked at the Ministry of Natural Resources. We lived in North Bay, about two hours from my Reserve. I was born when my parents were in their 40s and not expecting anymore children. For all of my childhood my father was away fighting forest fires and doing other sorts of work for the Ministry of Natural Resources. When I was a child my siblings were teenagers with their own lives, two of them off at college and university, and the other in high-school. My mother and I, therefore, spent lots of time together, just the two of us on many adventures to see my mother's sisters or my Grandmother (whom we affectionately called "Nanny"). Thus, I was able to learn about my Anishinaabe identity via my mother, her aunties, my aunties, and cousins.

I have many memories of traveling to my aunties' (my mother's sisters) homes and getting on the Greyhound bus to go to my Grannie's home in Sturgeon Falls or getting on the ferry boat called the "Chief Commanda," which traveled across Lake Nipissing and down the French River in order to get to my Reserve. My early childhood is filled with memories of being grabbed by the hand by my grandmother, pulled to the kitchen counter, stood on a box crate, and shown how to knead bread. While I still cannot make bread without it turning into the consistency of a rock, I cherish the memory of how she made bread and the huge pantry she stocked with jams and pickled vegetables. The shelves were filled with vivid colours of oranges, reds, yellows, browns, and greens. I remember her knitting and quilting scattered around her home. At night, I remember those patchwork quilts weighting me down, pinning me to the bed, but which kept me warm. Today, I keep one of her quilts at the foot of my bed to keep me warm on cool nights. My grandmother died in 1986, but the lessons she taught me shaped my identity as an Anishinaabe-kwe.

My childhood in the mid-1980s was spent listening to the Anishinaabe women in my family on and off my Reserve. These women took responsibility for me, surrounding me with women's ways of knowing and being in the world. Hours were spent reminiscing, gossiping, recounting family stories, teaching, and instructing. Most of the time, as women do, they included me in the goings-on of daily life. One of the most striking lessons was their long fight to gain their "Indian status" back under Bill C-31. They would spend many years struggling to gather information to prove that their parents were both of First Nations ancestry, but it was worth it in the end.

Over the years, I spent time traveling with these women. I was surrounded by many women who I considered my mothers. We went from little Catholic churches to long forgotten graveyards or foundations of homes buried deep in the bush on Dokis Reserve and sometimes off our Reserve in tiny nearby towns or villages. Along the way, they fostered me in my Anishinaabe identity. Each church, village, and graveyard contained story after story about our ancestors' lives, which I heard in great detail from the women. While they worked diligently to gather marriage, death, and birth certificates, old letters, and photographs of their ancestors, I listened to them talk about their identities, government policies, government records, the history of our Reserve, the history of our family, and all the family's oral histories and stories. As my childhood went by, I learned how much they valued their identity as Anishinaabe women from Dokis Reserve and heard them refer to themselves as "French River Girls." What I witnessed was the strength of many Aboriginal women's voices working together to change their own lives and the lives of their family for the better. By gaining their status back, these sisters honoured their mother who had lost her status and for themselves gained some peace of mind. They taught me the importance of leading by example and how, despite the rigors of colonization, Anishinaabe women continue to carry on those vital traditions of mothering and motherhood.

Mythology of Indigenous Mothers in Canada

In both western and Indigenous frameworks, mothers have historically held an important role as the bearers of the next generation, the community, the Nation, and the future. The Euro-Canadian constructed image of Indigenous mothers, therefore, mirrors western attitudes towards mothers. Historically, the Canadian image of Indigenous mothers, motherhood, and mothering has been constructed within the context of control, conquest, possession, and exploitation. These attitudes have evolved along with the evolving relationship of Canadians to the lands and Indigenous territories Canada now resides on.

When Europeans first came to North America, they produced images of Indigenous "mother" to symbolize the bounty and richness they witnessed. These images were informed by an ideology based in White, male-centered Christian fundamentals. Cree/Métis scholar Kim Anderson refers to this time period as "the phase of the great mother, the Indian Queen" (100). Cherokee scholar Rayna Green describes how European arrivals saw Indigenous women of the Americas: "She was the familiar mother-goddess figure—full-bodied, powerful, nurturing but dangerous—embodying the wealth and danger of the New World" (19). Indigenous women came to represent the land, the earth, and the mode to "birthing" a new future for Europeans.

Indigenous women's femininity was manipulated into erotic and promiscuous symbols. She became the icon of virginity waiting to be won and conquered. The equation of Indigenous woman with "virgin land," open to consumption and possession, created a dangerous archetype of Indigenous women's femininity based on profit, violence, and men's pleasure. Sakimay-Saulteaux/Métis scholar Janice Acoose notes that these symbols have worked to inform the Canadian consciousness, leading to

> ...the perpetuation of stereotypic images of Indigenous women as promiscuous, and later as either Indian princesses or easy squaws. Our lives, as Indigenous women, are still constructed within this very male-centred white-european-christian, and now a white-eurocanadian, ideology. This ideology informs Canadian institutions which construct and reproduce stereotypical images of Indigeous women that are based on binary opposites: good and bad. (43).

Indigenous women face images, symbols, and stereotypes that are oversexualized and dangerous to their safety. The impact of this mythology has been damaging to Indigenous mothers in Canada. In her book, *Capturing Women: The Manipulation of Cultural Imagery in Canada's Prairie West*, Sarah Carter argues that the Canadian state promoted images of the "dirty squaw" or "drudge" in the late 1800s (158-193). Carter notes that these negative stereotypes provided justifications for repressive measures against the Indigenous population. As Indigenous peoples were moved or shuffled to new land, women lost their status and role as contributors to their societies, they were cast out. Indigenous mothers and motherhood became a tool to decrease and eventually exterminate the Indigenous population. If Indigenous women gave birth to children of mixed ancestry, they inherited the legal burden of effectively contributing to the killing of their Nations and their grandchildren who would eventually not be allowed to live on their traditional territories (on Reserve). Further, Indigenous women were portrayed as poor parents, making it excusable for the Canadian state to remove their children and place them in residential schools and foster homes, a legacy that has had a negative ripple effect through the generations that followed afterward.

Currently, we are burdened with the oversexualized projections that taint the images of our mothers, sisters, aunties, and grannies. I do not see the faces of the women who raised me in Disney's half-naked animated film, *Pocahontas,* or the in the recently released movie, *The New World* (2005), where Captain John Smith is portrayed as lusting after a very young Pocahontas. I am saddened and sickened that these images continue to be viewed by Canadians. These are not the role models of womanhood and motherhood that I want to see projected of Anishinaabe women. With the *Sisters in Spirit* initiative raising awareness about the many missing Indigenous women who have been killed or are lost across Canada, it angers me that Indigenous women are still trapped by the negative imagery.

Since the arrival of early Europeans in the sixteenth century, Indigenous women have been trapped within a western dichotomous worldview. Indigenous women are either good or bad; virtuous woman or slut; mother or whore. The Euro-Canadian constructed stereotypes of Indigenous women pose a real danger to our safety as Anishinaabe women. In the absence of respect and honour, Indigenous women have been painted as characters: the "mother-goddess," "the Indian Princess," and "easy squaw." In terms of Indigenous feminine identity, these concepts never acknowledge the complex understandings, roles, and responsibilities Indigenous womanhood, motherhood or mothering entails. This legacy of negative imagery continues to interfere with the lives of the many contemporary Anishinaabe women I see around me everyday.

Nurturing Anishinaabe Women

Anishinaabe women have passed down many traditions and knowledge about mothering practices and the actions that lead to motherhood. The significance of birth is celebrated, honoured, and respected. Colonization did much to destroy, damage, and send into hiding, those women's ways of knowing about motherhood. However, many of these traditions still carry on to this day. There are many ceremonies, traditions, and knowledge practices that continue to be used to teach women and girls their responsibilities as women.

Ojibwe Elder Edna Manitowabi interprets the sweat lodge ceremony as a metaphor for birth and mother, as in our birth mothers and our first mother, Mother Earth (Manitowabi, 2004, 2005). She equates the dome-shaped lodge with the womb of Mother Earth or going back into our own mothers' tummies. I feel that the warm atmosphere inside the lodge from the heated grandfathers and grandmothers (rocks) is akin to the energy of the womb. The lodge is dark, hot, and wet just like the womb that the baby is in for nine months. Even if there are other people all around you in the lodge, you feel very much like you are on your own personal journey. When you crawl out on your hands and knees, it is as if you are being born again into the world because you are weak, struggling, and helpless. A sweat lodge ceremony follows a course of events that connects us women back to the significance of birth, creation, and the process of lifegiving.

There are many Anishinaabe teachings around womanhood and the responsibilities that go along with becoming a woman and mother. Menstruation rituals and ceremonies remind women about the importance of motherhood and mothering. Those young women fortunate enough to have parents who support them in the traditional rituals of puberty learn key lessons about the responsibility of being women and men. Young girls are taught how to be a "good" woman. Manitowabi describes the importance of such ceremonies for girls entering into womanhood:

Celebrate that young girl who has just become a woman. That's a gift we are given! Celebrate that first flow, that is like the earth, when she's flowing in the springtime. It's the same thing. That's who we are as women. We all flow. We all bleed, and that's how we bring forth life. That's how we mould and shape life. That first blessing that was given to women is that you open the door and water issues forth. You are able to take that life into your arms, take her to your breast. Celebrate that miracle! (qtd. in Anderson 186)

Through ceremonies like the Berry-Fast (a year long fast from any berries) our Anishinaabe girls or young women are told about the importance of understanding and living the values of *respect, responsibility, reverence,* and *reciprocity.* The foundations of respecting a woman's ability to bring forth life with her body are vested in those four principles values, which are displayed in Diagram 1.

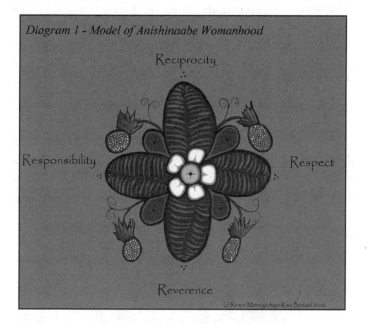

This diagram is a visual representation of my interpretation of an Anishinaabe woman's relationship to her ability to birth life. The diagram is a depiction of a strawberry plant, the heart-shaped fruit referred to in Anishinaabemowin *as Ode'miin,* and means the Creator's "heart" berry. If we open up that strawberry we will see what looks like a circle inside, and that circle represents the cycle of life, such as is the womb inside every Anishinaabe woman. That inner circle of the strawberry is considered sacred, just as the womb is considered a sacred space inside Anishinaabe women. The strawberry helps remind Anishinaabe women to honour their particular abilities to create, and to make the connection to an understanding of their central role in shaping the future of the Anishinaabe Nation. The dots inside the hearts represent the seeds on the strawberry, which ties into the teachings girls and young women receive about the eggs they carry in their wombs. Just as the strawberry loses seeds, women sacrifice an egg every month with each moon. Our roles as women are important to the health and well-being of our families, community, nation, and the world around us.

The four leaves in the diagram form a cross of the four directions and inscribe not only a fundamental image of cosmic order, but teachings about carrying out in our everyday lives those critical values of *reciprocity, respect, reverence,* and *responsibility* as women. Further, the leaves surrounding the berries remind us also that women are surrounded by family, and therefore we are not alone. Every strawberry plant sends out shoots creating more berry plants, however, the roots connect all the relations together to make a strong community of strawberry plants that work together, supporting each other through the root system. Like each berry, each woman is influenced by all their relations: family, clan, community, and nation.

As an Anishinaabe woman, these ceremonies that have been passed down, and in some places revitalized or re-established by women Elders, have continued to shape Anishinaabe women's sense of motherhood and mothering. I see myself becoming a mother in a few years and I am reminded of the importance of these cultural practices and knowledge. When I go out to ceremony or act as auntie to my nephew, I continue to be reminded of my relationship to womanhood, motherhood, and mothering. As an auntie to my three-year-old nephew, I try to fulfill those responsibilities as an Anishinaabe woman, to help him know his identity as an Anishinaabe. My responsibilities of my Anishinaabe womanhood are strengthened and celebrated when I see his little face. It is my responsibility and the responsibility of all Anishinaabe women to prepare the next generation to know our roles as Anishinaabe-kwe (women) and Anishinaabe-nini (men).

Anishinaabe-kwe Ideology of Motherhood

I grew up with a sense of a woman's responsibility for family, friends, and community. It is not just an Anishinaabe woman's responsibility to the children, instead we are raised with the knowledge of a greater responsibility to all our people, both women and men. As Anishinaabe-kwe, as women, we have to acknowledge this responsibility because we are life-givers and the nurturers of the next generation. Nothing is greater than motherhood or mothering. Anishinaabe women have a claim to authority under this ideology, for we not only birth the people, but we also have been given the responsibility of teaching, nurturing, and leading these children in a "good way."

As Anishinaabe women, our first teacher of motherhood and mothering is our first, true mother, Mother Earth. Mother Earth is cherished and honoured because she sustains us with beauty and nourishment. Mother Earth is an enduring and strong force in our lives. Mother Earth continues to be bountiful, sustaining all beings. Despite all the changes that are going on around us, the earth continues to give life. This consistency is a promise to the future, to those yet to be born. She shows generosity by giving and giving to us. She is like our own birth mother. Just as a mother gives birth to a child, Mother Earth nourishes her children, holds her child in her arms. She gives her child a place with her to live, safe and warm. She may give birth to other children, but to all she will give food, care, and a home. To each she gives a portion of herself. To each she assigns a place in her home. No child by virtue of priority of their birth or other attributes may demand more than her brothers or sisters. A mother gives equally amongst her children, from first to last, from strong to weak; makes no difference! All are entitled to a place near her, in her home and heart. Her gift as a mother never diminishes but increases and renews itself. Human beings live but a short time, and then pass on. As Anishinaabe, we are taught that Mother Earth remains whole, indivisible, and enduring into the future. As beneficiaries of their mother's care and love, children are obliged to look after their mother in her illness and decrepitude. Human beings owe our lives and the quality of living and existence to Mother Earth, our true mother, as well as to the mothers or women who raise us, nurture us, and sustain us into the future. As dutiful and loving children, we must honour our mother as we would Mother Earth. Therefore, the first teachings on motherhood relate to this relationship to the land and the life-giving gift given to Anishinaabe women. The ideology of motherhood and mothering begins with our first mother, Mother Earth.

Birthing and childrearing are celebrated as beautiful and cherished gifts from the Creator. The act of birthing and raising children represents a powerful act of survival for the future health and well-being of our Nation. Anderson argues that because of the importance of birthing to Indigenous peoples, motherhood and mothering is a complex web of relationships, which work to provide support and solidarity among women. The Anishinaabe ideology of mothering and motherhood holds that, like Mother Earth, we have a responsibility as women to foster and nurture the next generation and to allow others to assist in this process, such as aunties and grannies.

Some of the most important mothers are women in our families and communities who do not have biological children of their own, but take on the role of aunties, grannies, and even adoptee mothers. One does not have to be biologically related to a child to act as either auntie or grannie. Further, it is very common to adopt in Anishinaabe communities. Many family members often end up adopting other community members, family relations such as nieces, nephews or grandchildren. In Anishinaabe communities, mother, auntie and grannie are fluid and interchangeable roles, not biologically-defined identities. I was surrounded by aunties and older sisters who were all mothers to me. To this day, I still answer to my older sisters like some women answer to their mother. These sister-mother figures watch over me and guide me as my mother did when she was alive. Mothers do not have to just birth you, some take up the mantle of mothering out of sense of responsibility and love.

In order to teach, raise, and nurture, a woman does not have to have children biologically. Women in our families and communities often help raise the children of our sisters and daughters, sometimes even adopting them along the way. Anishinaabe women often hold up the familial structure by making sure that everyone has a place to live, food to eat, and clothes to wear. Being a mother and grandmother is about family, spirituality, and relationships. Being a mother is making sure that everyone will stay together and grow up together. These women are key to educating the next generation, as well as being responsible to the young women and young men who look up to them for guidance. Anderson writes:

> Educating both boys and girl[s] is equally important. Native women educate young women and girls so they can carry on building the nations of the future. Some women are doing this type of educational work as aunties and grannies. They work with traditional teachings and ceremonies to help girls learn self-worth, and self-respect…. Older women take the opportunity to use traditional ceremonies like the berry fasts to help our girls become the strong women that we want them to be in the future. (244)

There are significant differences between literal understandings of motherhood, mothering, and the Anishinaabe ideology of these words. Just as my mother, grannie, aunties, and sisters played an active role in guiding and directing my growth into a woman, I have also been surrounded by women throughout the years that have not been biologically connected to me, but who have nurtured my iden-tity nonetheless. Aboriginal women who have supported me from my community, in school, and the Elders I have met throughout the years have all mothered me. To be a mother, to adopt or to nurture is in my opinion, sacred work.

The Elders speak of *mino-bimaadiziwin*, meaning the "living the good life" as a human being. Motherhood and mothering speak to this philosophy of *mino-bimaadiziwin* because as Anishinaabe women, we are taught to follow a life based on teachings of love, honesty, respect, courage, kindness, wisdom, truth, and bravery, among others. As women, when we give our hearts, support, and knowledge to the birthing, raising, and nurturing of the next generation we begin to fulfill *mino-bimaadiziwin* and walk the good path in life. Our path as Anishinaabe women is to be givers. It is women who give and sustain, like Mother Earth who gives

A Daughter's Love, A Mother's Legacy

I am writing this contribution near Mother's Day and I am reminded of all the Anishinaabe mothers. This contribution was written as a tribute to my own mother who passed away, Shirley Ida Bédard, from Dokis First Nation, Marten Clan, as well as all my Anishinaabe-kwe sisters, aunties, and my grannie. I hope this chapter honours the mothers, aunties, and grannies, as well as celebrates the young girls who will be mothers some day. The knowledge, ideas, and concepts shared that have been presented in this contribution come from my Anishinaabe ancestors, the women in my family, and those women who helped teach me how to be a strong Anishinaabe-kwe. All that I speak of here is practical knowledge for our survival in the twenty-first century as Anishinaabe-kwewag (women). One of the great responsibilities we women have is building and maintaining these values and characteristics of our mothering and motherhood. As women, as mothers, aunties, and grannies, our influence over the family, community or nation determines the well being of the future generations. Gchi-Miigwech!

Renée Elizabeth Mzinegiizhigo-kwe Bédard is Anishinaabe-kwe (Ojibwe), Marten Clan, from Dokis First Nation, along the French River in northern Ontario. Currently, she is a Ph.D. candidate in the Indigenous Studies program at Trent University. As a scholar, painter, and craftswoman, she focuses her writing and art on issues that impact on the lives of Anishinaabe women, specifically their cultural traditions, their knowledge, and their roles and responsibilities as Anishinaabe-kwewag.

References

Acoose, Janice (Misko-Kìsikàwihkwè). *Iskwewak Kah' Ki Yaw Ni Wahkomakanak. Neither Indian Princesses Nor Easy Squaws.* Toronto: Women's Press, 1995.

Anderson, Kim. *A Recognition of Being: Reconstructing Native Womanhood.* Toronto: Second Story Press, 2000.

Carter, Sarah. *Capturing Women: The Manipulation of Cultural Imagery in Canada's Prairie West.* Montreal: McGill-Queen's University Press, 1997.

Green, Rayna. "The Pocahontas Perplex: The Image of the Indian Women in American Culture," *Sweetgrass* (July-August 1984): 17-23.

Manitowabi, Edna. Seminar on Indigenous Knowledge (NAST-410). (Fall/ Winter 2004). Trent University, Peterborough, Ontario, 2004.

Manitowabi, Edna. *Personal Conversation*, October 2005.

Solomon, Art . "The Woman's Part." *Native Woman — "A Voice of Many Nations": Recognizing Our Own.* Ottawa: Native Women's Association of Canada, 1985. ii-iv.

Power Mothering

The Haudenosaunee Model

JAN NOEL

Canadian "maternal feminists" such as Nellie McClung tried to project motherly nurturing and concern for social justice out into the wider world. Their limited success contrasts with that of Haudenosaunee (Iroquois) mothers in eighteenth-century settlements in what are today New York, Quebec, and Ontario. New work by Haudenosaunee and other scholars reasserts the extensive nature of this mothering. This was accompanied by a remarkably equitable distribution of wealth, including food and shelter of which women were the primary providers. Female elders, the clan mothers or gantowisas, carried maternal responsibilities even further. Not confined to the "clearings" of longhouse and surrounding fields, they were involved in choosing and deposing chiefs, in council deliberations and diplomacy.

By extending the concept of mothering to the highest political levels, the Haudenosaunee created an illuminating model of what mothering can mean in a society without patriarchy.

> *Some say, untruthfully, that suffrage for women would destroy the home. It will only destroy the narrowness of the home; it will spread the home spirit until it finds its way into every corner of the world.... Men alone cannot make just laws for men and women, just as any class of people cannot legislate justly for another class....*
> —Nellie McClung (early twentieth century)
> (qtd. in Savage 80-83)

> *It takes a village to raise a child.*
> —Hillary Clinton (late twentieth century) (1)

> *Brother, our ancestors considered it a great offense to reject the counsels of their women, particularly of the female governesses. Who, said our fore-fathers, bring us into being? Who cultivate our lands, kindle our fires and*

76

boil our pots, if not the women? ... They are the life of the nation.
—Oneida Woman's Speaker Agwerondongwas (1788) (qtd. in Beauchamp 1)

It was the custom of our ancestors for the women, by their moderation, to heal up all animosities.
—Mohawk leader Thayendanegea (1802) (qtd. in Beauchamp 44)

The Haudenosaunee, otherwise known as the Iroquois, developed a form of motherhood that other people could only dream of. North American feminists throughout the twentieth century called for better direction of community resources to meet basic human needs of food, clothing, shelter and healthcare. They also called for more involvement by women in the affairs of state. As early Canadian feminist Nellie McClung said, "I am a firm believer in women—in their ability to do things and in their influence and power. Women set the standards of the world, and it is for us ... to set the standards high" (Savage 48). Few would claim though, that feminists who entered the political sphere realized their goals. McClung was bitterly disappointed that enfranchised females failed to transform the system. American Presidential wife Hillary Clinton's efforts a half-century later to reform the American medicare system came to naught, and resentment of her ambitions dogged her subsequent career as Senator from New York. Yet, as some early feminists pointed out, on that same New York soil 200 years earlier, Haudenosaunee clan mothers had spoken up in councils and directed longhouses. The classic formulation is that the "clearings" (the village and outlying fields) were the domain of women, the "forests" (hunting, warfare, external diplomacy) the domain of men. However, recent research on the Haudenosaunee women makes it clearer than ever that some ventured beyond the villages to assume an active role in all levels of politics, diplomacy and warfare of their nation. Theirs was not the familiar "motherhood" we know so well, caring for the young in obscurity while public figures (usually male) decide what small measure of state resources might be directed towards family needs. Records drawn from the mid-seventeenth to the mid-nineteenth century indicate the Haudenosaunee had a profoundly empowered concept of mothering.

An outsider who approaches this topic must do so with caution and respect. It is too easy for a non-Aboriginal feminist historian such as myself to misread or oversimplify situations. There is particular danger when the discussion veers towards concepts of "power," "ownership," and "rights" drawn from European traditions but without precise parallels in Aboriginal ones. The slope is made even more slippery by the fact that interaction with Europeans caused arrangements to change over time, especially in an area so charged with meaning as gender relations. In European eyes, gender relations were hierarchical; dominance was all too often integral to male honour, making a powerful woman a rival to be disarmed. In contrast, there is evidence that the Haudenosaunee, at least as late as the eighteenth century, saw male and female roles in terms of reciprocal relationships that did not require power struggles. The traditional stories avoid western binaries and valorize complex pairings (such as the two successive pairs of females and males responsible for fashioning the earth) and unusual relational lines (especially bonds with maternal aunts and uncles, considered virtual parents in a matriliny). For a non-Aboriginal author to begin to grasp such viewpoints she needs familiarity with Aboriginal worldviews, traditions, and written accounts, and preferably linguistic fluency in the relevant languages. Entirely unable to claim the latter, I can only humbly approach the subject, doing my best to access Aboriginal knowledge and remaining open to suggestion and correction. To this end I have tried to consult as many Aboriginal sources as possible, ranging from colonial voices to current-day feminist Haudenosaunee scholars such as Barbara Alice Mann.

As has often been pointed out, outside observers of Aboriginal societies have always seen what they were prepared to see, influenced by goals that were sometimes imperialist, sometimes concerned with reforming their home societies. No one is immune to misperceptions, since there is no "view from nowhere," no completely "accurate" view of Iroquoia. Some question whether a unitary view is even a worthwhile goal. However, if one believes some conceptions do approach past realities more closely than others, one might also believe something happened to the western imagination in the last half century to draw us a little closer to Haudenosaunee notions. There are grounds for believing that western society has been moving, of late, towards an ability to conceive of both gender equality and a more respectful approach to the natural environment.

Non-Aboriginal writers have long disagreed about the extent of Iroquoian women's powers. In the eighteenth century the Jesuit Joseph-Francois Lafitau identified a matriarchy while fellow Jesuit Pierre F. X. Charlevoix thought some female councillors were just figureheads, kept in the dark about key issues. Nineteenth-century ethnographers, of whom the best known is Lewis H. Morgan, were generally struck by women's unusual authority, but they disagreed (in Morgan's case, even within his own body of work) on how extensive it was. In the 1970s, ethnographer Elizabeth Tooker's[1] all-too-popular debunking of the value of female agriculture, property rights, and political roles contrasted with later, somewhat perfunctory acceptance of those powers by scholar Daniel Richter (2001, 1992); and, at the turn of twenty-first century, full acknowledgement of them by anthropologist Roland Viau.[2] We begin the present analysis by accepting as fundamentally true the numerous reports over the centuries that, at least as late as the eighteenth century, Haudenosaunee mothers and grandmothers had unusual powers. Our own quest is twofold. First, we want to summarize the most reliable information we can find about the precise *ways* this group of Aboriginal mothers was empowered. Secondly, in this rare instance when mothers were able to shape the nation, what kind of nation resulted from it?

The position of mature Iroquois women (who were typically mothers or grandmothers) *was* highly unusual. Their formal powers were outlined in Aboriginal writings collected throughout the nineteenth century in early field studies such as those of Ely and Arthur Parker, Henry Schoolcraft, Lewis H. Morgan, Seth Newhouse and others. Fairly extensive powers were recorded, despite their erosion through more than two centuries of contact with surrounding North American patriarchial cultures. Fortunately there are also oral traditions and (our focus here) numerous written sources from the seventeenth and eighteenth centuries when the Five Nations flourished in their settlements in present-day New York, Quebec and (after 1784) Ontario. Up until the American Revolution, the Haudenosaunee were a formidable people, courted by colonial powers in search of trade and military alliances. A trove of information about them was left by explorers, missionaries, colonial officials, and travellers. One of the most knowledgeable commentators was early eighteenth century Jesuit missionary Joseph-Francois Lafitau, who lived for five years among the Iroquois at the mission outside Montreal now known as Kahnawahke. While not of course in a pre-contact state, these key military allies of the French retained considerable cultural autonomy. Lafitau supplemented his own observations with those of earlier missionaries and reports of pre-contact practices. The result was a thousand page ethnographic study. Lafitau's familiar summation is a foundational text for all subsequent scholars of Haudenosaunee gender. It attests female *hegemony* in so many specific areas, and stands in such startling contrast to what we understand about women in most societies, that it bears repeating:

> Nothing is more real than this superiority of the women. It is of them that the nation really consists; and it is through them that the nobility of the blood, the genealogical tree and the families are perpetuated. All real authority is vested in them. The land, the fields and their harvest all belong to them. They are the souls of the Councils, the arbiters of peace and of war. They have charge of the public treasury. To them are given the slaves. They arrange marriages. The children are their domain, and it is through their blood that the order of succession is transmitted. (I, 66-7)

Two recent full-length books on Haudenosaunee women offer considerable support for Lafitau's astonishing claims. An extensively researched work published in 2000 by Haudenosaunee scholar Barbara Alice Mann, *Iroquoian Women: The*

Gantowisas analyzes four centuries of Euro-american and Aboriginal source material, including Iroquoian "tellings" including "women's tellings," often drawn from nineteenth and twentieth century writings from elders and Aboriginal ethnographers. One might be tempted to believe Mann supports Lafitau's portrayal of a matriarchy, since she too assigns women superiority at councils as well as in the longhouse. However, Mann never employs the terms such as gynocracy[3] and Empire of Women that are found in Lafitau. She claims the Iroquois mindset rejects the kind of binary thinking that assumes one sex or the other must prevail. Another important voice on this question is that of award-winning Université de Montréal anthropologist Roland Viau, whose *Femmes de Personne: Sexes, genres et pouvoirs en Iroquoisie ancienne* reaffirms the highly un-usual position of Haudenosaunee mothers. The primacy of Sky Woman in the Iroquoian creation myth, the religious celebration of the Three Sisters (the beans, corn and squash which women cultivated), the frequency of marriages in which brides were older than grooms, and the preference for female infants all attest to women's status. So unusual was the gender balance that Viau singles out Iroquoia as "the human society which, from an anthropological point of view, appears to have come the closest to the definition of a matriarchy" (108). But gender mastery was not an issue. There was, Viau believes, a rough equality of the sexes, with power not decided along gender lines at all. Since it was *elders* of both sexes who held the most authority, Viau believes the society is most accurately seen as a gerontocracy.[4] Probably Lafitau went too far in attributing "all real authority" to women, given that male chiefs and elders (likely underrepresented in Lafitau's Kahnawake village)[5] played key roles too. In the same vein it seems too strong to claim that clan mothers alone were "the arbiters of peace and war." Our goal is to analyze Haudenosaunee mothering in a way that acknowledges its importance but avoids any triumphialism: there was no battle of the sexes, and neither sex "won." In some senses, as we shall see, *everybody* won.

Mother as Empowered Parent

In village and longhouse settings, the mother was clearly the most powerful parent. Haudenosaunee villages housed from about a hundred to as many as a two thousand people. The people were monogamous, although some polyandry was practiced among the Seneca. Pre-marital chastity was not expected of either sex. Older women often arranged marriages of their young, to which the latter generally assented. Unsuccessful marriages could be ended relatively easily by either spouse, but apparently social pressure weighed against it. Though there was some variation, new husbands seem generally to have moved into the wife's longhouse. Multiple families (typically 25-60 people) grouped around the fires were related though the maternal line. "Mother" was the highest term in a lineage, and names, titles, longhouses and most of their contents were transmitted through the maternal line. Of particular significance were female rights to the cache of goods or "treasury," which expanded greatly at harvest time when maize and produce of all kinds were crammed into the longhouses along with the dried meat and fish, furs, and wampum belts stored there in casks or pits. Iroquois women, as Judith K. Brown observed, controlled food distribution, allowing them to exert considerable control over daily life, including denial of shelter to husbands who did not bring in products of the hunt, or otherwise caused offense (Reverend Ashur Wright cited by Morgan 18).[6]

What about children? Male and female children were considered to belong to the mother; if a marriage ended, they stayed with her. French sources reported very tender mother-child relations in which errant children were never struck (though they were sometimes splashed with water). Nurturing is evident in reports of children being trained to carry little bundles of sticks and fetch small vessels of water from the river, and in archeological evidence of games and of toy "practice pots" likely made under the indulgent tutelage of female kin.

Mother as Farmer and Guardian of Land

Women were the chief horticulturalists among the Haudenosaunee, and the maize they grew is estimated to have supplied about 65 per cent of the diet (Delage 50).[7] The earth's bounty itself was traced to a woman. Sky Woman's daughter was said to lie buried just beneath the soil, and tobacco grew from her head, corn from her breasts, squash from her abdomen, beans from her fingers, potatoes from her toes. Women worked in teams under supervision of an older kinswoman, taking children and captives to the fields to help. Seneca adoptee Mary Jemison reported that this self-directed fieldwork was not particularly arduous (Seaver). Even frail Grannies found a niche, sitting on platforms in the fields to scare off crows and animal predators.

There is much support for the tradition that women not only tilled the soil but were its owners or guardians. For example, Seneca women asserted to a United States agent in 1791 that "we are the owners of this land, and it is ours. It is we who plant it for our and their use" (Carr 19). In the "Constitution of the Five Nations," transcribed by Seneca scholar Arthur Parker in 1910 from documents and wampum belts at the reserve near Brantford, Ontario, provision 44 states that, "Women shall be considered the progenitors of the Nation. They shall own the land and the soil" (42). Doctoral research done by Trent University Aboriginal scholar Susan Hill affirms the concept of women as guardians of the soil is reflected in council records from the Ontario Haudenosaunee during the eighteenth and nineteenth centuries.[8] The contention of Lafitau and many other sources, that lands and harvests belonged to women, seems correct.

Clan Mothers in Political Roles

The oldest woman in a maternal lineage, who typically would have been a grandmother, served as clan mother or matron. Alongside the hereditary aspect there was room for merit. A matron might resign due to age or illness in favour of an unusually able kinswoman, not necessarily the eldest daughter. The office was important, for it bestowed the right to choose various kinds of chiefs[9] as well as to depose or "dehorn" chiefs who ignored a twice-repeated warning that they were thought to be misusing their office. The women in a matrilinage could convene their own councils, which might then raise an issue with the whole village or with the tribal council, for possible referral to the grand council of all the chiefs of the Confederacy. All political powers, male and female, were based on expectations of extensive consultation and allowance for dissenters. There was a search for consensus in lieu of votes or ultimatums, and a tendency to postpone decisions until general agreement was reached. These flexible arrangements make comparison with modern states difficult. However, there is no question that the voices of mothers and grandmothers were built into the political structures of the Haudenosaunee.

Many observers noted women's political prominence. Marie de l'Incarnation, Ursuline Superior at Quebec, a woman of no small clout herself, was intrigued by the "capitainesses" who, she recorded, "have a deliberative voice at the councils, who reach conclusions as the men do, they even selected the first ambassadors who made peace with the French (in 1653)."[10] To this Lafitau added that women stood up at Council meetings and decided whether or not war would be waged. Father Claude Dablon recorded in the late seventeenth century that Mohawk matrons "are greatly respected; they hold council, and the Elders decide no affair of consequence without their opinion" (cited in Viau 93). An account apparently written by veteran missionary Pierre Millet reveals the great secrecy that surrounded Councils of Elders, councils in which he said women and men exercised the same powers (Viau 93-4).[11] Mid-eighteenth century French commanders and agents also observed the importance of Iroquois women at councils and in choosing a clan's civil and spiritual leaders. Adopted Mohawk John Norton indicated that at the Grand River settlement women attended the chiefs' council fire and were entitled to speak there (cited in Johnston 28-29). A number of ethnographers from Schoolcraft and Morgan onward, noted unusual female prerogatives of one form or another. For example, the early twentieth century scholar Lucien Carr reported to the Peabody Museum the pre-eminence of women not only domestically but "also around the council fire ... her influence was absolutely paramount..." while the Men's Grand Council "acted as attorneys for the women rather than independently and of their own volition" (Carr 13, 30).[12]

In sum, there was wide acknowledgement that matrons had power to select and depose peace chiefs, and to deliberate both in councils of their own and in councils with male chiefs and elders.

This idea is reaffirmed in the new monographs on Haudenosaunee women. Barbara Alice Mann observes that despite all the evidence, there have always been people who just could not conceive of women actually determining council decisions and questions relating to war. Notwithstanding the numerous primary sources attesting these motherly and grandmotherly offices, "academic discussions of the League as a political entity almost exclusively concentrate on the men's Grand Council. The contrapuntal Clan Mothers' councils are studiously ignored, not because they were unimportant to the League ... but because western scholars are following the prescriptions of male dominance so central to European political history" (Mann 117).[13] Sceptics can find some support for their views in the sources; some colonial witnesses spoke of women being present at various trade and political delegations but staying in the background, or being kept there by proprietorial husbands. Mann sees this as a misreading based on the political marginality and confinement of women in their own patriarchal culture. They did not understand that Haudenosaunee etiquette required a woman's council to delegate a male speaker to address men, just as men's councils would delegate a female speaker to address women. Since the European delegates were male, they were always addressed by one of their own sex, sometimes through a formal male Woman's Speaker, who dressed in a skirt and carried a corn pounder, in order to convey the wishes of the Women's Council. Indeed it was carried on to the extent that in one whole nation, the Lenape (Delaware), the men were chosen to wear skirts and take on the function of representing the women's council. Mann claims that the Lenape considered this feminization an honour, until westerners "enlightened" them that it was not.[14] Not labouring under such prejudices, Roland Viau identifies some eleven terms used by seventeenth-and eighteenth-century European observers to indicate Iroquoian female leaders, terms such as "femme considerable", "matrone," "captainesse," and "dame du conseil" and "femme de qualité." Writing in the wake of four decades when feminism had a major political impact, scholars are tending to remove the last logjams obscuring our view of one of the best-documented non-patriarchal societies in the human past.

Participation of Mothers in War and Diplomacy

In thinking about female powers, it is important to acknowledge a sphere that extended beyond the village clearings. Women bent on various missions appear in colonial records. For example, at her Quebec convent Marie de l'Incarnation parlayed with a female chief who came with other ambassadors from the Seneca. Dutch New Yorker Harmen van den Bogaert encountered three women, probably

Oneida, who had journeyed six days to sell salmon and tobacco to the Mohawks. The ledger book of Albany merchant Robert Sanders named Kahnawake women who regularly brought furs along an 800-kilometre circuit from Canada. Young Konwatsi'tsiaenni (Molly Brant) apparently accompanied a party of New York Iroquois negotiators travelling to Philadelphia (Marshall 216-17, 222-23; Gehring and Starna 6; Library and Archives Canada; *Dictionary of Canadian Biography* IV).

Those were not isolated cases. Whatever traditional association there may have been of male initiative in forest activities and female initiative in the clearings, it did not confine even the more ordinary kinds of wives and mothers. Though Iroquois men roamed afar for war, hunting and trade, women too were regular denizens of the forest, from which they derived much of their livelihood. They foraged for spruce and maple sap, medicinal plants, nuts, as well as berries, mushrooms, firewood and small game. There are numerous reports of their trading, fishing, hunting trips (including those of "temporary wives" whose work was essential in processing and transporting game). Whole families travelled with diplomatic parties to strengthen their negotiators' positions by the presence of a crowd.[15] Women accompanied some war parties as well, serving as provisioners and exhorting the men to bravery. Both youths and older men fought harder, according to adopted Mohawk John Norton, when the women were present.[16] When Haudenosaunee women discussed policy, they did it with firsthand experience of distant forests, foreign peoples, and the gore of battle.

Providing goods and services in villages was another integral aspect of statecraft. This lay mainly in the hands of mothers. The League of Five (later Six) Nations rested on good communications, including trained relay runners who (according to Morgan) could transmit information a hundred miles a day. Hospitality was essential to maintaining such a system. Runners and diplomats, traders and warriors too, could count on food, shelter and other necessities being supplied to them by the longhouse matrons. Travelling clan members knew to head to a longhouse marked with the animal emblem of their clan. The matrons also made decisions about whether, and how, dried corn and moccasins would be used to provision war parties. As controllers of the stored goods, they made decisions about the "gifting" that constituted diplomacy with other nations. Matrons had an impact too, when they forbade male relatives to go to war, and chiefs would enlist their help in curbing the overzealous. Did women's creation of wampum belts that served as historical and treaty records perhaps offer opportunities to shape that process too? Lest it be thought they were always an influence for peace, let us note that women presented wampum strings to warriors outside their kin group as an invitation to go to war to secure prisoners to replace fallen relatives.

A further aspect of war and diplomacy was assimilation of enemies. Haudenosaunee men were renowned warriors, and in the seventeenth century the original villagers were sometimes outnumbered by captives from many nations.

This was important, because early in that century European epidemics had reduced the Five Nations population by perhaps one-half. It was women who decided the fate of all these newcomers, the choice whether to kill captives or (more commonly) to keep them as slaves or adoptees being their prerogative. This made sense because women were considered the givers of life, and they were the ones who would supervise the newcomers in longhouses and fields.

The Mothered Community

Along with the economic and political roles women held, unusual social practices complete the picture of empowered motherhood. The frequency of older brides/ younger grooms and the existence of polyandry among one Iroquoian nation (the Seneca) affirm Viau's contention that "Iroquoian societies were strongly feminine. Their regime of maternal rights indicates as clearly as can be that in their social formations, authority did not necessarily belong to men" (243). Men certainly occupied esteemed positions as chiefs, councillors, warriors, and hunters; but these were not seen as being more important than the positions women occupied. Not all was rosy here: both sexes shared also in activities that were clearly *un*delightful, such as instigation of warfare and torture of prisoners. What is refreshingly different is the way relations between the sexes do not seem to have been founded on exploitation or dependence. In this case, neither sex commanded the other. Once one accepts that Haudenosaunee society was not patriarchal, one can begin to perceive an alternative vision of human relations. One sees unfamiliar kinds of bonds between children and uncles, siblings, twinned pairs that rest on neither hierarchy nor rivalry; one gets a little closer to non-western forms of responsibility. One catches a glimpse (is our civilization yet ready to believe it?) of resentment-free respect by males of female authority, indeed of *mutual* respect and a culture based on sharing, though it necessarily sounds utopian to our jaded minds. On that subject, Barbara Alice Mann's aboriginal sarcasm holds a pithy truth at its core:

> [Some] posit…the way things fell out historically in Europe as *The Only Possible Path of History Given Human Nature*. Capitalism, they argue (as Marxism argued before them), is the inevitable next stage of economic history. Scarcity just happens. So does inequality..… Greed may appear inborn to a materialistic culture, with its created scarcities and carefully crafted inequities, but only because bully-boy economics are allowed to ride roughshod over all else. It is not incidental that the roots of European economics stretch back to a warlord system of plunder run by heavily armed young men whose levels of testosterone vastly exceeded their levels of maturity. In the final analysis, capitalism is nothing more than a sophisticated expression of a pubescent boy's explanation of the uni-

verse: Mine's bigger; I get yours.

...Among the Iroquois, half-grown men were subject to their grandparents, male and female elders who had the wisdom and experience to
lift their eyes beyond self-aggrandizement to the welfare of the whole
community. Grandmother was high on the list of public officials to
whom youth was required to defer.... (Mann 231)[17]

This latter point is not fantasy; a scholarly biography of eighteenth-century
Mohawk Loyalist Konwatsi'tsiaenni (Molly Brant) for example, reveals she was
"head of a society of Six Nations matrons which was particularly influential among
the young warriors,"[18] and British and American officials on three different
occasions attested that she was able to direct the wartime conduct of such men.
Such political power had spiritual underpinnings: young men learned about Sky
Woman (not "Adam") as the first human, gazed up and saw Grandmother Moon
where neighbouring settlers saw the Man in the Moon. Iroquois youths heeded
shamans and healers who could be either female or male, wore masks to
impersonate Husk Face Women, attended ceremonies organized around female
activities such as berry harvests, female deities such as the Three Sisters.

What kind of conduct did "grandmother" decree? Some scholars, influenced by
late twentieth century ecological awareness, have shown an ability to appreciate the
ways in which non-Aboriginal societies could be less grasping and more in
harmony with nature in ways that surprised newcomers. Placing new trade goods
in graves to accompany the dead to the spirit world (where it was thought such
novelties were scarce) suggests spiritual concerns outweighed acquisitiveness for
the here and now. Denys Delage in *Bitter Feast: Amerindians and Europeans in
Eastern North America* argues that Iroquoians lived in greater harmony (in terms
of human relations *and* the environment) than Europeans did. Delage quotes
missionaries who were struck that "a whole village must be without corn, before
any individual can be obliged to endure privation. They divide the produce of their
fishery equally with all who come;" that "It is wonderful how well they agree
among themselves (no one displaying) ... an imperious or dictatorial manner. If
so many families were together in our France, there would be nothing but disputes,
quarrels and revilings."[19] Delage also stresses the ability of Amerindian societies to
sustain ecological balance for thousands of years. Europeans arrived and all too
quickly reaped their harvest, soon depleting the fertile soil and virgin timber, the
teeming fish and game. The physical stature and strength of Iroquoians that so
impressed Europeans was a function of both the women's unusually high-yield
agriculture and their redistribution systems that left no one hungry. The code of
hospitality was so clear on the latter point that a hungry person, after announcing
the intention, was entitled to take food from another person's field. (This was at
a time when stealing another person's pig could result in a death sentence under

English Common law). Delage's work reaffirms how radically successful Iroquoian society was in terms of providing and distributing nourishment. The full-length studies of Haudenosaunee women published at the dawn of the twenty-first century by Viau and Mann affirm that they were indeed, as Lafitau and a number of other observers had recorded, the authorities over the longhouses, children, marriages, and slaves. They did in fact control lands, fields and harvests and did speak up on matters of state. Scholars such as Delage help us appreciate the remarkable ecological balance that accompanied the remarkable gender balance.

Conclusion

We have seen that recent Aboriginal and non-Aboriginal scholarship affirms (old but contested) notions about Haudenosaunee mothers and grandmothers. Indeed, post-1960 movements advancing feminist, native, and ecological viewpoints permit a view of Iroquoian women that is surely closer to the truth than views that could not imagine women anywhere but in the shadow of males, tied by their apron strings to the "clearings." What Roland Viau called a "strongly feminine" culture shines through in the fact that both father and mother were considered to be pregnant and needing to take special precautions when a child was on its way. It shines through too, in the inauguration ceremony exhorting the federal chief to govern with special care for "the children who, running to and fro, sport around him" as well as the children who are creeping, the children in cradle boards and finally, "even those unborn children who, with faces turned this way, are on their way hither below the surface of the earth" (Hewitt 67). How different things would be if governments everywhere made tiny citizens, and future generations, their foremost concern! Among the Haudenosaunee or Iroquois, we have seen that, first of all, mothers did hold a very unusual degree of authority; secondly, they oversaw practices that were both egalitarian and ecologically sustainable. Even *before* the Europeans arrived, this was no utopia; but the accomplishments were impressive. Men apparently formed intense and loyal friendships among themselves,[20] and women intensely loved their children. Festivals, preparation of fields, harvesting of fish and crops, and fall hunting brought men and women together for happily remembered events that doubtless included courting. Putting all these elements together, one perceives a social system shaped by empowered mothers that was highly successful in producing and distributing the necessities of life.

This situation contrasts with the ill-fated attempts of North American feminists to project motherly nurturing and concern for social justice into public affairs; despite some successes, they were unable to remove the onus on the young to adopt competitive, patriarchal values if they pursued ambitions in the wider world. In contrast, the extensive powers of Haudenosaunee mothers and grandmothers allow us to appreciate the full potential of "mothering," to see a society that was constructed around the concept of nurturing, around responsibilities rather than rights, around political direction by both male and female elders. Matrilineal and matrilocal customs, control of longhouses and children, and guardianship of land and agricultural production buttressed female authority in the villages. A growing body of contemporary scholarship affirms eighteenth-century sources claiming that matrons shaped the "public", political life of their people. Placed in the hands of those responsible for daily nurturing, the distribution of essential resources of food, shelter and clothing was accomplished in a remarkably equitable manner. Out beyond the villages, clan mothers and many a more ordinary mother too, travelled extensively. Respected grandmothers served as elders, council members, religious figures and diplomats, just as grandfathers did. Haudenosaunee motherhood provides a model of which many have dreamed but few have attained. It allows us to see how powerful "mothering" can be in a society that is not patriarchal.

Jan Noel teaches Canadian History and Gender Studies at the University of Toronto at Mississauga. She won the Canadian Historical Association's Macdonald Prize for her book Canada Dry: Temperance Crusades before Confederation. *She is currently completing a study of the gantowisas and a book about women in early French Canada.*

[1]Elisabeth Tooker's "Women in Iroquois Society" was first delivered as a conference paper in 1975. Some have had difficulty conceiving of Iroquoian matrons as anything other than thoroughly marginalized and deeply domestic. Eighteenth-century traveller Father Pierre-Francois-Xavier de Charlevoix recorded being told by veteran missionaries that women had the chief authority in this group, that the male chiefs "are no more than their lieutenants." However, he could not resist editorializing: "They have indeed assured me that the women deliberate first on what will be proposed to Council, and that they then give their conclusions to the Chiefs, who report it to the General Council of Elders; but it certainly looks as though all that is for the sake of form and with restrictions...." For close analysis of these and other views of Charlevoix, see Viau (94-95).

Evincing similar scepticism was Tooker, who wrote:

> Council meetings were the work of men, and council decisions the work of men, not women—no matter how interested women might be in them. Men were the orators.... Women could, of course, and did attempt to influence the opinion of men. (One suspects women have always and everywhere tried to defend their own interests in ways that they could, as men have also attempted to defend their own interests.)

This is attested by occasional references in the literature to women advising chiefs and to particular men being asked to speak for women … taken to mean that women wielded considerable political power. Such an interpretation is usually not applied to comparable kinds of indirect influence women exerted in, say, nineteenth-century England or America…. (203)

The argument is the essentialist one that women are all pretty much the same; that what happened in nineteenth-century England and America represented a timeless reality for women across cultures and millennia: the best women can do is work behind the scenes. This ignores the fact that Iroquoian women had formal power to choose and depose chiefs, to serve on the Women's Council, and worked alongside men as shamans and in the Council of Elders. On the economic front, after conceding the women grew "a monotonous but balanced" diet, the men's viands leap in Tooker's article from being of "more than casual interest" to being (no evidence given) "as significant or almost as significant as that of the women" (206). In the same vein, women's ownership-through use of longhouses, fields, and tools is downplayed as property that "lacked durability and hence great economic worth" (Tooker 206)—factors of little consideration to someone hungry or seeking shelter in February!

Domestic stereotypes have enjoyed a long life, so much so that Tooker's essay was still reprinted without comment or counterweight in a 1995 collection of articles about women's history, *Canadian Women: A Reader* (Mitchinson *et al.*). That said something about the dearth of scholarship on a subject of primary significance to anyone interested in gender. In the wake of Morgan's influential nineteenth century work, there have been short studies and articles discussing the unusual powers of Iroquois women by scholars such as J. N. B. Hewitt, Cara Richards, and Nancy Bonvillain and in 1990, W. G.Spittal's important edited collection of essays on the subject. However, some leading scholars (especially Tooker) recoiled at assertions of Iroquoian powers when they were articulated by a new generation of scholars influenced by feminism, particularly at the powerful analysis Judith K. Brown published in *Ethnohistory* in 1970. Another strategy was simply to ignore the issue and discuss the men as the political actors. Francis Jennings' various works, that did so much to advance understanding of Iroquois diplomacy, was struck by the fact that female metaphors were not pejorative in that society; but he himself had little to say about its female half. Dean Snow's 1994 *The Iroquois* had a promising heading: "The Role of Women in the League." The section turned out to consist of *one paragraph!* A leading Iroquoianist, Daniel Richter, in his 1992 *Ordeal of the Longhouse,* conceded that "the workings of female clans and village councils" had been ignored by European observers, and he acknowledged considerable political influence of women as documented by early observers. But he did not return to the subject in his 2001 *Facing East from Indian Country*, though the primary sources include numerous recorded forest activities and travels of Haudenosaunee women.

[2]Viau deems ancient Iroquoia "la société humaine qui, du point de vue de l'anthropologie, paraitra avoir été la plus proche de la définition du matiarchat." This position makes his parody of Judith K. Brown and other feminist writers (52-3), some of whom make lesser claims for feminine power than he does, gratuitous.

[3]"Gynocracy" was also a term used by mid-nineteenth century scholar Lewis H.Morgan, rather surprisingly in view of the somewhat lesser (and inconsistent) evaluation Morgan made of the status of Haudenosaunee women.

[4]Viau notes a gerontocracy. He also considers male and female roles "relatively egalitarian despite a rigid division of tasks." Viau believes female powers expanded in the period after 1650 and remained strong until about 1850, a view shared by some other scholars including Cara Richards (reprinted in the Spittal collection). Some of the newer archeological evidence suggests a growth in matrilocality over time (see Engelbrecht 85-6). One theory is that men's deaths and absences in the context of colonial trade and warfare left village governance increasingly in the hands of women. However, the argument rests largely on negative evidence, the fact that the few early seventeenth-century accounts we possess have little to say about female powers. Those sources have the additional shortcoming that they usually deal with the related Wendat (Hurons), not with the Haudenosaunee (Five Nations) among whom women's powers were most striking. Regardless of whether female authority remained constant or expanded somewhat after contact, what ones sees in the seventeenth- and eighteenth century-records is clearly an astonishing departure from familiar patriarchal practices. Long-established pre-contact oral and religious traditions that placed women on at least a par with men in creation and other stories and in the ceremonial cycle suggest their high status was not a sudden or drastic innovation after 1600.

[5]The French regularly recruited them for war parties; many of the men there also joined long trading expeditions.

[6]Adopted Mohawk John Norton's eighteenth-century account also supports this idea, see Johnston (30).

[7]The book is a translation of Delage's *Le pays renversé* (Montreal: Boreal, 1985). On nutrition see also Richter (2001: 55-56).

[8]Chapter Four discusses women.

[9]A key function of a chief was to make decisions regarding war, peace and intertribal agreements. J. N. B. Hewitt reporting in 1932 to the Smithsonian Institute, distinguished between tribal and federal chiefs. Morgan, for example, refers to sachems and their assistants. A matron would consult with the other women in the clan and submit her choice to the council, which generally accepted it. Hewitt also refers, rather idiosyncratically, to one or more ohwachira (people

tracing descent from a common mother; perhaps the equivalent of what Morgan and Carr call a "gens"). Mothers and adult females of the ohwachira gave their consent to actions the ohwachira took, but its male warriors might be consulted too. The governing body had about 49 male members and 49 female ones. Hewitt (who provides extensive and specific detail, but little documentation) insists on female primacy in the political structure. He also speaks of the decision making powers of female "federal trustees" and male "federal chieftains." The most convenient place to access a variety of useful writers on the subject of political powers is the Spittal collection, which reprints important studies by William Beauchamp, Lucien Carr, J. N. B. Hewitt, Ann Shafer and Judith K. Brown.

[10]One version of Marie de l'Incarnation's statement appears in Marshall (216-17). On the Onondaga woman Teotonharason, who was reputed to be noble, wealthy and highly esteemed, *and* went with her people's ambassadors to Quebec with some of her slaves, see Beauchamp (43).

[11]Along these lines, the dearth of observations about the manufacture of pottery strengthens the case that male outsiders simply failed to perceive important female activities.

[12]Parker's "Constitution of the Five Nations" also alludes to equal female and male rights in clan council (55).

[13]Mann does note exceptions such as Paul Wallace, Nancy Bonvillain, Renée Jacobs and Roger Keesing (see pp. 121-4). One of Mann's examples of the obscuring of female actions is New France Governor Denonville's humiliating defeat in 1687-90. Although French Canadian sources speak of this as a defeat at the hands of "the Iroquois," Mann cites Haudenosaunee commemoration of this as a French defeat by a great female chief, the *Jigonsaseh*—a topic that warrants fuller investigation.

[14]The same line of thinking might lead to reassessing that when Iroquoians called Europeans "women," this was not the insult that European ears heard, but a more neutral remark about assuming a role usually assigned to members of the other sex. On the Lenape, see Caffrey.

[15]As Daniel Richter noted, the "same women who cultivated the fields also collected wild plants from far-flung locations"; and treaty councils "typically ... attracted dozens if not hundreds of men, women and children"(2001: 57, 139). For a long list of forest tasks of women, see Viau (174-7).

[16]Eighteenth-century adopted Mohawk John Norton described the impact of women on war parties (cited in Johnston 33).

[17]Certain flaws weaken Mann's enlightening text, for example a mistranslation of women having *beaucoup d'autorité* as women having a *surfeit* of authority.

[18]"Konwatsi'tsiaenni" (Mary Brant) (see *DCB IV*).

[19]See Thwaites 271-3 (Father Rageneau on the Iroquois) and Delage 67 (Father Le Jeune on the Huron)

Jan Noel

[20]See Spittal (121, note 38) for a discussion of this.

References

Beauchamp, William. "Iroquois Women." *Iroquois Women: An Anthology.* Ed. W. G. Spittal. Ohsweken, ON: Iroqrafts, 1990. 38-50.

Bonvillain, Nancy. *Studies on Iroquoian Culture.* Rindge, NH: Department of Anthropology, Franklin Pearce College, 1980.

Brown, Judith K. "Economic Organization and the Position of Women Among the Iroquois." *Ethnohistory* 17 (1970): 151-67.

Caffrey, Margaret M. "Complementary Power: Men and Women of the Lenni Lenape." *American Indian Quarterly* 24 (2000): 44-63.

Carr, Lucien. "On the Social and Political Position of Women among the Huron-Iroquois Tribes." *Iroquois Women: An Anthology.* Ed. W. G. Spittal. Ohsweken, ON: Iroqrafts, 1990. 9-37.

Charlevoix, Pierre F. X. *Journal d'un voyage fait par order du roi dans l'Amerique septentrionale.* Ed. Pierre Berthiaume. Montreal: Press de l'Université de Montréal, 1761. 2 vols.

Clinton, Hilary. *It Takes a Village.* New York: Touchstone, 1996.

Delage, Denys. *Bitter Feast: Amerindians and Europeans in Eastern North America.* Vancouver: University of British Columbia Press, 1993.

Dictionary of Canadian Biography IV (DCB IV). Toronto: University of Toronto Press, 1979.

Engelbrecht, William. *Iroquoia: The Development of a Native World.* Syracuse, University of Syracuse Press, 2003.

Gehring, Charles and William Starna, *A Journey into Mohawk and Oneida Country, 1634-1635: The Journal of Harmen Meyndertsz van den Bogaert.* Syracuse: Syracuse University Press, 1988.

Hewitt, J. N. B. "Status of Woman in Iroquois Polity Before 1784." *Iroquois Women: An Anthology.* Ed. W. G. Spittal. Ohsweken, ON: Iroqrafts, 1990. 53-70.

Hill, Susan. "The Clay We Are Made Of: An Examination of Haudenosaunee Land Tenure on the Grand River Territory." Unpublished dissertation. Trent University, 2005.

Jennings, Francis. *The Ambiguous Iroquois Empire: The Covenant Chain Confederation of Indian Tribes with English Colonies from its Beginnings to the Lancaster Treaty of 1744.* New York: Norton, 1984.

Johnston, Charles. *The Valley of the Six Nations.* Toronto: Champlain Society Publications, University of Toronto Press, 1965.

Lafitau, Joseph-Francois. *Moeurs des sauvages Ameriquains comparées aux moeurs des premieres temps.* Paris: Saugrain, 1724.

Library and Archives Canada. "Konwatsi'tsiaenni (Mary Brant)." *Robert Sanders Letterbook Manuscript.*

Mann, Barbara Alice. *Iroquoian Women: The Gantowisas.* New York, Peter Lang, 2000.

Marshall, Joyce, ed, *Word from New France: Selected Letters of Marie de l'Incarnation.* Toronto: Oxford University Press, 1967.

Mitchinson, Wendy, Paul Bourne, Alison Prentice, Gail Cuthbert Brandt, Beth Light and Naomi Black, eds. *Canadian Women: A Reader.* Toronto: Prentice Hall, 1996.

Morgan, Lewis H. *League of the Haudenosaunee.* Rochester: Sage, 1851.

Parker, Arthur C. "The Constitution of the Five Nations, or The Iroquois Book of the Great Law." *Parker on the Iroquois.* Ed. William Fenton. Syracuse: Syracuse University Press, 1968. 7-60.

Richards, Cara. "Matriarchy or Mistake: The Role of Iroquois Women Through Time." *Iroquois Women: An Anthology.* Ed. W. G. Spittal. Ohsweken, ON: Iroqrafts, 1990. 9-37.

Richter, Daniel. *Facing East from Indian Country.* Cambridge: Harvard Univeristy Press, 2001.

Richter, Daniel. *The Ordeal of the Longhouse.* Chapel Hill: University of North Carolina Press, 1992.

Rodham, Hillary Clinton. *It Takes a Village.* Darby, PA: DIANE Publishing, 1996.

Savage, Candace, ed. *Our Nell: A Scrapbook Biography of Nellie L. McClung.* Saskatoon: Western Producer Prairie Books, 1979.

Seaver, James E. *Life of Mary Jemison: Dehewamis.* Buffalo: Matthews and Bryant, 1880.

Shafer, Ann E. "The Status of Iroquois Women." *Iroquois Women: An Anthology.* Ed. W. G. Spittal. Ohsweken, ON: Iroqrafts, 1990. 72-114.

Snow, Dean. *The Iroquois.* Pennsylvania State University, 1996.

Spittal, W. G., ed. *Iroquois Women: An Anthology.* Ohsweken, ON: Iroqrafts, 1990.

Thwaites, Reuben, ed. *The Jesuit Relations and Allied Documents.* Vol. 43. Cleveland: Burrows Brothers, 1899.

Tooker, Elisabeth. "Women in Iroquois Society." *Iroquois Women: An Anthology.* Ed. W. G. Spittal. Ohswekan, ON: Iroqrafts, 1990. 199-216.

Viau, Roland. *Femmes de personne: Sexes, genres et pouvoirs en Iroquoisie ancienne.* Montréal, Boréal, 2000.

Dances With Cougar

Learning from Traditional Parenting Skills Programs

JOANNE ARNOTT

I used to collect clippings of stories I liked, that I found in newspapers: the sea turtle who kept a sailor aloft in the sea for days, brought on board ship and honoured and feasted, and marked with words like, "Do Not Harm! This is a Saviour of Man," before being released to the sea (*Globe and Mail*). The daycare teacher whose children were sought and found by a cougar, who went up against the hungry cat and fought for the lives of the children, standing arm to arm in argument against the big cat, and winning (*The Vancouver Sun; The Province*). These stories hit deep, and inspired me. These stories helped me through a troubled time.

Tides pass through our lives. Sometimes we feel like we're strong swimmers, even coasting across the top of the waves with the whole world carrying us. Other times we're riding low in the water, alternating gulps of ocean and air, living waves of panic. Sometimes, we're walking along the bottom of the ocean, don't even notice the difference between here and there.

As a mixed-race girl-woman and (I hoped) a literary artist, I began giving tongue to the painful contradictions of my upbringing, at the same time that I began walking along the road as a giver of life. Some balance was created, and some relief. Sympathetic audiences and many people whose lives were very much like mine brought consolation, and a sense of connection. Imbalance was also created. Troubles brewed in the present until they gushed ... a swift river which might leave me dead, or naked in a place unfamiliar, washed through.

I don't often tell the story of the time that guy strangled me into unconsciousness, in a tent, in the bush, in Alberta. But I wrote about it. It is the kind of story that brings sympathy, empathy, fellow feelings sometimes, shared rage against the bad guys in this world.

There was a time, a decade or so after that assault, when I was very pregnant. Each school day, I put my toddler on my back, and I held the hand of my five-year-old child, and I walked him through the bush to school. His was a half-day kindergarten program, and so, I would walk home again, share a snack with the little one, write or do housework for an hour. Then I'd put my little boy onto my back again, walk to the school again, rest in a chair in the classroom, and talk with the teacher. Then, toddler on back, five-year-old child in hand, we'd walk home again.

I had a lot on my mind in those days, a lot in my heart. Pressures from my original family, my common-law husband, my literary career, my household tasks, all pressed down upon me. From the inside pressing out, was a whole lot of everything else: I was mainly writing about what was wrong in my life, and the bad old days. I was shaking the bones of every bad thing I'd lived through, waking all the ghosts, and I had only a so-so ability to set it all aside.

The past and the present came together, from time to time, in an ugly way. Once, twice, three times, I was captured by an overwhelming urge, on the path that wound between home and school, to strangle my son, for some unimportant, childish impertinence. Alone in the bush with my charges, I was overcome by a rage as big, as powerful, as any feeling I had ever felt, including childbirth. It took all of my strength to fight, to dance with, to overcome these feelings.

Some people might see a traditional parenting course offered in their community, and take it out of curiosity, to expand the way they think about and do everyday life with their children. I highly recommend this approach, I encourage you to it. Many, many of us, however, wait until we have plunged ourselves and our families deep into crisis, before considering what such gatherings might bring into our lives.

Although I moved back and forth between programs and agencies, beginning in 1996, I have grouped my reflections by agencies, in the order that I met them.

The first traditional parents group I attended was the first one offered through the Vancouver Aboriginal Child and Family Services, then in Gastown, in Vancouver. When I arrived on the first day, the place was packed. I saw familiar faces from the community, and many new faces, too. I was a ball of misery, myself, and the people I knew looked to me to range from worried to distraught—not just us client parents, either, the leaders too!

Maybe it was just my skewed perspective, but doing something new—pulling together a program for the first time, putting your untried plans into action and seeing how it goes—is stressful, and how you interpret the excitement, and how that shows on your face, in your body language, all that varies, too. It must be a challenge for even the greatest optimist to stand wholesome and strong in the midst of a room filled with people in high states of distress. It takes a profoundly kind person, even to consider taking on the job.

When people become parents, and when parents become troubled, the threats can be overwhelming. I felt despair at my wobbling ability to master my anger. I felt resentment, despondence at the uneven skills I'd picked up from my family, and rage at the dearth of support. I felt shame at not having floated past the obvious traps of abusive behaviour, and panic—*I'm running out of time to get this right.* More than everything else all together, I experienced a seemingly endless, overflowing grief.

All of the external threats, the possibilities or outright promises of loss, played up against this inside story, demanding change: stripped of our children, we are stripped of meaning, and there is something unbearable in that kind and level of threat. In the case of death, we simply have to bear it, we simply have to find new meaning, or go on without. In the case of other kinds of loss, however, there is a profound motivation to make change, and hunger for guidance.

Some of us had come along to the group in hopes of finding our way through the tangles of our lives. Some of us had been ordered to come or lose custody of our children, usually by social workers. But all of us had some degree of faith in the course, the organization, the leaders and the counsellors: this was an example of a community helping itself, and we were all willing.

I had shared grief too recently, though, with many of these people. I was overwhelmed physically, with the challenges of pregnancy/breastfeeding/pregnancy/breastfeeding/stress ever mounting. I was unable to absorb what I needed to, the strength of community and good leadership and good energies. I was unable to deflect what I needed to, the stories of rage, of despair, of abuses lived and struggled with; I gathered them into my body and stored them, along with my own.

It was too soon for me. I withdrew from the program, and regrouped for a while—life spinning further out of balance—at home.

Until I became homeless.

Through the next two years, I struggled to know what was real and what was illusion; what was within my power and what was beyond my control; how to be gracious with an alarm bell ringing in my ear at a profound pitch; how to hold my head up through shaming and loss; and most importantly, how to hold onto what was good in my life—my children—through all of this.

The second traditional parenting program I participated in, Traditional Mothers, was offered by the Indian Homemakers Association, then on East Broadway, also in Vancouver. The Indian Homemakers Association had been up and running since the 1960s, and their Mothers' Group had been offered for several years, as well.

I spent a lot of time thinking about the name of this organization, and I concluded that it was exact, and it was good. "Indian" is a misnomer, it's gone out of fashion, it isn't correct—it's also what people have been calling themselves for a few generations, a country person's word, maybe, plainspeaking. "Association" is a group, structured, organized, people together. "Homemakers" carries a sense of plainspeaking, too, a word and a self-definition that's gone out of fashion.

An artist can define herself any way she likes, I suppose, but I was the first to acknowledge that there were gaps in my upbringing, my training, my abilities—that's all I ever wrote about! The word "Homemakers," contemplated from a place of homelessness, brought many riches.

Can a feminist poet want to be a homemaker? *Should she? Is she allowed to?*

What can a smarty-pants learn from modest traditionalists?

This was a time when my inner parts were striving for reconciliation—the Catholic girl with her ethics and morals, the happy child with her natural buoyance, the angry child lashing out, the young person who liked to use words like sharp sticks. I had to let a lot of things go at this time in my life, including the endless either/or choices I had surrounded myself with.

The idea of home-making, for any person in the world, and especially for any person who has one way and another wandered from or been sundered from a sense of community, where the how-to of life is passed on in a wholistic way, seemed to reveal something fundamental to me.

If I am to be at home in the world, I need to understand how home is made.

Once I have understood what home is, how home is made, then I may be forever after empowered to make home again, to gather home around me, to construct home out of whatever materials come to hand. This is no small thing: the predations of life can mean loss of home, for anyone, at any time. To hold the understanding of home, to be able to invent home, to have the power of recreating home as often as necessary and in the face of whatever life throws at me, this is a skill that, if I am to survive, I must have.

The Traditional Mothering program, when I attended, was facilitated by two experienced leaders, Grandma Harris (Margaret Harris), and Ellen Antoine. Each of them has entered my heart in the same way, and on the same level, that the mothers, sisters, aunties, and grandmothers of my blood and family have done.

The group was set up for mothers only, a full-time day program, and there was no childcare on-site. Very small children could attend from time to time, but basically the participants needed to have childcare organized, safe and consistent, in order to attend. Between balancing childcare and other demands of life, I was only able to participate on a part-time basis. After my second round with the group, they presented me with a certificate of graduation, with the words "part-time program," pencilled in.

The circle of women was established physically, the first and every day, by seating ourselves in a rough circle of chairs, arm chairs, and couches. Our activities through days, weeks, and months together, helped weave fullness into our senses of ourselves and of one another. Rituals, like smudging, and routines, like a tea break, grounded our time together, gave rhythm and a sense of safety, made our days—at least our days on site—predictable.

We spoke of our lives. We learned to drum. We studied the medicine wheel, and we learned to sing. We heard traditional stories, and we learned how to dance them. We visited the museum, at the university, to examine our people's clothes, and we learned how to sew. Never in my life can I hope to create something as fine, something as beautiful, as the artful making and beadwork of some of those old Métis clothes.

Every day was new and different, and every action we were invited to take was a gift to ourselves. While there were opportunities to share heartbreak, to ask for advice, to request some specific resource or teaching, we were all the while driven toward action, toward helping one another by sharing our knowledge and experience, toward becoming a helping force in our own lives, families, and communities.

Givers of life, you have already shown courage. Be grateful for what you have. Each child is a gift.

Givers of life, you must take care of yourselves, if you hope to care for others. Each experience that life provides us is a teacher, is a gift.

Acceptance: each of us is a gift.

Moving through shared song and traditional dances, slowly we reinhabit our full bodies.

Learning by doing: make yourself moccasins, a shawl, a belt, a dress, whatever your traditional clothes may be, and self-decoration; make a bag, to keep them all in.

Take everything out of the bag, now, put them on, and perform: at benefits, rallies, gatherings of every kind, supporting other organizations, inviting new women in, carrying traditions forward into the world. The Traditional Mothers' Dance Group, a public expression of private, personal, and collective healing.

Ellen Antoine spoke in a soft, clear voice. Auntie, mother, elder sister, she has book learning and quiet wisdom, leading us through the rounds of our days, often beaming. For me, personally, she is forever associated with a generous gift of fish. She is a joker, too, she teased us. We basked in the warmth of her attention, and when she spoke, we listened:

Think good thoughts.
Think good thoughts, while you make things.
Think good thoughts.

One day, Grandma Harris spoke of residential school, of being punished into learning to do housework quickly and thoroughly, and how today that is a skill she appreciates, freeing up her time to do all kinds of other things. While I laboured over my first pair of moccasins, she teased me about my "big, ugly stitches." She told me later, she had been teased with these same words.

I can't tell you how many needles I broke, clutching them with all the power of my being, trying to force my will upon them, to make things right. I learned to ease up a little, to be a little more aware of my own power, to be a little more trusting, too, of what may come.

One of my sister-mothers told me about her counsellor; she loved her counsellor, they'd been working together for a long time. I contacted the agency she mentioned, and I started to see a counsellor, too, right away. It wasn't the same woman that she saw, but it turned out to be exactly the right woman for me. I'd seen many counsellors over the years, some very helpful and some less so, but this was the first time that I worked with a counsellor where we both brought to bear a solid and continuous focus on what is, and on my everyday life as a parent. We worked together for two years, weekly, then bi-weekly, long enough for her to catch me at all of my tricks, and to show them to me, one at a time. I learned to see them, and to deal with them, myself; this was her enduring gift.

There is a song and a dance that we learned, that was particularly healing for me. An old story, about a prophet and what he foresaw, and how his foresight was received by his community. I wept a lot of tears learning that song, breathing it in. Right here, in a B.C. landscape, the coming of the whites was predicted, many of the changes were predicted, long ago. The changes continue to unfurl, and will continue to do so, however we may feel about it all. Thus, this, being a mixed race person, is not a mistake. It just is.

Between the daily struggles of rebuilding my life, step by step, I had some people to laugh with. I had good advice, sympathy, or a kick in the pants, whatever seemed needed. I had the opportunity to swirl around the room, doing the goose dance, and it was good. I only performed publicly with the group a couple of times, because I couldn't manage the time away from my family.

I remembered my long history of making homes, for myself, for others. Pictures torn from magazines, drawings I was pleased with, taped to the wall beside my bed, when I was young. A shelf in my place in a rooming-house, when I was eighteen, concocted from tooth-floss, thumb-tacks, and a light slice of wood. Other, later, more substantial things: a room for a child to enjoy himself in, a room for myself to rest in, a rhythm of snacks and meals served to the young. I remembered the pleasure taken in this sort of invention, this problem-solving, this rhythm making.

The sense of the world collapsing behind me, every time I stepped through a doorway, became less of a threat. One realization, among many others: I am a homemaker, actually.

The third traditional parenting program I attended, sponsored by Burnaby Life, met less often, perhaps once a week, once a month. I didn't attend very often, and at the time—again, the program was in its beginning stages—few others did, either. What has stayed in my mind most powerfully, in fact, was the intake interview, conducted by a handsome man in good humour.

Among the many questions asked, there was one that seemed to be a favourite of the day: how many siblings did I have, and where was I in the birth order? I gave a long, rambling version of my parents' marriage, eight children, divorce, my father's second marriage, his ninth child—a half-brother I felt attached to, but had never lived with. He listened. I'm not sure whether he is simply a light-hearted man, or if my storytelling powers were particularly ticklish that day, but he did seem amused.

When I was done, he was quiet for a moment, and then he simplified my life forever.

"Let's just say," he said, "there are nine children in your family. That puts you right in the middle."

I carried this off like a bright trinket, and I was thrilled by it. I played with it for days.

I have eight siblings, four elder, and four younger. I am in the middle.

I have four sons.

I am at centre, all my relations unfurling around me.

Restored was a child's natural sense of belonging: a balanced gait.

I am here in the middle of everything, aren't I?

The fourth Traditional Parenting Program I attended was run by the Urban First Nations Society, on Carnarvon Street, in New Westminster. They had received funding for on-site childcare, and so I brought my two littlest ones with me, and if I had to nurse or console, I could do that, and if the little ones decided to sit in to smudge, to take part in the talking circle or a class discussion, they were welcome to do so. Sometimes, the need to care for them and the need to become immersed in the group presented problems, but not usually. As more parents brought their children, friendships grew. Eventually, the space was re-organized, so that the little ones and the adults were physically further apart, and both groups were able to operate more independently. Both ways had their advantages.

The Urban First Nations Society, later known as the First Nations Urban Society, ran a variety of programs, including a school in another part of the building. I attended several therapy groups, an anger management course, and a life skills course, before moving on. Both the school and the parenting and other programs hosted many healing ceremonies, as well as regular social gatherings. It was a good place to go, a place of opportunity, and a place of healing.

The first course I attended was facilitated by Corinne Stone and Sally Lee. We met three days a week, a mix of men and women, all bringing in our real life stories. The heart of the program was, again, the smudge and the talking circle. Together, we worked through a course of studies that examined traditional practices of childrearing, and then invited us to think and reflect on our families, the ways we do or can apply the old ways, and the benefits of doing so.

We worked together, too, sometimes making craft projects to share with our children, sometimes preparing ourselves for ceremony and learning, always learning. We exist inside of history, and we are empowered to act, within our own lives, and to choose our path. Making good choices, for ourselves, our children, for all of our loved ones: making hard choices, sometimes, and seeing the good that may come.

I had, it's true, a few things to learn about being a parent. But the greatest changes came in my relationships with the adults in my life, my original family members, and my children's father—adding necessary distances in some relationships, and opening up the closed gates between myself and some others. It was necessary for me to find a new set of advisors, to restore the flow of love and communication between myself and my father, and to overcome the limiting belief, often heard from my mother, that raising many children is "impossible."

Corinne and Sally passed into my heart, two sister-teachers. I had days of extreme discouragement, days of optimism, days of confusion. Some days, I was only going through the motions. I learned about leadership, both as a parent and as a person in the world, by spending time with these two women, in the parenting group. When you agree to lead others with an open heart, when you do your best, and when you are honest, you are feeding the hungry, just by walking into work every day. By sharing your life experience and your hard-won wisdom, everything—even your mistakes, your sorrows, your feelings of inadequacy, along with your sense of humour, your sense of proportion, your curiosity and your appetite for life—all become food for the broken hearted, to take in, to heal with.

I took another anger management course, at another agency, but that first one, presented by Gayle, was a wonder to me. To see the rush of emotion and the random lashing out slowed down, plotted on a scale, explained: to be shown other diagrams, with the same cycle drawn, and all the possible points of interruption mapped in. Change takes time, and I knew that, but here was something I needed, that I could bring home with me. Guidelines. Food for thought.

Sarah Thomas, a fellow mom-participant, also stayed on at Urban First Nations. While I took course after course, she worked as a volunteer, then became a staff member. We spent a lot of time, talking together, and we shared some happy days, our families around us.

Ray, a teacher at the school, took an interest in me. We went, one day, on an outing to visit a Job Fair, a group of students, parents, life-skills participants, and Ray. I was ripe for this activity: I was soaking it in. I moved slowly through the rooms, examined every poster, every display from every school program, every employment option. My arms steadily filled with brochures, calendars, fridge magnets, pens: my talismans.

I was invited to picture myself as a medical professional, working on a northern reserve: I could do that.

B.C. Hydro is hiring and training linesmen, women and Aboriginals encouraged to apply: I'd love that job!

Train to be a counsellor, a teacher, an environmental assessor, a computer technician: why not? I'm ready!

Every table promised baptism and a new life, glowing futures.

As I was immersed in this experience, every once in a while I'd hear a whisper at my shoulder—"You already have a job."

A little while later, "You already have a career."

Two tables on, "You are a writer."

Ray!

Sometimes, he didn't even whisper, just waited across the room, within my line of vision, until I surfaced, looked up, focussed: an eyebrow, then, or a look.

I felt profoundly irritated by Ray's antics.

I went home, after, and I cried for a long time.

I hung around at Urban First Nations until my life had re-stabilized, my custody battles done, our new routines as a family established. At the Life Skills graduation ceremony, a visitor made a comment to me, about me: "I thought you were a teacher." Soon, I heard this comment repeated by others. No one had ever questioned my role, in those first two years;: it was clear to everyone then, what I was doing there!

I'd healed enough, it seemed, to pass as a teacher. Time to move on.

What drove me into healing as a full-time occupation was loss of home, and the need to negotiate powerfully for my children's rights to be mothered, and my own right/responsibility to mother them. A few honest words from my eldest son, confirmed my new direction: "I didn't know we were that important to you." To free myself as a mother, so that my love of my children and my good parenting shone through, I had to redraw the boundaries between myself and every other person, and I needed to reform my ways of relating to my family, and to myself.

The Medicine Wheel is a fundamental guide to healing, that we can use to begin a process of re-weaving our splintered experiences and finding a wholesome way to be in the world.

Begin with the colour of the road you are on: I am on black, or red? It's not about my ideals or how I would like things to be, but my actual presence in the world, the impact of my hours and days on those around me, and on those who will come along after.

Are the faces around me relaxed, interested, healthy?

Are the faces around me protected, raging, fearful?

Once I know the colour of the road I am on, I can decide if that is really how and where I want to be. But I have to notice, first.

The black road: *am I picking fights, ripping people off, drugging myself, delusional? Do I go roaring through life, never noticing who gets knocked aside by my passage? Do my children know how essential they are to me, or do they feel like excess baggage? Do they feel safe with me?*

The good red road: *am I living with respect for myself and for others? Do I take care of and nourish myself, my children, my elders, my ancestors, my children's children, my community, Mother Earth, all of Her Children?*

What does it mean when I say, All My Relations?

The Medicine Wheel includes the four directions, those fundamental elements of life. We were encouraged to look at how all of the four directions are, and can be, expressed in this human life. It was the beginning of understanding—locating the lack that becomes driving need, locating the excesses that, unchecked, will defeat me.

The thing about life—whether you're a mom, or a student, or deep into a career, or into parties, mainly, or all that and more—the thing about life is, you make it up as you go along. Life is a work of the imagination, and the limits of imagination are the real, what you've seen and been before, because that is the basis of new growth, new life.

Whatever I do today, as a parent or as an artist, depends on what is already around me, and it depends on what I've seen others do in times past. Being aware of the need for balance and for good influences, we learn to look for them. Today, I have six children, and the ties of love and affection are strong, and they flow in all directions. Conflicts, we know, can be resolved peacefully, and respectful behaviour is expected, from all of us.

One day I returned, as a writer/mom, to visit a new group of mothers participating in the Traditional Mothers program at the Indian Homemakers. I made my presentation, then invited questions from the gathering. Grandma Harris piped up, and cheerfully invited me to tell the mothers all about the times I used to walk my son to school, through the bush. *Tell them what happened.*

I felt such a flush of embarrassment. It isn't a story I like.

But I did. I remembered to use "I" statements.

Traditional Parenting Skills Programs are, for me, a gift from the sea: the generous, patient sea turtle, who carried me aloft for a time, so I could keep breathing. Beyond refuge, essential in itself when we are in crisis, parents benefit from having old ways, and new ways, brought to our attention, modelled and demonstrated to us. Becoming ourselves immersed in old/new ways, expands our bases of knowledge, provides us with a wider sense of what is possible, and what is real. They can carry us, for a time, until the tides of our lives have changed, and we have regained our own buoyancy.

I learned that I can face down threats to my children, threats from inside of me, and threats from the outside. I can do this without (permanently) disappearing from their lives. I can deal with what is. Like the indigenous caregiver whose children were stalked and mauled by a cougar, I can respond appropriately and with sufficient power.

With this essay, I hope to honour and feast all of those people who give of themselves, in a helping way. A lot of years, many generations, went into bringing us to this place. There is no quick fix. Patience and sincerity, as displayed by our "modest traditionalists," are necessary. It is good to remember, too, when facing life's challenges: compassion and victory are both natural possibilities.

Deep thanks to Marie-Micheline Hamelin, for her help with this essay.

Joanne Arnott is a Metis/mixed blood writer, originally from Manitoba. Joanne worked for many years as an Unlearning Racism facilitator, and has performed readings and given writing workshops across much of southern Canada and in Australia. She lives with her family in Richmond, B.C. Joanne's most recent book is Steepy Mountain: Love Poetry *(Kegedonce Press, Cape Croker, 2004). Forthcoming is* Mother Time, *a collection of pregnancy, birth, and mother-related poetry (spring 2007, Ronsdale Press). I would like to invite other indigenous mothers and writers who have an interest in birth stories and birth practices to contact me, to develop diverse projects and collaborations: Joanne.Arnott+birth.stories@gmail.com*

Back to Basics

Mothering and Grandmothering in the Context of Urban Ghana

BRENDA F. MCGADNEY-DOUGLASS, NANA ARABA APT AND
RICHARD L. DOUGLASS

Raising children and ensuring the future has always been the fundamental biological mandate of being human. In the best of times providing parenting to our offspring has also been a daunting task that is part biological, but increasingly cultural, social, economic, political, and eventually historical within each life and within the fabric of each family. In contrast, the worst of times has been imposed on countless nations by colonization, centuries of warfare, and economic or actual enslavement. History has not been equally generous to all people but most grievously unjust to indigenous peoples who have been subjected to conquest, subjugation, marginalization, exploitation, policies that have sought assimilation, and intentional efforts that aimed at annihilation. Aboriginal mothering has been the fail-safe for indigenous peoples that thwarted such historical efforts and those that persist today.

The purpose of this chapter is to discuss the challenges and victories of indigenous grandmothers and other senior women who, we believe, have been, and are still today, elemental in the survival of many cultures. At the micro-level, each narrative of survival begins with the survival of the children. To demonstrate the universality of Aboriginal mothering it is necessary to first describe the threats to such survival and mothering, and the particular roles of women as collectives within Aboriginal cultures. Then, after a presentation of the larger framework of the social-historical concept of Aboriginal grandmothering we will provide illustrations from our field observations. These illustrations will be based on the narratives of such women who confronted malnutrition in the ethnic Ga communities in urban Accra, Ghana.

The Meaning of Aboriginal Mothering: Mothering in the Context of Post-Colonial, Post-Conquest or Post-Emancipation Marginalization and Subjugation

We have taken the liberty of adopting the term "Aboriginal" to refer to people in any place who have been conquered, colonized or transplanted against their will and then subjugated by an alien, majority culture. For the last 400 years such subjugation of indigenous peoples has almost always been at the hands of "eurarmericans," as used by Lisa Udel in her specific reference to Native American women in the U.S. whose resistance to assimilation into "European" or "American" culture is a coined term that is in many ways equivalent to the concept of "western" versus traditional, indigenous, or eastern. Udel's descriptions were of women in whom there has been a renewal of their roles as the protectors of the future. The future, of course, is best demonstrated by the survival of children who accept their own roles as carriers of their culture.

The domination of conquered or enslaved peoples who were both essential resources and then, ultimately, viewed as inconveniences to the invaders, is a traumatic history that others have documented in depth. In addition, the roles of traditional women were foreign to the conquering forces, as noted by the British in the eighteenth century in the Americas:

> ...native American women stood at the center of the great circle of life, revered and sometimes even feared. Their capacity to ring forth new life and to grow the crops and harvest the wild plants that sustained the community made them essential. They considered themselves "part of" rather than "dependent upon" which gave them a dignity of bearing and an endurance wholly unfamiliar to Europeans of the contact period. (Fleet 79)

Lisa Udel cited Patricia Monture-Angus with the observation that the centrality of childbearing and determination of the future provided First Nations women respect that was unique (Udel 43). But the history of conquest and oppression of Aboriginal women, and therefore Aboriginal mothers, is thick with a sorry saga of exploitation of the Aboriginal women for sex, reproduction, and labour while the Euramerican, white women generally experienced an insidious marginalization that took the form of infantilization and isolated dependence.

Then, in the shadows of history, large proportions of the conquered or transplanted indigenous people nearly disappeared. Some became fully assimilated. Others, however, survived as distinct, albeit, reduced populations who struggled to claim their own place in a different world. In most cases the surviving indigenous people, whom we here call Aboriginal, continued to face a variety of forms of oppression and to struggle for identity, even survival, within the context of hostile majority populations.

It is the Aboriginal survivors' worldviews, especially a compelling common denominator of collectivism, therefore, that accepted the challenge to keep their children alive, with or without men and without the essential intervention of a governmental power, or the state. We will provide, here, a contexualized, central theme in the mothering of Aboriginal children that transcends the continents, historical time, and ethnicity. This mothering, as we have observed by the grandmothers and senior Ga women in urban Ghana, defies the lasting effects of colonial powers, overlords or conquerors to be assimilated or eliminated; instrumentally through the defiant protection and nurture of their children (McGadney-Douglass *et al.* 2005).

For present purposes we want to identify such populations as inclusive of First Nation Peoples, Indigenous Peoples, Aborigines, Natives, American Indians, Native Americans, African Americans, and other designations that distinguish the marginalized, resilient, original or forcibly transplanted inhabitants in much of the industrialized and post-colonial world. These people, from their traditions and timeless values, have found ways to keep their children alive and ensure the future despite the majority population's direct or subtle efforts to make them disappear. We will draw from the experiences of Aboriginal mothers, families, and documentation from Canada, the U.S., Australia, and especially former colonized nations in Africa as our concept of Aboriginal mothering takes form.

It would be too great a simplification to claim that the European conquest of the Americas was uniform or homogeneous regarding the consequences on Native Americans or First Nations people. I would be just as excessive to claim that these conquests and subsequent tawdry histories were identical to the experience of African slaves in the Americas, the colonization and conquest of most of Africa, parts of Asia or the assimilation of Australia. Within these domains, as Lauren Morris MacLean noted in a comparison of Ghana and Cote d'Ivoire, colonialism often had different lasting effects in different places. Despite these historical distinctions, however, the essential elements of marginalization, translocation from advantaged lands to disadvantaged lands, epidemic diseases and military- or civilian-led violence, subjugation and exploitation remain common denominators. These historical themes link these populations, both in the past and today, within our concept of Aboriginal.

In the case of Africans who were stolen from their homes for the slave trade in the Americas, indigent cultures were transported along with the labour force for overlords who treated slaves as subhuman, and often even more harshly than the Native American Aboriginal people.

Much of contemporary views regarding African American mothering roles, from the U.S., as noted by W. E. B. Du Bois in his "Damnation of Women" (see Reiland) has been identified as illustrative of the strength and values, hallmarks of culture, and raw survival skills of African American women's legacy from slavery. Lawrie Balfour noted that this independence and strength illustrates the autonomous and liberated roles that many women now seek. Clearly in response to the demasculination of Aboriginal men, be they Native American,

Figure 1: Layers of Challenge to the Survival of Children in Contemporary Urban Aboriginal Circumstances

Paternalism and other consequences of colonialism or conquest-related domination. Overcoming self-identification as inferior.

Cultural Hostility, economic marginalization, intentional destruction by the State of traditional family social structures, language, values, and cultural identity

Issues of Childhood Survival:
Poverty, multi-generational households with co-dependence on grandmothers, lack of traditional oral history and tools, cultural ambivalence, economic and vocational discrimination, isolation among a dominant culture, resurgence of aboriginal (ethnic and historical) identity, adaptation of traditional identification and problem solving (including pragmatic identification of resources and means), feminization of family units within communities that limit or constrain gender-based equality of opportunity, and collectivist responsibility for raising the children.

Immediate Threats to Overcome:
•Inferior infrastructures and exposures to disease, bad water quality, toxic waste, poor housing and crowding;
•Lack of predictable resources for minimum nutritional and health care expectations;
•Less adequate access to education or affordable transportation;
•Family configurations that can skip generations, exclude gender-based role models, and fail to provide alternative vocational or educational options.

African American slave, or servants of colonial powers by Euramerican men, collectivist, multi-generational women, have been the ones that raised and protected the children. While contemporary society may dismiss or corrupt this historical truth, in fact it is a cornerstone of Aboriginal mothering in every oppressed population. As summarized by Balfour, Du Bois demanded that [we] attend to the accomplishments of African American women "in the face of violent exclusion." This, we contend, has been the experience of Aboriginal women in the roles of motherhood, throughout the world today. To the extent that conquered people, post-colonial people, and displaced people live in marginalized circumstances, or in continuing threat by a majority population, the skills that have historically helped them to survive will continue to be essential; and therefore deserving of our attention.

In the discussion that follows we will present a model of the challenges to the survival of children in contemporary, urban circumstances that are faced by Aboriginal people. In this model there are fundamental "layers' of challenge that begin with paternalism and other consequences of colonialism or conquest-related domination that requires an active effort to overcome the majority-imposed self-identification as inferior. The model, based on historical and contemporary observations, displays phases over the passage of time of how successful Aboriginal mothering must confront cultural hostility, economic marginalization, intentional destruction by the State (the majority and oppressing population) of traditional family social structures, language, values, and cultural identity.

Child Survival in Threatening Places

It is our contention that Aboriginal children in places where original populations have been suppressed, as discussed above, are also places where there are broader and more widespread threats to child survival. The oppression by a majority population, if historically designed to marginalize to the point of annihilation, takes its toll first on the children. In Africa's previously colonized nations, inclusive of both Aboriginals as we use the term and fully assimilated people, it has long been recognized that children face high odds against reaching adulthood. Within the context of providing care to colonized Ghanaians, for example Cicely Williams, a British pediatrician, introduced the category of protein-caloric deficiency diseases to the medical lexicon with the Ga phrase *kwashiorkor*, meaning "what happens when the second child is born." This endemic form of malnutrition currently accounts for about 3.5 per cent of childhood, under age-five, mortality in Ghana and persists despite over 70 years of British and post-colonial programs directed to toddler nutrition. (Douglass; McGadney-Douglass, Douglass, Apt and Antwi) The difficulty, as noted by Christine Oppong (2004) in this, as well as

Brenda McGadney-Douglass, Nana Araba Apt and Richard L. Douglass

other child killing conditions in West Africa such as diarrhea from bad drinking water, has as much to do with the imposition of chaotic social structures and the persistent destruction of traditional social stability that encouraged breast feeding and child spacing. Migration from rural places into cities in hopes of improved economics has also caused women to spend much more time in market activity, less time with their children, and to become more dependent on others, as isolated surrogates, to care for the young. Rural women who have been displaced or transplanted into urban areas may not have familial support systems upon whom to depend, and the parenting role becomes one that is apart-from, rather than integrated with, the collective experience and multigenerational perspective of the traditional community that was left behind. This pattern of social upheaval that has also been witnessed in Aboriginal populations throughout the world as majority populations push, or tempt, traditional people to survive within un-healthy and unstable circumstances. As summarized by Oppong (2004), the workload of mothers in the form of tasks that are added to mothering in order to survive, without the traditional embrace of extended kinship and family structure, has had a destructive impact on child survival. Child survival is the essential role of Aboriginal mothering:

> If we knew that African babies in the historical past were well fed at the time that systems of kinship and marriage were functioning to provide strict rules and practices regarding sexual congress and birth spacing and to ensure ample social and material support to nursing mothers, our hypothesis linking disruptions in support with truncated care and hunger would be further supported. ... [The problems were in] migrant (urban) populations, where the traditional social support and norms (social capital) had broken down to a large extent. They were populations characterized by dislocation of peoples, scattering of kin, separation of spouses. Such movements were typically brought about by the introduc-tion of a cash nexus and the commoditization of labour and most needed resources. What is also important there was the breakdown of traditional community sanctions, ensuring common norms and individual behav-iour, designed to support and promote safe and successful reproduc-tion.... This resulted in mothers alone trying to cope with too many different and often conflicting role demands with too little support (conjugal or kin) and few resources and too closely spaced births. (Oppong 2004: 7)

The movement, by force or economic incentive, of whole populations has been a common denominator of Aboriginal peoples' experiences with invading, colo-nizing, or conquering majority domination. We can conclude that it is still

110

associated with preventable childhood morbidity and mortality because in all displaced Aboriginal populations there is an excess of preventable child deaths. We will return to the specific question of *kwashiorkor* and the role of Aboriginal values and practices in child survival. Our point here is that the disruption in traditions that historically served the needs of childhood survival, and the "future" of Aboriginal people has been associated with significant and persistent child mortality in colonized places and among conquered, dislocated peoples.

Each population of Aboriginal people has faced a sequence of common experiences that have challenged their ability to retain traditions that were wholesome for their children or, indeed, to reproduce at all. Native women in Canada and the U.S. have faced involuntary sterilization by government sponsored health services. In Australia the sterilization of women who are Aboriginal has also been documented. But historically, it is also true that African slaves throughout the Americas were used essentially for unaccountable sexual pleasure or for outright breeding purposes to increase the supply of cheap labour for white people's agriculture and domestic work. Historically, Aboriginal women who partnered with white men have had more children and less time between births than those who remained tied to their indigenous community. Although inconsistent, the sexual treatment of Aboriginal women highlights the centrality of women's reproductive lives in the discussion of Aboriginal policies and practices. (Udel; Lowe, Kerridge and Mitchell; Looking Horse; Berland). This legacy is evident today, and follows a long and tragic history, among Native Americans on U.S. government reservations[1], in First Nations in Canada, Aboriginals in Australia, in most former British or French colonies in Africa, and among African Americans in U.S. cities.

In recent years the revitalization of Aboriginal values has been identified as a key element in Aboriginal survival and, perhaps, for the rest of us too. Kim Anderson and Bonita Lawrence provided a sober assessment of the spectrum of how traditions, including those corrupted by Christian patriarchy and gender role-definitions, however, are not universally to be associated with community revitalization. For over 400 years Aboriginal mothering, and the collectivist community mentality associated with Aboriginal mothering, has been an important defense of native peoples from extermination by Euramerican cultural expansion. As we will also discuss below, the lessons to be learned from this inclusive view of Aboriginal mothering could serve contemporary Euramerican cultures well, especially in emerging nations that struggle with culture conflicts, aging, and multi-generational societies. Gwendolyn Mikell discussed how African feminism, from ten different nations, has resurrected traditions of female independence and child-focus, with distinctly non-western (non-Euramerican) models, which she and her contributors call survival strategies.

Most European colonization included the corruption of traditional life styles, economic and family structures. Most post-independence African nations have adopted many of the economic and social structures that were imposed on them during colonial domination that has had lasting consequences, particularly for the most severely marginalized people. Although not all colonial or post-colonial governments in Africa sought to replace extended family-based, decentralized social policies with centralized government services and bureaucracies because these social structures were often used to pit one ethnic group against another for the benefit of the colonial overlords. Ghana, for instance has been more decentralized and family-oriented than has been Cote d'Ivoire, and also relatively more tolerant of informal institutions and traditional, ethnicity-based systems of community support and development than its next-door neighbor. Both of these West African nations were subjected to hundreds of years of slaving, exploitation and colonial rule (MacLean). Civil wars and economic chaos, however, in these two countries have forced millions of people to leave traditional settings in search of economic opportunities that rarely live up to their hopes and expectations. Similarly traditional peoples in Australia, elsewhere in Africa, and among First Nations and Native Americans have experienced the destruction of essential traditions and social fabric when they are relocated by force or economics to urban settings or remote, isolated reservations (Douglass; Hope).

The history of Aboriginal people as largely documented by Euramerican writers consistently demonstrates how these populations have been swept into geographical dislocation or migration and disruptions in culture and tradition. The traditional roles of men and women, and the corruption of historical patterns of equity and gender respect, have been documented in the eighteenth and nineteenth centuries and have often been reinvented by Aboriginal peoples who are disconnected from their kindred and their actual histories. Within contemporary efforts at the national level this has taken the form of "…the top-down and bureaucratic push for multiculturalism"; further "Aboriginal women must also confront the legacy of colonialism that contours the personal and political terrain of their everyday lives" (Naples and Dobson116-117). The marginalization of Native men and male roles, complicated by poor education and employment opportunities, the introduction of abusive drugs and beverage alcohol and other historical methods of control by the majority population, has not served Aboriginal children or their mothers well. In most Aboriginal communities, alcohol and drug abuse, unemployment and high mortality are hallmarks of the male population, as is abandonment of mothers and young children by the fathers. Although some of the families in which we studied cases of malnutrition in our work in Ghana had male presence in the home, the majority of cases had no ongoing contribution or assistance from any men. In this sense, then, we see Aboriginal mothering within the contexts of marginalization, largely to be the work of women, alone.

Aboriginal Expectations and the Roles of Strong, Older Women

The documentation of historical and contemporary roles of older women and the raising of Aboriginal children, as we are using the concept, is substantial. More limited, however, is the specific discussion of just what grandmothers and other older women do regarding the survival of children, why these roles are abdicated or delegated by the mothers and fathers, and what, if any, public recognition and support is available to help the grandparents in the face of such responsibility. We contend that the return to Aboriginal values of familial resource allocation, or as Oppong (2004) considered it "social capital," is not so much an intentional application of tradition for tradition's sake, as much as it is a pragmatic and communal decision to survive with the most effective distribution of tasks and responsibilities among the family members who are available to assume such assignments. Mhairi Gibson and Ruth Mace in their discussion of kin selection and parental investment argue that grandmothers had a positive influence on child survival. In the Gambia, Rebecca Sear, Mhairi Gibson and Ian McGregor distinguished the influence of maternal grandmothers from paternal grandmothers with improved nutrition, survival, and physical development of children. These authors also indicated that paternal grandmothers' influence was negligible compared to the maternal grandmothers, as also was the influence of grandmothers who, themselves, were still reproductively active. In Ghana, Nana Apt documented specific activities and responsibilities that grandmothers have assumed in a spectrum of ethnic groups, and our recent work between 1999 and 2002, among the urban Ga, clearly identified the instrumentality of the grandmothers in survival of toddlers diagnosed with *kwashiorkor* (McGadney-Douglass, Douglass, Antwi, Owusu and Garrison 1999; McGadney-Douglass *et al.* 2005).

Distractions and Urgencies Facing Young Women and Mothers

It is part of our thesis that the migration, dislocation or transplantation of Aboriginal people has been an historical common denominator that has challenged motherhood, child survival and the collective responsibility of families and kinship systems to raise children. In South Africa, as a result of large population movements, mortality from HIV/AIDS, splintered home lives due to work opportunities in distant locations and segregated housing within mining and metropolitan areas, the post-Apartheid period has experienced grandmothers and other available family members doing much of the child rearing and routine childcare. In these black South African homes both the mothers and fathers are often compelled to seek paid work in order for the families to survive. In these contexts of translocation, extreme poverty, and marginalization, the parents, mothers in particular, are obligated to devote their time and attention to market and paid work instead of to their children and families. We found the same to be true among the urban Ga women whose children had suffered from *kwashiorkor*. Grandmothers, in particular, provided the domestic work while parent(s) made economic contributions. This is a multi-generation image that is mirrored in Aboriginal populations that have found themselves in urban settings throughout Sub-Saharan Africa, Canada, the U.S. and Australia; we expect that similar observations would be made in any place where parental roles were replaced, or supplanted, because the parents could not be attentive to domestic needs because of work and economic necessity.

Aboriginal mothering, like most of life's experiences at the individual level, is less an application of analytical decision making than it is the result of pragmatism and being realistic about task distribution within family contexts. The process of seeking the survival of children and families is not an opportunity for exhibiting one's allegiance to tradition as much as it is one of taking one day at a time and maximizing the import of minimal resources, both human and material. There is some evidence that this role, in the isolated context of marginalized people and those who have been displaced, is not without potential negative consequences for some of the oldest family members who have been reported to experience depression and alienation (Miller; Bozalek).

Contemporary urban settings are frequently places of high child morbidity and mortality relative to surrounding majority populations. Australian Aboriginals in urban settings face substantially documented risks to infants, for instance, smoking exposure to children, maternal smoking during pregnancy, and close residential quarters which increases the level of second-hand tobacco exposure (described by Sandra Eades and Anne Read). This study also noted a 68 per cent shared bed exposure of children to adults. Cynthia Garcia Coll, Janet Surrey, Kathy Weingarten, and Mary Watkin's book, *Mothering Against the Odds: Diverse Voices of Contemporary Mothers*, is illustrative of the large literature that exemplifies the challenges of African American women in urban environments. This work is in the spirit of Du Bois and his less heralded contemporaries such as Anna Julia Cooper (Haywood) or Ida B. Wells-Barnett (Schechter) and modern scholars including Patricia Morton, Dorothy Roberts, Hazel Carby and others (see Balfour). This literature concludes that it is necessary for those who survive to be more than assertive in employment, child rearing and child spacing, and to embrace a mindset of collectivism as bearers of the future. These survivors, historically or in oppressed circumstances throughout the United States, then, are also practitioners of Aboriginal mothering in response to marginalization as "free women"; this is a situation that has been common yet inadequately recognized for nearly 150 years since emancipation from slavery in the U.S.

Pragmatics, Practicality and Accessing Formal Resources: Pathways to Child Survival

Poverty and ignorance, without extended family members, especially those with age and more experience, can increase the vulnerability of children. Marginalized people have usually experienced multi-generational poverty, layers of economic, education, health care, housing and transportation discrimination that are associated with critical disparities in both opportunity and personal accomplishment. At the same time traditional beliefs are not universally effective (for instance, in areas of nutrition or folk medicines) and can have unwanted consequences if practiced without sufficient consideration of alternatives. The use of traditional folk medicines is not always appropriate or sufficient to deal with actual medical problems. When traditional healers are substituted for medical services, for instance, because health care infrastructures are not available or because the families lack the resources to access legitimate medical care, the outcomes can be very bad, especially for young children. Among our cases in Ghana, the successful rehabilitation of malnourished children was always associated with the family's participation in formal health care and community health programs and the avoidance of traditional healers in the neighborhoods (McGadney-Douglass *et al.* 2005). Similarly, as noted by Udel in reference to Native Americans:

> …an emphasis on Native traditions does not preclude the integration of old and new. While recognizing the value of traditional culture and practice, Native activists and feminists do not blindly embrace behaviour simply because it may be called "traditional," especially if it is oppressive to women. Just who determines what is to be called "traditional" and therefore valuable is also under scrutiny. (Monture-Angus qtd. in Udel 55)

Economic and other barriers to access of acceptable health care services, including transportation or mistrust of non-Aboriginal care givers, can also delay or prevent vulnerable children from getting the health care that they need even when it is clear and apparent to the family that modern medicine, the Ministry Health Service, or a medical referral are important. Without access, by way of insurance, cash, transportation, or formal service provisions, the barriers to health care for high-risk children can be insurmountable. If, in addition to these barriers there is a history of mistrust, bad experiences, abuse, or neglectfulness by formal health providers, precious time can be lost while a hesitant mother or extended family decide that "it is serious enough," to warrant attempting to receive care from the majority culture (Wardman, Clement and Quantz).

Traditional collaborative family norms can be essential to child welfare when a child has need for health care or other interventions; this collaboration falls apart and the child's life can be at risk if women do not have such familial resources when they need them. As noted in Mali by Sangeetha Madhavan, the use of clinics for treating children's illnesses partly depends on a woman's ability to leave her other children with a responsible caretaker or to obtain cash for medicines and transportation from others. The lack of appropriate and accessible childcare has frequently emerged as a variable that prevents women from economic, personal, and role success; this includes the success of having your child survive. This, of course, is a challenge that is faced by both Aboriginal and majority populations in many nations today.

It is the knowledge, communal understanding, the deliberateness of seeking advice from elders and the mutual distribution of resources that gives Aboriginal mothering strength in challenging times and threatening environments. This communality rested on the shoulders of the grandmothers in our field studies of child survival. Our work in Ghana revealed that younger and more isolated mothers were often late to suspect serious malnutrition in their children because they did not have the personal history to know what the signs and symptoms were. The older women did know, however, and their experience-based knowledge was frequently the key in the ultimate referral of the child to appropriate medical care, rehabilitation and survival. Poverty, isolation (both geographic and cultural within chaotic urban settings), the dissipation of family systems, and deteriorated (or never established) health care infrastructures can lead to desperation when there is a health care crisis, particularly when a young child is ill or not thriving. We have seen in the field that desperate people often do desperate things; but desperate people who can turn to a wise and experienced elder make fewer mistakes or bad decisions (McGadney-Douglass *et al.* 2005). In Nigeria, Jasper Chiwuzie and Chike Okolocha found similar results while studying the health status of pregnant women who accessed traditional healing rather than appropriate, modern, medical care. Rayna Green eloquently explains the position of a young American Aboriginal woman:

> Women like me are going to blow it in the role of mother if left to the narrow, biological role. But in Indian country, that role was never understood necessarily only as a biological role; grandma was never understood as a biological role; sister and aunt were never understood in the narrow confines of genetic kinship. (qtd. in Udel 66)

Kwashiorkor and Child Malnutrition as a Special Case of Child Survival Threat

Kwashiorkor is one of the major manifestations of childhood malnutrition that claims high rates morbidity and mortality throughout the developing world, and among Aboriginal populations within many economically and industrially developed nations. In particular, where there is widespread poverty and over-population, in marginalized Aboriginal populations it is likely that childhood malnutrition will serve as a sentinel to many other public health and personal health problems. The Ga term, *Kwashiorkor,*[2] essentially means, "What happens when the second child is born." What "happens," of course, is that the first child, now a toddler, is taken off the breast too soon because of the new pregnancy and then the birth of a sibling. The first child then is given substitutes for breast milk that are deficient in protein and other essential nutrients and a slow and quiet progressive deterioration will lead to the clinical condition. The *kwashiorkor*-afflicted child often has a swollen belly, reddish hair or the loss of hair due to the deficiency in essential dietary proteins, often the child is stunted and small for their age, and usually lethargic. Because the child is not demanding attention, as is the case in the infant condition of early stage *marasmas,* which is frank starvation, the child with *kwashiorkor* is often assumed to be a "good child," leaving the mother's attention free to be devoted to the new child in the home. Ultimately, without recognition and intervention, the child's condition will cause fatal system failures and death. Recent statistics from Ghana document that six per cent of childhood deaths in that post-colonial nation are due to *marasmas* and *kwashiorkor,* nearly evenly divided between the infants' *marasmas* and the toddlers *kwashiorkor.* Because one of the elements of the complex etiology of *kwashiorkor* is child spacing, the survival of children with this condition makes an excellent illustration of the role of Aboriginal mothering. It has been repeatedly demonstrated that Euramerican values and cultural impositions on Aboriginal people shortens the spacing of children and increases the per-woman fertility rates. Aboriginal peoples' movements to urban communities, and the frequent breakdown of traditional, collective childrearing leads to isolation and the lack of experience and knowledge to young mothers whose children are in trouble.

Our work in Ghana began in 1999 with a simple, but poorly researched question. We did not seek to study Aboriginal people's childrearing, grandmothers, or even to focus on mothering. The research question at that time was to determine if those children who survived *kwashiorkor* were able to become independent, productive adults. (McGadney-Douglass *et al.* 1999). This research question was quickly addressed and replaced by more complex questions. We found that the young adults, who we interviewed in the company of the mothers and grandmothers who raised them, were normal in nearly every way when compared to other youth in the same communities who had not had *kwashiorkor.* The question, for us, became focused on the specific roles, responsibilities and the decisions of the adults that led to the survival of the children from a condition that is, worldwide, nearly 80 per cent fatal (McGadney-Douglass *et al.* 2000).

Our fieldwork was continued in 2001-2002 in the Ga communities of Accra, Ghana and included detailed interviews with families. Interviews included all of the circumstances of the recognition, referral, care and keeping of the malnourished children, the children's growth and development, and individual roles of each of the adults who were involved. We determined that it was the older women, usually the maternal grandmothers or aunts, who were directly involved in recognizing that the children were sick and not just lethargic. To be sure, there were some paternal grandmothers and aunts involved too, and a handful of the families had men who were directly involved; but few men were directly involved with childcare, or managing to get the afflicted child to months of rehabilitation at the local polyclinic. (McGadney-Douglass *et al.* 2005).

Our interviews revealed that the grandmothers and older women realized the true nature of a *kwashiorkor* case before the mothers because their life experience gave them the experiential basis to really know what was going on. The older women then were instrumental in deciding to obtain medical care, to participate fully in the Ministry of Health rehabilitation programs, and to also assist the family in ways that set these successful cases apart from those without collective child rearing capabilities. The grandmothers and older women provided transportation, prayer, childcare, economic and market support, housing, knowledge and many other kinds of support that, we believe, were essential for these children to have survived. While we were in the field our participants frequently told us of cases that were contemporaneous with their own, where the child died; the distinctions were clearly the Aboriginal value of the collective, pragmatic, and effective decision making that was associated with a direct role of one or more older women.

A woman's value in marginalized, post-colonized, or conquered populations, due in part to the imposition of paternalistic role expectations, is directly associated with her role as a producer of children, independent of her other contributions. Christine Oppong observed that in much of Africa's high fertility populations a woman's status is at least partly dependant upon her reproductive success (1989). In communities where traditional familial social structures, gender and generational isolation, and such fecundity-based personal worth are common, the contributions of older women, within a context of collective mothering, are reduced or absent. Often missing from the formula for child survival are the gifts of the older women who are bearers of tradition, holders of history, and who have the ability to diagnose/recognize situations, or medical conditions, that are beyond the experience of isolated mothers. As a collective, this Aboriginal mothering increases the availability and effectiveness of problem solving and increases the family resources to the advantage of the children who are at risk. Moreover, the grandmothers and older women, as directly involved participants in childrearing are role models of strength and persistence; our cases often produced remarkable quotations that essentially underscored the conclusion that were it not for the contributions of grandmother, or auntie, the child would probably have died (McGadney-Douglass *et al.* 2005).

Discussion and Conclusions

This most important message that we hope to be shared by this chapter is that the experience of Aboriginal people, those who have been conquered, enslaved, marginalized, colonized and controlled in the Americas, Africa and Australia, at least, have had many common denominators including the collectivist presumption in childrearing and the important roles of grandmothers and older women. These roles are not played-out as interested, but distant, observers as is often the role of grandparents and older adults in European or American families. Instead this collectivism is manifested in these women as critical and involved decision-makers, co-parents, and full participants in childrearing, and, indeed in child survival. This was described by Madhavan as traditions of cooperation and collective decision-making about most familial decisions affecting reproduction or childrearing in Sub-Saharan Africa; we suggest that it applies broadly to Aboriginal peoples. We would further argue that because child survival is the fundamental basis of cultural survival, among indigenous people the roles of powerful senior women is essential for these oppressed cultures and ethnic distinctions to survive. This conclusion has substantial implications. Oppression of minority populations, subsequent to conquest or other forms of domination, will not be a likely candidate for extinction in the geopolitical future. This, combined with the ultimate success of public health and economic developments in developing nations, suggests that more effective supports should be implemented for senior women who may literally carry these populations into the future.

In El Salvador, after decades of military and political oppression, the rural "Christian Base Communities' movement have a song, *No Basta Rezar*, which includes the verse, "*No, no, no, Basta Rezar, hacen falta muchas cosas para conseguir la paz.*" or, "No, no, no, it is not enough to pray; there are a lot of things missing to obtain peace" (Jordan). In other words, with no intention of minimizing the importance of prayer and beliefs for intercession and help, it is also essential to be actively involved in creating the future in ways that are fully reflected in the direct roles of senior women in child, and therefore cultural, survival. We would contend that among all Aboriginal peoples, it is not enough to pray, there are a lot of things that need to be done to survive and raise the children; and all of it is more effective when you do not do it alone. The Euromerican model of isolated, nuclear families, characterized by paternalism and competition that are expected to be self-sufficient has not worked well for Aboriginal, native people.

Traditions that emphasize cooperation and collaboration, as well as pragmatism and good decision-making for common goals, have time-tested value; as we have tried to document to a broad and diverse, yet experientially distinct, part of the human family. Problems such as *kwashiorkor* "should not" be prevalent in any community where there is an abundance of food such as in contemporary Accra, Ghana, but ignorance and other causal explanations suggest that these and similar challenges to child survival will continue to plague the future. Complex etiologies aside, however, when models of child-rearing that are based on meaningful collectivism within families is called into play the negative consequences of many threats to children can be mitigated. Isolation, lack of inter-generational supports and the loss of co-parental involvement, and other consequences of Aboriginal marginalization, post-colonial exploitation, and post-emancipation discrimination are associated with failed mothering, absent fathering, and an inability to succeed in the fundamental motherhood role of ensuring the future. From a larger perspective family structures that emphasize competition and fail to nurture meaningful contributions between generations may encourage poor economic and social development, high rates of preventable adult and child morbidity, and poor prospects for child development and survival.

Brenda F. McGadney-Douglass received her Ph.D. from the University of Chicago. Her career in applied social work practice, undergraduate and graduate education, research, and academic administration spans three decades in the United States, Ghana, and other locations in West Africa. She has focused the majority of her research and teaching on applied gerentology, international social work, health care for the poor and underserved, and the international legal and social issues of refugees and aslylum-seekers. Her field research in Ghana began in 1999 and has been continuous to the present time with field data collection in 1999, 2001/02 and 2005. She served as Visiting Scholar at the University of Ghana in 2001-2002, and taught again at the Legion campus in 2005.

Nana Araba Apt, Ph.D., is an internationally recognized scholar and expert on aging in Africa, poverty, and human development. Currently, she is the Dean of Academic Affairs at Ashesi University, a private university in Accra. She is a frequent consultant to many international human development organizations including UN organizations, the World Bank, and African Union. She was the founding director of the Centre for Social Policy Studies at the University of Ghana, and founder of the African Gerentology Society. She has published widely on aging, family, and children issues in Africa.

Richard L. Douglass is a social epidemiologist who has been directly involved in quantitative and qualitative research, field studies, and public policy analysis in public health since 1972. He received his Ph.D. in Public Health Administration from the

Univeristy of Michigan. The focus of his research has been on the impact of social and health policy and health care for the poor and underserved. His work in Ghana has been continuous since 1991 and he served as Senior Fulbright Scholar and Visiting Scholar at the University of Ghana-Legion during the 2001/02 academic year.

[1]Colonialism and post-colonial government ineptness, post-emancipation marginalization of African Americans, translocation and repression of Native Americans, Australian Aborigines, and comparable treatment of First Nations in Canada have had similar long-term consequences on these populations (see for instance Lowe, Kerridge and Mitchell; Mulholland; Fenn, Morris and Black; Black, Morris and Bryce; Bryce and Victora). Although it is clear that formerly colonized populations can enjoy significantly reduced child mortality, these advances can only be realized if governments and other sponsors are sufficiently motivated and resourced to do the job well. Aboriginal people often find that the promise of resources and services is greater than the delivery and then child mortality is either unchanged or worsens. If you add epidemics and wars to such situations, then communities become chaotic, which has been experienced by marginalized Aboriginal people. (Asenso-Okyere, Ahiadeke, Osei-Akoto and Duncan; Brockerhoff and Derose; Sall and Sylia). In addition, Aboriginal resistance against assimilation and encroachment by the majority population has often led to retaliation that has contributed to the absence or ineffectiveness of service delivery, economic development, or infrastructure management. (Elias; Udel). In some situations Aboriginal people have asserted their independence and rights and the majority power structures have punished them with fewer resources, delayed or insufficient infrastructure development, or more mistreatment. Programs for Aboriginal mistreatment are not only in remote history, but recent events that are seldom in the consciousness by majority populations, such as the experiences of Algonquin people in Quebec, or the mistreatment of Lakota People in South Dakota. Udel noted that:

> The involuntary sterilization of Native women (as well as Mexican American and African American women) is common knowledge among those communities affected but remains largely unknown to those outside the communities. A [U.S.] federal government investigation in 1976 discovered that in the four-year period between 1973 and 1976 more than three thousand Native women were involuntarily sterilized. Of the 3,406 women sterilized, 3,001 were between the ages of fifteen and forty-four, a clear violation of the 1974 Department of Health, Education and Welfare (DHEW) guidelines prohibiting involuntary sterilization of minors … the estimated number of women sterilized either coercively (often through the illegal threat of withholding govern-

ment aid or the removal of existing children), or without their knowledge, during the period is estimated at twelve thousand" (Miller [1978] and England [1997] qtd. in Udel 18-20).

[2]In the Ga language *kwashi* means the first child; *orkor* means the second child. Together the phrase takes on the meaning, "What happens when the second child is born."

References

Asenso-Okyere, W. K., C. Ahiadeke, I. Osei-Akoto and B. A. A. Duncan. *The 2000 Situation Analysis of Children and Women in Ghana.* Legon, Accra, Ghana: ISSER, The University of Ghana. 2001.

Anderson, K. and B. Lawrence, eds. *Strong Women Stories: Native Vision and Community Survival.* Toronto: Sumach Press, 2000.

Apt, N. A. *Coping with Old Age in a Changing Africa: Social Change and the Elderly Ghanaian.* Brookfield, VT: Avebury Press, 1996.

Balfour, L. "Representative Women: Slavery, Citizenship, and Feminist Theory in Du Bois's 'Damnation of Women.'" *Hypatia* 20 (3) (2005): 127-148, 238.

Berland, L. *The Queen of America Goes to Washington City: Essays on Sex and Citizenship.* Durham, N.C. Duke University Press, 1997.

Black, R. E., S. S. Morris, and J. Bryce. "Where and why are 10 million children dying every year?" *The Lancet* 361 (June 28, 2003): 2226-2234.

Bozalek, V. "Contextualizing Caring in Black South African Families." *Social Politics* 6 (1) (1999): 85-99.

Brockerhoff, M. and L. F. Derose. "Child Survival in East Africa: The Impact of Preventative Health Care." *World Development* 24 (12) (1996): 1841-1857.

Bryce, J. and C. G. Victora. "Child survival: Countdown to 2015." *The Lancet* 365(9478) (June 25-July 1, 2005): 2153-2154.

Chiwuzie, J. and C. Okolocha. "Traditional Belief Systems and Maternal Mortality in a Semi-Urban Community in Southern Nigeria." *African Journal of Reproductive Health* 5 (1) (2001): 75-82.

Coll, C. G., J. L. Surrey, K. Weingarten and M. Watkins. *Mothering Against the Odds: Diverse Voices of Contemporary Mothering.* New York: The Guilford Press, 1998.

Douglass R. L. "Social Factors Affecting Infectious and Communicable Diseases in Ghana." *Behinderung und Dritte Welt* 1 (2003): 4-8.

Du Bois, W. E. B. *Darkwater: Voices from Within the Veil Mineola.* New York: Dover Press, 1999 [1920].

Eades, S. J. and A. W. Read. "Infant Care Practices in a Metropolitan Aboriginal

Population." *Journal of Paediatrics and Child Health* 35 (6) (1999): 541-544.

Elias, P. D. "Models of Aboriginal Communities in Canada's North." *International Journal of Social Economics* 24 (11) (1997): 1241-1255.]

Fenn, B., S. Morris and R. E. Black. "Co-Morbidity in Childhood in Northern Ghana: Magnitude, Associated Factors, and Impact on Mortality." *International Journal of Epidemiology* 34(2005): 368-375.

Fleet, C. *First Nations – Firsthand.* Rowayton, CT: Saraband Inc., 1997.

Gibson, M. A. and R. Mace. "Helpful Grandmothers in Rural Ethiopia: A Study of the Effect of Kin on Child Survival and Hrowth." *Evolution and Human Behaviour* 26 (6) (2005): 469-482.

Green, R. "American Indian Women: Diverse Leadership for Social Change." *Bridges of Power: Women's Multicultural Alliances.* Eds. L. Albrecht and R. M. Brewer. Philadelphia, PA: New Society Publishers, 1990. 63-64, 71.

Haywood, A. J. *Voice from the South.* Xenia, Ohio: Aldine Publishing, 1892.

Hope, K. R., Sr. "Child Survival, Poverty, and Labour in Africa." *Journal of Children and Poverty* 11 (1) (2005): 19-42.

Jordan, E. R. Personal correspondence (with R Douglass), 2006.

Lawrence, J. "The Indian Health Service and the Sterilization of Native American Women." The American Indian Quarterly 24 (3) (2000): 400-419.

Looking Horse, K. Personal interview (with B. McGadney-Douglass). Pine Ridge, SD., 2004.

Lowe, M., I. H. Kerridge and K. R. Mitchell. "'These Sorts of People Don't Do Very Well': Race and Allocation of Health Care Resources." *Journal of Medical Ethics* 21 (6) (1995): 356-360.

MacLean, L. M. "Constructing a Social Safety Net in Africa: An Institutional Analysis of Colonial Rule and State Social Policies in Ghana and Cote d'Ivoire." *Studies in Comparative International Development* 37 (3) (2002): 64-90.

Madhavan, S. "Female Relationships and Demographic Outcomes in Sub-Saharan Africa." *Sociological Forum* 16 (3) (2001): 503-527.

McGadney-Douglass, B. F., R. L. Douglass, P. Antwi, B. Owusu and E. Garrison. "Social and Behavioural Characteristics of Long-Term Survivors of *Kwashiorkor* in Ghana." Paper presented at the African Studies Association, Philadelphia, November 1999.

McGadney-Douglass, B. F., R. L. Douglass, P. Antwi, B. Owusu and E. Garrison. "The Role of Grandmothers in the Survival of Children with *Kwashiorkor* in Ghana." Paper presented at the Michigan Academy of Science, Arts and Letters, Saginaw, March 2000.

McGadney-Douglass, B. F., R. L. Douglass, N. A. Apt, and P. Antwi. "Ghanaian Mothers Helping Adult Daughters: The Survival of Malnourished Grandchildren." *Journal of the Association for Research on Mothering* 7 (2) (2005): 112-124.

Mikell, G., ed. *African Feminism: The Politics of Survival in Sub-Saharan Africa.*

Philadelphia: University of Pennsylvania Press, 2002 [1997].

Miller, M "Native American Peoples on the Trail of Tears Once More: Indian Health Service and Coerced Sterilization." *America* 139 (1978) :422-425.

Mollar, V. "Intergenerational Relations and Time Use in Urban Black South African Households." *Social Indicators Research* 37 (3) (1996): 303-332.

Monture-Angus, Patricia. *Thunder in My Soul: A Mohawk Woman Speaks.* Halifax: Fernwood Publishing, 1995.

Morton, Patricia. *Disfigured Images: The Historical Assault on Afro-American Women.* New York: Greenwood Press, 1991.

Mulholland, K. "Commentary: Comorbidity as a Factor in Child Health and Child Survival in Developing Countries." *International Journal of Epidemiology* 34 (2) (2005): 375-377.

Naples, N. A. and M. Dobson. "Feminists and the Welfare State: Aboriginal Health Care Workers and U.S. Community Workers of Color." *National Women's Studies Association Journal* 13 (3) (2002): 116-137.

Oppong, C. "Social Capital and Systems of Care: Some Contrasting Evidence." Research report. *Research Review Supplement 16. Children at Risk in Ghana: Family Care Under Review* (University of Ghana-Legon, Institute of African Studies, 2004. 1-15.

Oppong, C. *Sex Roles, Population and Development in West Africa.* Portsmouth, NH: Heinemann Press. 1989.

Reiland, R. "W. E. B. Du Bois and 'The Damnation of Women': An Essay on African Anti-Sexist Critical Social Theory." *Journal of African American Studies* 7 (2003): 37-60.

Roberts, D. "Welfare's Ban on Poor Motherhood." *Whose Welfare?* Ed. G. Mink. Ithaca, NY: Cornell University Press, 1999. 152-170.

Sall, M. and J. Sylia. "African Prime Ministers take lead in child survival." *The Lancet* 366 (9502) (December 10-16, 2005): 1988-1989.

Schechter, P. *Ida B. Wells-Barnett and American Reform, 1880-1930.* Chapel Hill, Univeristy of North Carolina Press, 2001.

Sear, R., R. Mace, and I. A. McGregor. "Maternal Grandmothers Improve Nutritional Status and Survival of Children in Rural Gambia." *Proceedings of the Royal Society of London, Series B-Biological Sciences* 267 (14530) (2000): 1641-1647.

Udel, L. J. "Revision and Resistance: The Politics of Native Women's Motherwork." *Frontiers* 2 (2) (2001): 43-62.

Wardman, D., K. Clement, and D. Quantz. "Access and Utilization of Health Services by British Columbia's Rural Aboriginal Population." *Leadership in Health Services* 18 (2) (2005): 26-31.

Williams, C. D. "Kwashiorkor: A nutritional disease of children associated with a maize diet." *Lancet* 229 (1935): 1151-1152.

Aboriginal Mothering

An Australian Perspective

BELINDA WHEELER

[I]t is from those who have suffered the sentence of history—subjugation, domination, diaspora, displacement—that we learn our most enduring lessons for living and thinking.

—Bhabha (1992: 438)

Growing up as part of the white majority in Australia, I was somewhat aware of the Aborigines and their assigned position in white society. It was not until I started researching their history that I began to understand parts of their fascinating culture and some of the relationships that occurred within their tribes. As a woman, I was especially intrigued by the role of the Aboriginal mother. I discovered that, traditionally, the bond between an Australian Aboriginal mother and her children was strong, with the mother undertaking multiple responsibilities, including nurturer, protector, and educator. Since the colonization of Australia, however, legislation by white culture stripped Aboriginal mothers of this traditional role. Numerous acts by the government, especially between 1905 and 1970, forcibly and permanently removed tens of thousands of Aboriginal children from their families. In order to "civilize" them, by forcing them to assimilate into white society, the children were placed in institutions or homes of white Australians. This event had a traumatic affect on all Aborigines, especially mothers and their children. Stolen away from loved ones and all they knew, these children are known today as the "Stolen Generation."

This chapter will review case studies, government legislation, and the recent literature produced by mothers and daughters from the Stolen Generation to show the numerous setbacks Aboriginal mothers have endured since Australia was colonized. Furthermore, the chapter argues that despite many obstacles, Aboriginal mothers are starting to rally together and reclaim their voices. This process is helping Aboriginal women recover their identity, helping them return to their traditional role, and helping them ensure the white majority understands what happened to them so that similar events never occur again.

Anthropological Case Studies

Since the First Settlers arrived in Australia in 1788, there has been increasing interaction between the Australian Aborigines and whites. While some reports have claimed that the relationship between the two groups was friendly, there have been conflicting reports stating their relations were hostile. Regardless of what opinions are to be believed, early anthropological reports from the 1800s onwards describe how foreign the natives seemed to the whites and what little research was conducted in order to truly understand the Aboriginal culture. Instead, sweeping statements from an ill-informed white majority appear to have set the stage for an openly hostile forum of discussion. Furthermore, the lack of research regarding Aboriginal women highlights just how little the white majority valued them.

Given the little regard whites had for the Aborigines, it was no surprise that much of the research highlighted the inferiority of the native peoples. Deeming Aborigines as "the most uncivilized of the races of mankind" (Wake 1867: cv-cvi), many whites viewed these savages as "nearer than most existing peoples to the anthropoid apes" (Bonwick 202). Painting them as "mere children" (79), Charles Staniland Wake stated:

> [t]o speak … of intellectual phenomena in relation to the Australian aborigines is somewhat of a misnomer. This race presents, in fact, hardly any of what are usually understood as the phenomena of intellect. Nor could it be otherwise with savages who … have no aim in life but the continuance of their existence and the gratification of their passions. … (1872: 74)

Therefore, continued Wake, "the low position I have assigned to the Australian aborigines, a position which their moral defects … requires for them" is deserved (1872: 76).

Further research highlights how most of the "critical revisions [centered] around issues of cultural difference," perpetuating the belief that Aborigines were inferior to whites (Bhabha 1992: 437). Believing in the Dreamtime, "the time when the great mythical beings established the foundations of human socio-cultural existence, formed the physical features of the environment and created human beings and animals," rather than Christianity, Aborigines were considered to be immoral and immature (Choo 29). Also, because they were nomads who felt a close connection to the land and chose to forage for food rather than cultivate the earth for crops as Europeans did, they were deemed uncivilized. These negative views of the Aborigines, because of their different cultural beliefs, were used to paint them as a lower class of being.

As more research was conducted in the 1900s, many anthropologists continued viewing Australian Aborigines as others. As anthropologist Henry Taylor Parker states, "The Australian aborigine is a race apart.... [He represents] a more generalized type of man than is to be found in any other part of the world ... [and] remains in a very primitive state" (57). Even less than 60 years ago, the Aborigine was seen as "other." Physical anthropologists in the late 1950s went into the field taking blood pressures, hair and blood samples for laboratory assessment, as well as photographing the Aborigines naked (Abbie 96-97). Thus, more than 150 years since Australia was colonized, Australian Aborigines continued to be seen as others who were valued only as a source of study rather than as equals.

While there was much discussion in earlier reports about the Aborigine, anthropologists gave little attention to women and their role within the tribe. As scholar Marie Reay states, male anthropologists provided "a sketchy impression of the women's activities. Consequently most of the standard accounts present a somewhat unbalanced view of Aboriginal society" (319). These sketchy impressions by the white male anthropologists reveal how little attention was afforded to Aboriginal women.

From the piecemeal information that was available from the late 1800s and early 1900s, it is evident that the white male anthropologists saw Aboriginal women as greatly oppressed individuals who were biologically different from white counterparts. Referring to the woman's place within the Aboriginal community, many anthropologists reported the Australian Aborigines were "the greatest oppressors of women on earth," keeping them in a role "of abject slavery" (Westermarck 408). Similarly, believing Aboriginal women were treated heartlessly by their community, Wake stated, "[t]he favoured classes are the old or the strong, who obtain their advantages at the expense of the female sex, the young, and the weak, who are condemned to 'a hopeless state of degradation'" (1872: 77). For the first 50 years of anthropological research regarding Aboriginal reproduction, many researchers painted Aboriginal women as biologically different from white women. During this time, it was thought that when an Aboriginal woman copulated with a white man and produced a child, she would no longer be able to reproduce with Aboriginal men. It was not until an investigation undertaken by surgeon T. R. H. Thomson in 1854 that this theory was discredited. Thus, from these examples it is clear how little was known about Aboriginal women at the time.

Role of the Aboriginal Mother

While earlier anthropological cases make it appear that the women were oppressed members within the Aboriginal community, or led unimportant lives, this was far from the case. The work by noted anthropologist Phyllis Kaberry overturned previous data and highlighted the rich lives Aboriginal women had both within their families and their tribes. In her 1939 study, Kaberry "disposed of the prevailing view that the women were mere drudges, revealed the part they played in the economic exchanges of this area, and presented generally a new picture of the place and function of women in the economic life of the Aborigines" (McCarthy 176). Kaberry also noted the role the mother had in her children's lives, acting as educator, protector, and nurturer. Debunking the previous view that only Aboriginal men held rituals, Kaberry pointed out that the women had a rich ceremonial life of their own, performing various rituals, both private and secret, including birth corroborees (Aborigine ceremonies that involve singing and dancing) and "love magic" rituals that tied them closer to one another and their tribe. After spending close to three years in the field, Kaberry concluded, the Aboriginal woman "is a complex social personality, having her own prerogatives, duties, problems, beliefs, rituals, and point of view ... and at the same time exercising a certain freedom of choice in matters affecting her own interests and desires" (ix).

Traditionally, Aboriginal women passed along stories of their rituals and beliefs from generation to generation; this activity by the women helped ensure their native culture survived. As scholar Christine Choo states, by keeping alive "the memory and oral tradition of their families and communities" Aboriginal women "constitute the backbone of Aboriginal society" (1). Narratives by Aboriginal daughters demonstrate the important lessons mothers have passed on to their children. Talking from personal experience Betty Lockyer notes, "The old women taught us what fruits and plants to eat and what not to eat, the poisonous ones and the medicinal ones... they taught us survival skills" (30). Reflecting on her relationship with her mother, Tazuko Kaino reveals, "Mum took me to corroborees, cockling, collecting oysters, etc., to teach me how to live off the land and look after it" (90). Thus, through the medium of oral stories, or practical application, Aboriginal mothers passed on valuable advice to their children, keeping the traditions alive for future generations.

Government Legislation

Disregarding the importance of the Aboriginal race, their culture, or the roles each person held within their community, especially women, the government began proposing legislation regarding the treatment of the native people. Concerned about the increasing numbers of the half-caste (mixed race—one white, one Aboriginal parent) population, the government started implementing radical legislation in the late 1800s to deal with this new class of Aboriginal. Believing the half-castes were superior to the full-blood Aborigines (a belief fostered through the theory of Social Darwinism), state governments throughout the nation set about identifying Aborigines as either "full-blood, half-caste, quarter-caste, according to the amount of Aboriginal blood in their veins" (Fraser 266), and began enforcing legislation that would forever change their traditional way of life.

One of the most powerful pieces of legislation that had a dramatic impact on the Aboriginal population was the *Aborigines Act of 1905*, implemented by the Western Australian Government. Reflecting the belief of Social Darwinism at the time, the Act identified "aboriginality to be a biological rather than a cultural matter," consequently "anyone with more than twenty-five per cent [sic] aboriginal blood was included within its terms" (Tillbrook qtd. in Turner 535). The *Aborigines Act of 1905* assigned a Chief Protector of Aborigines who "was declared legal guardian of all aboriginal children" and given various powers including the authority to "separate children from their families and move aborigines among settlements at will" (Tillbrook qtd. in Turner 535).

A major focus of the *Aborigines Act of 1905* was the removal of half-caste children from their families. Legislation by governments reflected the belief that because of their mixed parentage half-caste children felt displaced from society and were consequently "deprived of the moral and social standards of either black or white" (Parker 63). Removing children from what was seen as the negative influence of their Aboriginal family and community it was believed the half-castes would forget their past and develop into civilized beings. With these goals in mind the government enacted legislation that sought the removal of half-caste children so they could be taught in the ways of the white culture, learn the values of Christianity as opposed to the Dreamtime, and become trained as domestic servants and laborers for their eventual release at the age of sixteen into the white community. By integrating the half-castes into white culture, it was also hoped that they would marry white Australians and eventually through the process of reproduction throughout future generations, the Aboriginal blood would be bred out and cease to exist.

Along with the removal of the half-caste children, the government also hoped the *Aborigines Act of 1905* would overturn the rising half-caste population. In order to reduce the increasing numbers, the government started limiting the interaction between full-blood Aborigines and whites, hoping to reduce the opportunity for the two parties to reproduce. A way the government set about achieving this goal was to make it illegal for non-Aborigines to socialize with Aborigines, unless they were in possession of a social permit. The government also made it harder for Aborigines and non-Aborigines to marry. If such a union was desired the white male or female had to fill out various forms requesting permission from the Chief Protector, as well as pay a significant fee. This application could be denied at any stage of the process and there was no means of appeal. The implication of these policies reflects the radical steps the government was willing to take to reduce the half-caste population.

Recognizing the dramatic and favorable effect of the Western Australian legislation, other states throughout Australia began implementing similar policies.

Examples of this include the *Aborigines Protection Act,* which was implemented in 1909 by the state of New South Wales. This Act included empowering police to remove children from their family and send them to training homes, begin legal proceedings against parents who resisted their children's removal, and expel light-colored people from areas frequented by Aborigines, such as reserves. Similarly, the *Aborigines (Training for Children) Act* of 1923 implemented in South Australia also called for the removal of half-caste children from their families, whereby they would be transported to institutions until their wardship expired. In accordance with legislation by the states, children were either relocated to government settlements, missions run by religious institutions, or placed into foster care. Legislation like the abovementioned had a devastating effect on the Aboriginal population between 1910 and 1970, with estimates close to 100,000 half-caste children being forcibly removed and placed into the various types of facilities. These conditions existed until the 1970s when the federal government overturned states' legislation, thereby ending the removal of half-caste children.

Women's Stories

Before the federal government intervened in the 1970s Aboriginal mothers suffered in silence while their children were stolen away from them. Overpowered by the states' legislation, mothers had no platform to speak out or raise their voices in protest. The states' legislation, therefore, not only severed the connection between mothers and their children, but it also severed the connection between the older and younger generations of Aborigines. Responding to the silence they were forced to maintain during this time, many Aborigines, especially mothers, have started reclaiming their voices. They are beginning to retell their native stories as well as discuss the incidents that happened to them while their children were stolen away from their families, their native homeland, and their culture. "[T]hese narratives," according to Kay Schaffer, have become "a forum for indigenous people to speak in their own behalf, thus mediating 200 years of being spoken about by anthropologists, historians, linguists, missionaries, government officials, artists, novelists, and filmmakers" (5). Reflecting on the Aboriginal stories becoming available, Australian Aboriginal Rita Huggins states, "I like the sad stories coming out because it helps people. It gives Aboriginal people confidence to speak about our lives and to be listened to. I think it's good that Aboriginal people are writing down these stories. We've got a lot of things to say to the migaloos (whites)" (qtd. in Schaffer 5).

While the legislation enacted between 1905 and 1970 significantly affected mothers, it also had serious repercussions for their children. When placed in the care of foster homes, missions or dormitories, the Aboriginal children were stripped of their heritage and forced to adopt the European system. Under the care of the government, they were taught how to read and write, to be obedient, to work, to value Christianity, and told to forget the ways of the past. As a person who was forcibly removed from her family, Tazuko Kaino reports, "The police used to take the half-caste children away from their full-blood mothers and place them in an orphanage, to be brought up in the white-man system. They were told not to remember their mothers and families" (89). The children were not allowed to speak their native tongue, to practice any of their own rituals, or follow any of their own belief systems. Author of the novel *Rabbit-Proof Fence*, Doris Pilkington, relates that her mother and aunts were told, "'You girls can't talk blackfulla language here, you know. You gotta forget it and talk English all the time'" (72). This act of silencing a voice, according to bell hooks, "particularly the girl child," was "intended to suppress all possibility that [a girl] ... would create [her] ... own speech. That speech was to be suppressed so that the 'right speech of womanhood' would emerge" (6). Thus, the Aboriginal children, especially girls, were only allowed to speak if their speech reflected the beliefs and ideals of the white majority.

The narratives that have been published since the 1970s vary with some women describing their experiences in the dormitories or missions, and others recounting the incidents that occurred while living in foster care. Living in the dormitory since she was eight, Elsie Roughsey recalls being locked up between the hours of seven in the evening until seven in the morning (qtd. in Huffer 36). While her experience was not as traumatic as many other children, Roughsey recalled that many young children were brought to the dormitory when they were three to four years of age. These children, states Roughsey "never saw their parents again and they would cry and cry" (qtd. in Huffer 36). Recalling her experience at the dormitory, Catherine Elong reports "The dorm was good, but not a happy place" (qtd. in Huffer 84). Elong stayed at the dormitory until a missionary asked her if she would like to marry a man that had been raised in the dormitory for boys, an act which goes against the traditional Aboriginal belief that the child's parents find a suitable wife or husband for their child. Reflecting on the marriage Elong states, "I married him to get my freedom from the dormitory. The marriage was never any good. It was with someone I never loved" (qtd. in Huffer 85).

While most Aboriginal children never saw their families again, for those fortunate enough to be allowed to maintain contact with their families, it was under strict rules. Meeting with families on an allocated day, the children would be separated from their families by a fence. This fence, remembers Stolen Generation member, Betty Lockyer was "like cattle yard fences, which kept animals at bay" (24). Further highlighting how little the Aborigines were trusted, the reunions would always be overseen by either a nun or priest until the visits were over (Lockyer 24). The effects of being forcibly removed or having little or no contact with their families was evident. As Lockyer recalls, "the kids I grew up with at the mission, and later on at the orphanage in Broome, were like lost souls, plucked out from loved ones' arms, herded like cattle into holding yards and then dumped with strangers in a frightening environment" (24-25).

While living in the missions and dormitories was traumatic for many Aboriginal children, so was the experience of many children brought up in foster care. Removed from the family home in 1961, Rosalie Fraser and her siblings were placed into various foster care homes (210). Fraser recounts, "we had no idea where our parents were, we never saw or heard from them and we were unaware of what efforts they might be making to get us back.... The separation was total; our new life was the only one we knew" (12). In her heart-wrenching narrative entitled *Shadow Child*, Fraser recalls numerous times of both verbal and physical abuse she and her sister Bev endured. Called such names as "fuckers, bastards, pair of bastards ... or boongs," Fraser recalls her foster family rarely using their real names (24). Fraser also remembers her foster mother grabbing her "by the back of the neck and pushing [her towards] ... the mirror, and saying, 'Now look! Look how ugly you are, you dirty boong—you're nothing but shit.'" (27). These experiences left Fraser feeling like she was ugly, unworthy of love, and not fully accepted as human, hence the title of her book.

Apart from the verbal abuse she endured, Fraser and her younger sister also suffered horrific physical abuse. This abuse varied, including being nearly drowned while taking a bath, having limbs broken, or parts of their bodies burned on the kitchen stove. More chilling, however, was a horrendous event that occurred after Fraser and her sister had been playing. Pretending to cook food for her sister out of mud, the preschoolers Fraser and Bev sat down to their dinner when they were called inside. Seeing the mud over Fraser's hands and mud all over Bev's face, their foster mother flew into a violent rage grabbing both girls. Fraser recalls, "My foster mother dragged me by the leg, screaming.... She laid me over her knee, ripped my pants off, forced my legs apart and pushed something long and sharp inside me [which Fraser later determined was a knitting needle], moving it around inside me ... the pain was shocking" (19). After pushing Fraser to the floor, her foster mother demanded she get up. Unable to do so, Fraser was then told that if she did not get up from the blood-soaked floor, her foster mother would kill her. With her younger sister helplessly watching on, Fraser, in agony, pulled herself up to her feet, but with the blood flowing more profusely from her body she soon passed out (19-20). After spending eight days in hospital, Fraser was sent back to her foster home (22). Recalling her story, Fraser states, "I tell you, for the life of me I never spoke to a single soul about what happened to me, not even to my own little sister, even though I knew she had seen what happened" (22). Thus, for part of her life, the abuse Fraser sustained silenced her voice. It was not until Fraser was writing the book, a process she believes allowed her to reclaim her voice, she learned that while she was in hospital, her sister, Bev, sustained similar injuries and was also admitted to hospital. Recalling past events, Fraser laments, "I believe we were just one family amongst many, many thousands who suffered from the implications of the *1905 Aborigines Act*" (265).

Like the narratives being published recently, the 1997 Human Rights and Equal Opportunities Commission (HREOC) Report, entitled *Bringing them Home*, also provided Aborigines the chance to let their voices be heard. This report, states Schaffer, "documents the history, effects, and the consequences of the government's assimilationist policies on Indigenous children who were forcibly removed from their families between 1910 and 1970" (5). Containing over 500 personal stories, the HREOC report, like the personal narratives being published, "reveal shocking instances of racist oppression and violence, physical and sexual abuse, physical dislocation, loss of language, land and culture" (Schaffer 5-6). Regarding the impact of the stories contained in the report, Schaffer states, "The voices, juxtaposed with and framed within the public discourse of the Inquiry, enabled indigenous speakers a place and a space within a national culture they had not been able to occupy before" (6). Furthermore, the reports by hundreds of Aborigines in this document not only reflected the shocking types of abuse many Stolen Generation members suffered, but they also gave credibility to the personal narratives that had been published since the 1970s.

Effects on Mothering For Stolen Generation Members

While many of the women's stories vary, it is clear that the effects of forced separation were considerable. Not surprisingly, their traumatic experiences impacted the children later when they became mothers. When Fraser had her own baby she was terrified the government would take him away from her. She recalls, "I stayed at the hospital for only one day, because ... above all, I was terrified they were going to take my baby. I knew that the longer I stayed in hospital the less chance I would have of walking out with my new son" (Fraser 143). Even when she turned eighteen and received a letter from the Welfare department stating her "wardship had expired," Fraser recalls still feeling threatened by the government: "I did not trust them. I was always worried and believed I had to stay on my toes so I could keep my son" (153).

Other women from the Stolen Generation noted how difficult it was being a mother to their children, or similarly how difficult it was being the stolen daughters of their native mothers. As anthropologist Virginia Huffer noted, "Elsie [Roughsey] and many other mothers were deeply concerned about, but confused by, their offspring. They found discipline and control difficult" (137). Huffer believed many factors contributed to the problems mothers were having, including "the rapid transition in their way of life, from their polygynous tribal beginnings to the unique dormitory rearing, and then to marriage in a western-type family structure," which meant the women "had no prototype for the job of being parents in a settled family situation" (137-138). Similarly, the Aboriginal Legal Service has noted that, because of their institutionalized upbringing, many Aborigines have never had the chance to develop parenting skills (qtd. in Beresford and Omajl 213). Likewise, many children from the Stolen Generation have felt confused about their native parents, especially their mothers. As Kathy Richards discovered after being forcibly separated from her mother for most of her life, "[a]t times, I don't understand my real mother at all. Sometimes I get angry when I think about it" (215). Thus, by severing the relationships between mothers and their children, the various state governments' legislation between 1905 and 1970 effectively damaged many Aboriginal women's attempts to pass on the mothering role to future generations.

Raising their Voice

Despite all they have endured since the First Settlers arrived, Aboriginal women have started rallying together and begun raising their voices. This process, states theorist Homi Bhabha, shows "the crucial importance, for subordinated peoples, of asserting their indigenous cultural traditions and retrieving their repressed histories" (1994: 13). Whether it is through their published narratives, their reports to the HREOC, or their oral traditions they are beginning to retell within their own communities, Aboriginal women are making considerable strides to reconnect with their past. As Kaino proclaims, "I'm proud to say that I'm Aboriginal ... I would like ... [our] people to be recognized and not forgotten. We had a hard life in the 1800s and 1900s.... Now it's our time to be recognized and live ... in peace. The land and customs is always in our hearts and minds, we cannot forget what our mothers have taught us about how to live and respect our land" (91). Realizing the importance of ensuring their voices are never silenced again, Kaino notes, "my generation will keep on teaching and passing on what we know to our children" (91).

Similarly, women like Kathy Richards and Elsie Roughsey are raising their voices in an attempt to heal the wounds of the past and ensure others learn from their histories. Forcibly removed when she was four, Richards remained in the government's care until her wardship expired at eighteen. Discussing her past, Richards states "My real family got scattered all over the place and I am only just getting to know some of them now. We have all been affected in different ways.... We were all hurt, some more than others, but we are all doing what we can to live our lives as best we can" (215). Explaining why she chose to come forward and tell her story, Richards confesses, "I don't want to see the department return to the days of moving kids around all over the place. That's one reason for telling my story. The other is to say, despite all that has happened, I have survived" (215).

Likewise, Roughsey states, "I have nothing to be ashamed of and you [Virginia Huffer] have written about my life as I have known and lived it. I want the world to know what life is like on Mornington Island. If any student can learn anything from it, I will be pleased" (qtd. in Huffer vii). These stories by women such as Richards and Roughsey, therefore, are not only mending past wrongs within the Aboriginal community, but by sharing their stories with the white majority Aboriginal women are making considerable strides towards educating those that were not aware of what Aborigines have endured.

Conclusion

Looking at the lives Aboriginal women, it is evident how much Aboriginal mothers and their children have been forced to endure since white settlement. Early anthropological studies show how Aboriginal women were seen as mere drudges who led simplistic lives. When an interest was taken in the increasing half-caste population, the legislation by state governments had direct implications for Aboriginal mothers. Trying to strip them of their children, diminish their role within the community, and limit their social interaction with whites, the government hoped the half-caste population would be bred out and the traditional culture that Aboriginal mothers passed on to their children and the community would be stopped. Such is their resilient nature, however, that between 1905 and 1970 rather than die out, the mothers' voices lay dormant. Remembering all they had been taught by their mothers, the Aboriginal women waited until legislation was overturned, and when they no longer feared retribution they reclaimed their voices and started mending the wrongs of the past. Restoring the oral tradition, Aboriginal women have begun retelling stories from their historic past and passing on numerous teachings to future Aboriginal generations. This act has helped Aboriginal women reclaim their identity as the "backbone of Aboriginal society" and assisted them as they have tried to reconnect with their own children and families (Choo 1). More fascinating, however, is the Aboriginal women's decision to raise their voices to a wider audience. Rather than limit their voices to their own community, as had been done in the past, modern Aboriginal women are spreading their voices to include white culture as well. By taking this action in the world, Aboriginal women are claiming their identity and creating a space within white culture. By ensuring they are no longer seen as 'others' or "degenerate types on the basis of racial origin" (Bhabha 1992: 438), Aboriginal women are ensuring an ill-informed white majority learns from past events and never again strips away their important role as mothers or as invaluable members within the Aboriginal community.

Belinda Wheeler graduated with highest honours from Purdue University, Indiana,

USA. She is currently working toward a Ph.D. in English. A passionate Australian, Belinda feels strongly about the plight of Australian Aboriginals. She has presented numerous papers and won several awards for her writing.

References

Abbie, Andrew Arthur. "Physical Characteristics of Australian Aborigines." *Australian Aboriginal Studies: A Symposium of Papers Presented at the 1961 Research Conference.* Ed. W. E. H. Stanner. Melbourne: Oxford University Press, 1963. 96-97.

Beresford, Quentin and Paul Omajl. *Our State of Mind: Racial Planning and the Stolen Generations.* South Fremantle, W.A.: Fremantle Arts Centre Press, 1998.

Bhabha, Homi K. *The Location of Culture.* New York: Routledge, 1994.

Bhabha, Homi K. "Postcolonial Criticism." *Redrawing the Boundaries: The Transformation of English and American Literary Studies.* Eds. Stephen Greenblatt and Giles Gunn. New York: MLA, 1992. 437-465.

Bonwick, James. "The Australian Natives." *The Journal of the Anthropological Institute of Great Britain and Ireland* 16 (1887): 201-210.

Choo, Christine. *Mission Girls: Aboriginal Women on Catholic Missions in the Kimberley, Western Australia, 1900-1950.* Crawley, W.A.: University of Western Australia Press, 2001.

Fraser, Rosalie. *Shadow Child: A Memoir of the Stolen Generation.* Alexandria, NSW: Hale and Iremonger, 1998.

hooks, bell. *Talking Back: Thinking Feminist, Thinking Black.* Boston, MA: South End Press, 1989.

Huffer, Virginia. *The Sweetness of the Fig: Aboriginal Women in Transition.* Sydney: New South Wales University Press, 1980.

Human Rights and Equal Opportunity Commmission (HREOC). *Bringing Them Home: Report of the National Inquiry into the Separation of Aboriginal and Torres Strait Islander Children from Their Families.* Sydney: Australian Government Publishing Service, 1997.

Kaberry, Phyllis. *Aboriginal Woman, Sacred and Profane.* London: Routledge, 1939.

Kaino, Tazuko. "A Very Special Family." *Holding up the Sky: Aboriginal Women Speak.* Broome, WA: Magabala Books, 1999. 89-91.

Lockyer, Betty. "War Baby." *Holding up the Sky: Aboriginal Women Speak.* Broome, WA: Magabala Books, 1999. 24-30.

McCarthy, F. D. "Ecology, Equipment, Economy and Trade." *Australian Aboriginal Studies: A Symposium of Papers Presented at the 1961 Research Conference.* Ed. W. E. H. Stanner. Melbourne: Oxford University Press, 1963. 176-189.

Parker, Henry Taylor. "The Australian Aborigine." *The Journal of Negro Educa-*

tion 3 (1) (1934): 57-65.

Pilkington, Doris. *Rabbit-Proof Fence*. New York: Miramax Books, 2002.

Reay, Marie. "The Social Position of Women." *Australian Aboriginal Studies: A Symposium of Papers Presented at the 1961 Research Conference*. Ed. W. E. H. Stanner. Melbourne: Oxford University Press, 1963. 319-334

Richards, Kathy. "Nobody's Child." *Holding up the Sky: Aboriginal Women Speak*. Broome, WA: Magabala Books, 1999. 215.

Schaffer, Kay. "Stolen Generation Narratives in Local and Global Contexts." *Antipodes* 16 (1) (2002): 5-10.

Thomson, T. R. H. "Observations on the Reported Incompetency of the 'Gins' or Aboriginal Females of New Holland, to Procreate with a Native Male after Having Borne Half-Caste Children to a European or White." *Journal of the Ethnological Society of London* 3 (1854): 243-246.

Turner, David. "Nyungar Tradition. Glimpses of Aborigines of South-Western Australia, 1829-1914." *Pacific Affairs* 57 (3) (1984): 534-535.

Wake, Charles Staniland. "On the Antiquity of Man and Comparative Geology." *Journal of The Anthropological Society of London* 5 (1867): cv-cxvii.

Wake, Charles Staniland. "The Mental Characteristics of Primitive Man, as Exemplified by the Australian Aborigines." *The Journal of the Anthropological Institute of Great Britain and Ireland* 1 (1872): 74-84.

Westermarck, Edward. "The Position of Women in Early Civilization." *The American Journal of Sociology* 10 (3) (1904): 408-421.

"BIG MOTHER"

THE ROLE OF THE STATE IN THE PERFORMANCE OF MOTHERING

Aboriginal Mothering Under the State's Gaze

RANDI CULL

Aboriginal people, unlike any other race or ethnicity in Canada, are born political. Historically and currently, Aboriginal women in particular are used as political pawns of the state. In the late 1970s, Kathleen Jamieson wrote "to be born poor, an Indian, and a female is to be a member of the most disadvantaged minority in Canada today, a citizen minus" (qtd. Indian and Northern Affairs Canada 1). Almost three decades later, the status of Aboriginal women, especially mothers, has not changed significantly. For Aboriginal women, motherhood represents a core aspect of a woman's being and it constitutes a benchmark component of an Aboriginal community's well-being. Being an Aboriginal mother involves navigating parenthood under the pervasive, critical glare of the state. The theme that links the state's past and present treatment of Aboriginal mothers involves the non-empirically supported, implicit notion that Aboriginal women are "unfit" parents in need of state observation, guidance and at times, intervention. The state has been instrumental in creating a negative stereotype of Aboriginal women as being inherently "inferior" people and "unfit" parents. This stereotype justifies and legitimizes the state's inappropriate and unjust scrutiny of Aboriginal mothers.

The stereotype of Aboriginal women being "unfit" mothers has a long history and it has, over time, become an entrenched aspect of the Canadian social and state system, with often devastating consequences for Aboriginal women and their communities. To understand the significance of this stereotype, one needs to put Aboriginal women's collective experiences in historical context. The legacies of the *Indian Act* of 1876, assimilation initiatives, the residential school system, the eugenics movement, landmark legal decisions, and child protection policies have all served to nurture and sustain the negative stereotype of Aboriginal mothers. These will be elaborated upon in an attempt to deconstruct the complex nature of the negative stereotype of Aboriginal mothers that portrays them as inherently "unfit" and as threats as opposed to women who, overall, successfully manage motherhood against enormous odds.

141

Randi Cull

The Legacy of Colonization and the Creation of the "Indian"

Aboriginal motherhood needs to be appreciated juxtaposed with the experiences and legacy of colonization. Prior to European contact, Aboriginal women were revered for their roles as mothers. For the most part, Aboriginal clans and culture were matrilineal in nature and as such, Aboriginal women had considerable power and social status. Post-contact, the social structure changed to the patriarchal system that was standard among Europeans and the status and influence of Aboriginal women was dramatically altered. Aboriginal woman's roles as mothers became increasingly subject to state scrutiny and control.

European contact with Aboriginal peoples was not always negative or conflict ridden. At the end of the fifteenth century, relations between Aboriginals and non-Aboriginals were, overall, respectful and both parties were tolerant of one another (Bennett, Blackstock, and De La Ronde 10). The eighteenth century period witnessed the inception of pervasive conflict between the European settlers and the Aboriginal peoples. The post-eighteenth century was a bleak time marked by the decimation of Aboriginal populations. The Canadian government aggressively expropriated native land and implemented policies of segregation, oppression, and discrimination. Arguably, assimilation polices went too far and became extermination policies (Restoule 110). The state came to develop and entrench, especially with the passing of the *Indian Act* of 1876, a mandate that sought to enslave the Aboriginal peoples by enforcing a system of dependency. The *Indian Act* explicitly designated Aboriginal people wards or children of the state (Bennett, Blackstock, and De La Ronde 13). Every aspect of their lives became regulated to the degree that the Canadian government resolved to create, and to "own," the very identity of the "Indian" (Restoule 111). This identity involved the notion that Indians were inherently inferior; they were portrayed as being fundamentally unable to think for themselves and thus needed the Europeans, members of the "master race," to do it for them (Switlo 103; Bennettt, Blackstock, and De La Ronde 12). Indians became the "savages"; the "evolutionary throwbacks" in dire need of the guidance, influence, and intervention of the "benevolent" colonists.

Politics and resource accumulation is what drove the creation of the negative stereotype of the "Indian," not any identifiable, inherent traits. The negative identity of what it was to be an Indian was a necessary tactical maneuver for the state to secure land ownership. European sovereignty regulations involved the interpretation of the concept of the "doctrine of discovery" or *terra nullius* (i.e., land considered to be barren and uninhabited); if land was deemed barren, settlers had rights to the immediate sovereignty over the land (Bennett, Blackstock, and De La Ronde 11). If the land was found to be inhabited, sovereign ownership of land required "proof" that it was occupied by uncivilized people and to do this, it had to be shown that the original inhabitants were without government and social organization—"uncivilized" people were considered not capable of legitimately holding land (Bennett, Blackstock, and De La Ronde 11).

In reality, Aboriginal people had a well-established system of governance and a complex social structure. As noted, the pre-contact Aboriginal social structure was for the most part matrilineal. This was a sharp contrast to the established European patriarchal norms. Dismantling the traditional male-female social roles among Aboriginal peoples and devaluing their established system of social order was an essential tactic to "prove" the Indians were uncivilized (Bennett, Blackstock, and De La Rhonde 13). A critical aspect of the creation of the concept of the "Indian" was the re-development of the concept of the female Indian, especially their historically revered roles as mothers. A situation reminiscent of our modern situation, the state blamed Aboriginal women for their children's social and medical problems. Old government sessional reports dating back to the early twentieth century suggest that inadequate native mothering practices were the reasons for the prevalence of tuberculosis and high rates of infant mortality that were ravaging Indian communities. The mothers were considered to be the source of the problem as opposed to the dramatic changes in their lifestyles and the dire social conditions experienced since colonization (Moffat and Herring 1828). Mothers were portrayed as ignorant and unable to properly care for their children; as such, the state sought to "teach" the native mothers the proper way to care for children by setting up baby clinics (Moffat and Herring 1821). By the latter nineteeth century, the Aboriginal mother was "the bad mother, uncivilized and uncivilizing" (McGillivray and Comaskey 31). This depiction justified more aggressive tactics; hence, the implementation and proliferation of programs and policies that restricted and redefined Aboriginal women's capacity to parent.

Wounding the Soul: The Displacement of Aboriginal Children and Youth

The singularly most damaging action geared towards supporting the notion that Aboriginal females are inadequate nurturers has been the arbitrary removal of their children from their families, clans, communities, and culture. Definitions of what constitutes an "unfit" parent vary but having a child removed from your care or having restrictions placed on your autonomy and privacy as a parent are strong indicators that the state and the public perceive you as being "unfit." The most explicit indication that the state perceives Aboriginal mothers as "unfit" has been the over-surveillance and inappropriate state interference in their capacity as a parent.

State initiatives designed to facilitate the removal of Aboriginal children and youth from the influence of their Aboriginal mothers and their heritage initially involved placing them in industrial and residential schools and, starting in the

1960s, placing them in state care, predominantly with non-Aboriginal homes. This deliberate process has been so extreme that it has been identified as an act of "cultural genocide," as defined by international law (Chupik-Hall 13; Downey 57; Johnston xx). The removal of Aboriginal children and youth from their parents and communities has been linked to a host of social pathologies such as very high suicide rates, sexual exploitation, substance use and abuse, poverty, compromised educational attainment, and chronic unemployment. Exacerbating the situation, these outcomes have resulted in the ever-increasing surveillance and involvement of the criminal justice system and child protection agencies (Blackstock, Trocme, and Bennett 904).

Both the residential schools and the child protection system are instrumental tools of assimilation and control. Aboriginal people have always strongly resisted the removal of their children (Pettit iv) but the significant power differentials between the state and Aboriginal people, a population systemically disenfranchised, have disabled attempts to fight the system. In total, the esteemed bond between Aboriginal mothers and their children has been under attack for over five generations, the cumulative effects of which are largely non-quantifiable but undeniably devastating and unjust. The socialization process involved with exposing children and youth to Aboriginal parenting practices has also been precariously compromised

Assimilation policies created a situation in which each birth of an Aboriginal child implicitly violated the state's goal of dominating and at times exterminating the Aboriginal peoples (Restoule 110). With this type of ethos in place, the Aboriginal mother became, whether explicitly stated or not, an enemy of the state. Indirectly, the residential school experience re-enforced the idea that Aboriginal mothers were irresponsible and uncaring. The residential school system served to deny generations of Aboriginal children access to their families, communities, language, culture, and customs. They also exposed thousands of Aboriginal children to abuse and neglect. Although Aboriginal mothers are highly scrutinized and penalized for possibly exposing their children to "neglect" and "abuse," the Canadian government and religious institutions remain sheltered and enjoy relative immunity from their aggressive actions which continue to cause harm to Aboriginal children and youth.

Killing the Spirit: The Legacy of the "Sixties Scoop"

Although unknown to many Canadians, it is estimated that up to three times more Aboriginal children and youth are currently in state care than during the height of the residential school experience in the 1940s (Blackstock, Trocme, and Bennett 905). The involvement of the state in the removal of Aboriginal children and youth from their homes started in the late 1960s and continues today. The mass removals of Aboriginal children during this time came to be called the "Sixties Scoop." Although this event has not registered in the Canadian public's mind as the residential school experience has, it marks one of the darkest times in Canadian history. The "Sixties Scoop" coincided with the residential school experience and in many ways it continued where the residential system left off.

Similar to the residential school experience, the "Sixties Scoop," involved agents of the state entering Aboriginal communities, rounding up children, and relocating them away from their parents, siblings, families, communities, clans, language, customs, and culture. Although simple statistics cannot begin to tell the tale of the enormous damage done by the state's mass apprehension of Aboriginal children, they do speak of the dramatic impact a policy change can have on the lives of Aboriginal people. In 1955, less than one percent of children in state care were Aboriginal; by 1964, this figure had jumped to 34 percent (Johnston 23); by 1969, the number rose to 40 percent (Downey 56). The current situation has not significantly improved; researchers Cheryl Farris-Manning and Marietta Zandstra estimate that nationally, there were about 76,000 children and youth in out-of-home care and of those 40 percent were Aboriginal (cited in Blackstock, Trocme, and Bennett 901). Provincially, estimates range from a sobering 78 percent in Manitoba (Amnesty International 12) and 70 percent in Saskatchewan (Bennett, Blackstock, and De La Ronde 19) to a more moderate yet disturbing 32 percent in British Columbia (Office of the Provincial Health Officer 1).

The "Sixties Scoop" apprehension and relocation process involved placing children in distant locations and with non-Aboriginal families (Downey 56; Blackstock, Trocme, and Bennett 903). Many children and youths from Canada were shipped to the United States, never to be heard from again (Bennett, Blackstone and De La Ronde 20). Unlike the residential school era in which the churches kept reliable records, this was sadly not the case with the child protection agencies. Upon removal, names of children were changed, often multiple times and personal histories were essentially erased (Downey 57). This has cumulated in the creation of a "lost generation," a cohort of Aboriginal people removed from their homes without access to their roots.

The dramatic changes that facilitated the "Sixties Scoop" involved modification of jurisdictional duties; in 1951 the federal government revised the *Indian Act* allowing provinces increased control over the health and welfare of Aboriginal children and youth (Bennett, Blackstock, and De La Ronde 18; Downey 56). Acquiring funds was the primary catalyst for state involvement in the well-being of Aboriginal children, not necessarily findings of abuse and/or neglect, although the stereotype of the Aboriginal mother as being "unfit" served to justify and legitimize state intervention. When there was no funding, there was little, if any, interest or concern about the children (Johnston 3). Early on, money was exchanged for the children; Ottawa guaranteed payment for each child apprehended (Downey 56). Canadian child welfare services "sold" Aboriginal children to American adoption agencies at a cost of $5,000 to $10,000 per child (Bennett, Blackstone and De La Ronde 20).

Dismantling the State Justification for Child Apprehensions

For the most part, provincial child welfare agencies act autonomously and, in practice, with a lack of transparency. Very few independent researchers in Canada have been granted access to government files as they pertain to child protection services and their clients. Both departmental policies and the fragmentation of agencies and services serve to isolate child welfare agencies from systematic, critical assessments and evaluations. From what is known, a longstanding pattern has emerged that suggests Aboriginal children and youth have been and continue to be consistently overrepresented at each stage of investigation. (Blackstock, Trocme, and Bennett 908).

Removal from the home is legislated to be the option of last resort, yet with Aboriginal families it has too often been the primary mode of intervention (Blackstock, Trocme, and Bennett 904). This contradicts research findings, which indicate that even in situations of substantiated abuse, separation of the children from the parents and families has very serious consequences for the children, and as such it should be the option of last resort (Johnston 59). For Aboriginal children, these consequences are more severe because of the very tight knit nature of their communities and extended families and their unique culture. In a sense, they risk being lost between two worlds and may not feel accepted by either; the critical sense of belonging that we all seek is something that they have difficulty experiencing (Johnston 59-60).

The landmark 1996 *Royal Commission on Aboriginal People* concluded that the misinterpretation of conditions that Aboriginal people experience coupled with the forced application of Euro-Western values and beliefs, especially as reflected in social work pedagogy and practice, are the source reasons for the devastating mass removals of Aboriginal children and their placement in pre-dominantly non-Aboriginal homes (cited in Blackstock, Trocme, and Bennett 902). Aboriginal parenting, *per se*, is not the root of the problem. The Aboriginal women that come under the scrutiny of children protection agencies are being measured and judged by the standards of the ideal white, middle-class, nuclear family. The more a mother deviates from that norm, the more she is vulnerable to state observation and intervention.

It is now well established that aspects of parenting styles and customs that some Aboriginal people have differ from, and at times clash with, those recognized as "good parenting" by child welfare agencies. The differences in child rearing practices and beliefs can sometimes be profound (Johnston 68). A point of contention has been the Aboriginal emphasis on providing children with more freedom, independence, and autonomy. A more pacifist approach as opposed to an authoritarian approach is employed (Johnston 68). This gets misinterpreted as "overly permissive," "lax," "disorganized," and worse, "neglectful parenting" (Chupik-Hall 12; Bennett, Blackstock, and De La Ronde 18; Johnston 68). Cultural misunderstandings may help explain why neglect has been found to be the predominant reason why Aboriginal parents are investigated for abuse (Blackstock, Trocme, and Bennett 908).

The privileged nature of modern Canadian society involves the implicit notion that parental ability and capacity are linked to material goods and conditions. With child welfare agencies, parental "competence" is measured by variables such as the size and condition of a home, the number of people residing in the home, and even the number of bathrooms in the residence (Johnston 75). The compromised socioeconomic status of Aboriginal mothers places them in perpetual risk of state intervention; they live their lives in a society that essentially makes poverty a "quasi" crime and Aboriginal ethnicity a risk factor. Aboriginal mothers, especially impoverished, multiparous, young women, must prove that they are "fit" parents on a daily basis. In criminal law terms, they are guilty and must continually prove themselves innocent.

Legislating a Stereotype: How the Law Nurtures the Myth of the "Unfit" Mother

The *Indian Act* of 1876 has been one of the most influential and intrusive acts of legislation in Canadian history. This is a primary example of the state's active involvement in the lives of Aboriginal people, especially those of women and children. It not only created the "Indian" but also endeavored to destroy the Aboriginal peoples of Canada. Without consulting Aboriginal people, it provided the government control over Native affairs. It also fragmented Aboriginal people into arbitrary categories (e.g., registered Indian, Métis, Inuit, etc.). Rights and restrictions depended on the group you belonged to; it created a situation that broke the collective nature of the people (Bennett, Blackstock, and De La Ronde 14).

The *Indian Act* was particularly damaging for Aboriginal women. Their once esteemed status in the community was systematically devalued and their very status as an Indian became dependant on their matrimonial choices. If they chose to marry a non-Indian, they would loose their status, as would their children. This particularly controversial part of the *Indian Act* was altered with the passing of *Bill-31* in 1985 but irreparable damage had already taken place. With the status and land ownership stipulation, the government created a situation of blatant discrimination, and instead of resolving the situation in a way that ensured that the rights of Aboriginal women were protected, they handed over the control of band membership to individual bands knowing that racist, sexist attitudes and behaviours prevailed and women's rights were not necessarily going to be protected (Green 717). This policy essentially enforced a system of patriarchy that continues in the modern setting.

The *Indian Act* resulted in the displacement of the power and authority that Aboriginal women had prior to colonization. The residential school experience attempted to dismiss their esteemed roles as mothers. By the early twentieth century, Aboriginal women's very capacity to reproduce came under government scrutiny and with the eugenics movement, legislation was passed that allowed for the arbitrary involuntary sterilization of Aboriginal women and men.

For many, Canada's role in the eugenics movement was not known until Leilani Muir, an Aboriginal woman, successfully sued the Alberta government for wrongful confinement and the improper use of Alberta's *Sterilization Act* of 1928. In 1959, at the age of 14, she was sterilized without her knowledge (Cull 1). She was told she needed to have an appendectomy but was instead sterilized. She was made aware of the deception when, after having difficulty conceiving, a doctor informed her of the operation and of the irreparable damage that had taken place.

Two provinces—British Columbia (B.C.) and Alberta—passed eugenic laws that allowed the sterilization of people deemed "unfit" to procreate. In Alberta, 2,822 officially approved sterilizations took place; of these, 64 percent were females and 25 percent were Aboriginals even though Aboriginals only accounted for 2.5 percent of Alberta's population at the time (Cull 54).

The "official" number of women sterilized in B.C, whose sterilization law was much more restrictive than Alberta's, was much lower and race did not appear to play as significant a role in deciding who was sterilized. That being stated, Aboriginal women in B.C. were "unofficially" sterilized either without their permission or knowledge, the numbers of which remains unknown (Annett 96). Determining who was sterilized was influenced by the ideology that sustained the eugenics legislation and movement: the belief that some people are inherently inferior and as such, their ability to reproduce needed to be conceptualized and responded to as a threat to the wellbeing of society. The eugenics movement was about power and control. It targeted society's most marginalized citizens; Aboriginal women were highly vulnerable to its application because of their severely compromised social status.

Laws have had and continue to have an instrumental role in creating and sustaining social, cultural, and economic inequalities in Canada, especially as they pertain to Aboriginal mothers (Lessard 719); case law, or interpreting the practical application of legislated law, has played an equally decisive role in this process. In practice, case law is conducted in a contextual vacuum; it rarely acknowledges the complex nature of people's lives or how social, economic, and cultural factors influence behaviours and situations. Case law can determine the course of an Aboriginal mother and her children's lives but it denies them and the public their personal narratives. The cases cited in the following text involved marginalized, highly vulnerable women who were struggling with their roles as mothers on many levels—they were young, multiparous, and very poor. They had histories of violence, faced housing and employment barriers, had been previously been subjected to child welfare investigations, and had substance use and misuse issues. The cases also involved women who refused to give up on themselves and on their children. They fought difficult battles to demonstrate that they were worthy parents. With assistance, they made the necessary chances asked of them and regained custody of their child/children. These women, who speak for thousands of other women, would not have participated in this process and have been held up for such harsh criticism and scrutiny unless they were committed to their children and to being the best parent they could be given their circumstances and capacities.

With an estimated 40 percent of the children and youth in state care being Aboriginal, the legal ramifications of child welfare court cases are particularly salient for Aboriginal mothers. Case law involving child protection agencies and parents has at the core the principle that the state is acting in the "best interest of the children and youth." The "best interest" is, in theory, used to determine which option will be the "least detrimental" to the child. The courts have been reluctant to realize the Charter implications and constitutional relevance of familial relationships (Bala 1). The first time the Supreme Court of Canada (S.C.C.) recognized the constitutional relevance of the familial relationship was with the 1999 *G.(J)* case when the court determined that child protection proceedings represent a fundamental threat to an individual's "security of person." The court established that child protection legal proceedings need to be conducted according to the principles of fundamental justice, which in this case meant that the mother who could not afford a legal representation had the right to a state-paid lawyer (Bala 1). Prior to this decision, indigent Aboriginal women would not necessarily have had access to legal representation in situations involving the removal of their children. On a more practical level, this case was a victory for gender equality since a disproportionate number of parents subjected to child welfare intervention policies are impoverished, single mothers (Lessard 719). Poverty is not gender-neutral, meaning that women tend to be more adversely affected.

Winnipeg Child and Family Services (W.C.F.S) v. G (D.F.) (1997) was the infamous "glue sniffing" case that pitted the rights of the mother against the rights of the unborn child. The court case involved the W.C.F.S. requesting that D.F.G. be detained in a treatment centre for the duration of her pregnancy in an effort to protect the fetus from further drug exposure. The media was merciless with its portrayal of the mother as a selfish villain, the antithesis of the "good" mother. She was stigmatized, demonized, and ostracized. Lost amongst the media coverage and the public outrage were important facts such as the mother had voluntarily entered the treatment centre, and earlier, during her pregnancy, had sought treatment but was turned away due to lack of facilities (*S.C.C.* 1997: pp5). D.F.G. was seen as the "fetus abuser" and not as a woman with a long history of trauma who was struggling with an addiction and who was in need of and actively seeking help in an effort to create a better life for herself and her child.

In the legal sense, this case involved a conflict between a woman's autonomy and the best interests of the child, as determined by the state (Flagler, Baylis, and Rodgers 1730). De-emphasized were the contextual factors of these cases; the limited options available to women like D.F.G.; the overly coercive way the W.C.F.S. treat single parents; and how the legal system and the public frame addiction differently for poor women as opposed to the middle class. For middle-class people, addiction is a medical condition and their behaviours are conceived as being beyond their control; for poor, single mothers, especially for Aboriginal women, it is their rational choice, and thus justification for excessive state control and intervention.

In 2000 the S.C.C. quietly made one of their more ominous decisions. The court ruled that the W.C.F.S. can apprehend a child without a warrant in non-emergency situations if it is believed the child *might* be in danger. This ruling opens the door for "crystal ball" apprehensions; child welfare agents are provided the authority to "predict" whether abuse *might* occur. The onus is placed on the family, usually the mother, to provide evidence that the child is not in danger. With this court decision, the power differentials that exist between the state and clients of child protection services are magnified. The potential for child welfare agents to arbitrarily use this as a weapon against a parent is substantial. Aboriginal mothers have an elevated risk of inappropriate state intervention; legal rulings such as this facilitate the process.

The Social Context of Aboriginal Mothering

Problems experienced by Aboriginal women—racism, addiction, poverty, precarious social and medical status, violence, chronic social and legal persecution, and discrimination—need to be appreciated as being the tip of the iceberg, the body of which was developed a long time ago when Canada's colonization took root. From the time prior to the birth of her child, the average Aboriginal mother finds herself having to navigate parenthood through a minefield of chronic challenges. In general, Aboriginal women, in particular single mothers, live hard lives. The harsh and critical glare of the public and the chronic scrutiny of the state create and compound these challenges and make navigating them difficult. The social, economic, and health conditions of Aboriginal people are improving but the situation, when compared to that of non-Aboriginal people and in relation to the overall high standard of living enjoyed in Canada, is unforgivably tragic. The Department of Indian and Northern Affairs re-evaluated the coveted number one Human Development Index designation granted to Canada by the United Nations and applied it to Aboriginal people living on a reserve; the ranking fell from the number one position to a dismal and shocking 79th and 80th (Bennett, Blackstock, and De La Ronde 7).

In 2004, the United Nations reported that 60 percent of Aboriginal children and youths live below Canada's poverty line. In Winnipeg, the figure rises to 80 percent for inner city Aboriginal households (Amnesty International 10) making it Canada's child poverty capital (Skelton 133). One in four Aboriginal households in Canada lack the basic necessities such as adequate water and sewage systems (United Nations 36). The stereotype of Aboriginal people, especially lone mothers, of being "lazy" and "welfare dependent" is particularly injurious. Entrenched racist and sexist beliefs result in very real discrimination manifested as employment, education, and income barriers. The Labour Force Participation Rates (the percent of people actually working or looking for work) for Aboriginal people is relatively high and not significantly different than that of non-Aboriginal people (Kendall 45). It is not the case that Aboriginal mothers do not want to work. They face barriers that prevent them from working or keep them in dead-end, low-income occupations (Maxim, Beavon, and Whitehead 475). Until changes are made, Aboriginal mothers will be trapped in a circle of disadvantage that is very difficult to break.

The addiction issue is a particularly salient source of justification used to support the negative stereotype of Aboriginal people and in particular, mothers. The social stigma attached to substance abuse is significant for Aboriginals mothers. Already on the defense with having to prove they are worthy parents, having addiction issues further ostracizes them, forcing them to conceal their problems as opposed to constructively seeking assistance with managing their situation. Substance abuse issues involve both voluntary and involuntarily addictions. Certain substances, such as tranquilizers, have been over-prescribed to Aboriginal women for decades with the full knowledge and participation of the government. The British Columbia Centre for Excellence in Women's Health estimated that one in four Aboriginal women over 40 in Western Canada were using benzodiazepines, a highly addictive and dangerous tranquilizer (4). This type of involuntary chemical dependence can lead to and/or complicate polydrug use; it also pacifies Aboriginal women and shelters them from reality but at a tremendous cost.

The government and public take a passive stance when it comes to acknowledging the role of Aboriginal involuntary addiction but they are quick to acknowledge the role substance abuse has in Aboriginal communities (e.g. media coverage of glue sniffing addiction on reserves) because this information is congruent with the negative stereotypes held of Aboriginal people. The state is equally passive with regard to providing help to women addicted to substances but they are very aggressive when criminalizing substance use and misuse; of the $454 million spent on Canada's substance abuse strategy in 2000, 96 percent was spent on enforcement initiatives while a mere six percent had to be shared between prevention and treatment programs (Wood, Spittal, Li, Kerr, Miller Hogg, Montaner, and Schecter 750).

One of the most damaging and pervasive stereotypes Aboriginals must contend with is that of the "drunken Indian." A shift has occurred over the last two decades and increasingly, fetal alcohol exposure is becoming a class issue as well as a race issue. In Canada, it has become the "Native people's problem." However, research suggests that socioeconomic status and not race is the critical factor when evaluating harm to the fetus (Nanson 808). Factors related to a pregnant woman's compromised socioeconomic status (and not factors inherent to the individual or to a group) including inadequate nutrition, parity, social support, violence, unstable housing, and exposure to toxic, unsafe living and working environments are very detrimental to the healthy development of both the fetus and child yet these mutable variables are not receiving the same attention as addiction and consumption issues among certain races (Nanson 808). The decision to drink or to use drugs is embedded in complicated social contexts that cannot be ignored yet they consistently are (Wilson and Martell 36). Forgotten amongst the rhetoric that surrounds the emotive issue of prenatal substance use is the realization that it is rare for a woman to knowingly and willingly harm her unborn child.

Conclusion

Aboriginal mothers are required to walk a tightrope between being invisible and highly visible. Our perceptions of them as being "unfit" render their many victories and accomplishments invisible. The insidious nature of the negative stereotypes and racist beliefs held about Aboriginal people in general, results in a collective myopic vision—we notice that the intoxicated person panhandling is Aboriginal, but do not notice that the doctor at the walk-in clinic or the police officer who helped us in our time of need, are both Aboriginal. It results in Aboriginal women being over-policed and under-protected. When an Aboriginal person commits a violent act, the media and public are quick to make note of it yet an estimated 500 Aboriginal women have gone missing or have been murdered over the last 15 years (Amnesty International 15) with little if any national attention given to the tragic situation.

In a time that one would expect apprehensions of Aboriginal children to have decreased, the Department of Indian Affairs and Northern Development estimated that the number of children and youths in out-of-home care actually increased between 1995 and 2001 by 71.5 percent (Blackstock, Trocme, and Bennett 905). It is an unfortunate irony that Aboriginal children continue to be placed in out-of-home care in alarming numbers because state officials determine neglect is taking place in the home when it is the legacy of the government's gross neglect of the needs of the Aboriginal people (as defined by Aboriginal and not those in power) that continues to force Aboriginal families and communities to live in Third World conditions. In Canada's wealthiest province, Ontario, many Aboriginal communities do not even have access to clean, safe water, or education.

As it currently stands, child neglect is treated as a "quasi crime" but research suggests that it is a resource-based, poverty-related problem. As such, neglect needs to be re-conceptualized as a resource issue as opposed to an individual's personal problem and choice (Lessard 734). The pervasive racism and discrimination that Aboriginal women and their children contend with on a daily basis needs to stop. There is an expectation that the Canadian government will protect the rights of its citizens but the state neglects to do so with Aboriginal women. The human rights that most Canadians enjoy—the right to privacy, autonomy, security of person, justice, and a basic level of health—are precarious notions for Aboriginal women and in particular, mothers.

Previously, the state was explicit about determining the inferiority of Aboriginal women; in the modern setting, the Canadian political system continues to act on the premise that Aboriginal women's gender and ethnicity make them inferior but they do so in an implicit, insidious fashion (Green 737). The Canadian government has yet to take responsibility for its actions or to offer an apology to the Aboriginal women, children, families, and communities who were victims of the "Sixties Scoop" child protection policies (Downey 57). Doing so would provide the necessary platform to make the sweeping changes to policies and ideologies required to address the continued over-representation of Aboriginal children and youth in state care. The passive stance the government takes toward its involvement in this matter masks its active participation in maintaining the fallacious stereotype of Aboriginal women as inferior, inadequate, unfit parents.

The belief that Aboriginal mothers are "unfit" is not an empirically supported finding. It is a deleterious stereotype that continues to justify inappropriate and unjustified state intervention in the lives of Aboriginal women. There is over one hundred years of experience that documents how the state has done an appallingly bad job when acting as the parent or guardian of Aboriginal children. Focus needs to be taken off Aboriginal mothers and placed on the state's continued negligence with respect to providing for one of its most vulnerable groups of citizens: Aboriginal women and their children.

Aboriginal mothers live their lives under a state-controlled microscope and no one's life or behaviours look acceptable under that type of unnatural and unjust scrutiny. The state's creation and preservation of the "unfit" stereotype serves to deny the public the truth about Aboriginal mothers. The negative perception of Aboriginal mothers conceals their positive aspects, attributes, and achievements. There is much that non-Aboriginals could learn from Aboriginal parenting methods and philosophies. For the most part, Aboriginal mothers value their children above everything else. They successfully navigate motherhood and they raise good, decent, honest citizens. They are as different from one another as they are the same. These women struggle and they make mistakes but against enormous odds, they do not give up, and they are successful parents. Their resiliency, their sense of responsibility, and the love they have for their children help them cope with being under the constant critical gaze of an unforgiving and at times merciless public and state. Although not recognized as such, they are "citizens plus."

Randi Cull is in the process of completing her Ph.D. in Public Health Sciences at the University of Toronto. The focus of her doctoral work is on the health and social consequences of exposure to violence as it relates to Aboriginal women and children. Her background is in law, human rights, and women's health.

References

Amnesty International. *Stolen Sisters: A Human Rights Response to Discrimination and Violence Against Indigenous Women in Canada.* 2004

Annett, Kenneth. *Hidden from History: the Canadian Holocaust.* Vancouver: The Truth Commission into Genocide in Canada (2001).

Bala, Nicholas. "The Charter Rights and Child Welfare Law." 2004 Conduct of a Child Protection File. Law Society of Upper Canada, March 9, 2004.

Bennett, Marilyn, Cindy Blackstock, and Richard De La Ronde. *A Literature Review and Annotated Bibliography on Aspects of Aboriginal Child Welfare in Canada.* 2nd ed. The First Nations Site of the Centre of Excellence for Child Welfare and the First Nations Child and Family Caregiving Society of Canada, 2005

Blackstock, Cindy, Nico Trocme, and Marilyn Bennett (2004). "Child Maltreatment Investigations Among Aboriginal and Non-Aboriginal Families in Canada." *Violence Against Women* 10 (8) (2004): 901-916.

British Columbia Centre of Excellence for Women's Health. *Manufacturing Addiction: The Over-Prescription of Benzodiazepines and Sleeping Pills to Women in Canada.* Policy Series 1. Vancouver, 2004.

Chupik-Hall, Jessa. "'Good Families Do Not Just Happen': Indigenous People and Child Welfare Services in Canada, 1950-1965." Unpublished dissertation, Trent University, 2001.

Cull, Randi. "The Historical Legacies of Eugenical Sterilization Policies in British

Columbia and Canada." Unpublished dissertation, Simon Fraser University, 2002.

Downey, Michael. "Canada's Genocide." *Maclean's* 112 (17) (April 26, 1999): 56-59.

Flagler, Elizabeth, Francoise Baylis, and Sandra Rodgers. "Bioethics for Clinicians: 12 Ethical Dilemmas that Arise in the Care of Pregnant Women: Rethinking "Maternal-Fetal Conflicts." *Canadian Medical Association Journal* 156 (12) (1997): 1729-1732.

Green, Joyce "Canaries in the Mines of Citizenship: Indian Women in Canada." *Canadian Journal of Political Science* 4 (34) (2001): 715-738.

Indian and Northern Affairs Canada. *Aboriginal Single Mothers in Canada, 1996: A Statistical Profile.* Winnipeg, Manitoba: Department of Indian and Northern Development, 2001.

Johnston, Patrick. *Native Children and the Child Welfare System.* Toronto: Canadian Council on Social Development, 1983.

Kendall, Joan. "Circles of Disadvantage: Aboriginal Poverty and Underdevelopment in Canada." *The American Review of Canadian Studies* 31 (2001): 43-57.

Lessard, Hester. "The Empire of the Lone Mother: Parental Rights, Child Welfare Law, and State Restructuring." *Osgoode Hall Law Journal* 39 (4) (2002): 717-770.

Maxim, Paul S., Dan Beavon, and Paul C. Whitehead. "Dispersion and Polization of Income Among Aboriginal and Non-Aboriginal Canadians." *The Canadian Review of Sociology and Anthropology* 38 (4) (2001): 465-476.

McGillivray, Anne and Brenda Comaskey. *Black Eyes All of the Time.* Toronto: University of Toronto Press, 1999.

Moffat, Tina and Ann Herring. "The Historical Roots of High Rates of Infant Death in Aboriginal Communities in Canada in the Early Twentieth Century: The Case of Fisher River, Manitoba." *Social Science and Medicine* 48 (1999): 1821-1832.

Nanson, Josephine, L. "Binge Drinking During Pregnancy: Who Are the Women at Risk?" *Canadian Medical Association Journal* 156 (6) (1997): 807-808.

Office of the Provincial Health Officer. *Children and Youth In Care: An Epidemiological Review of Mortality, British Columbia, April 1974 to March 2000. A Technical Report of the Office of the Provincial Health Officer.* Victoria, British Columbia: Ministry of Health and Ministry Responsible for Seniors, May 2001.

Pettit, Jennifer L. "'To Christianize and Civilize': Native Industrial Schools in Canada." Unpublished dissertation, University of Calgary, 1997.

Restoule, Jean-Paul. "Aboriginal Identity: The Need for Historical and Contextual Perspectives." *Canadian Journal of Native Education* 24 (2) (2000): 102-112.

Skelton, Ian. "Residential Mobility of Aboriginal Single Mothers in Winnipeg: An Exploratory Study of Chronic Moving." *Journal of Housing and Built Environment* 17 (2002): 127-144.

Switlo, Janice, G. A. E. "Modern Day Colonialism—Canada's Continuing Attempts to Conquer Aboriginal Peoples." *International Journal on Minority and Group Rights* 9 (2002) 103-141.

United Nations. *Indigenous Issues. Human Rights and Indigenous Issues.* Commission on Human Rights. Sixty-first session. Item 15 of the provisional agenda, Dec 2, 2004.

Wilson, Sylvia A. and Rebecca Martell. "The Story of Fetal Alcohol Syndrome: A Canadian First Nation's Response." *Women and Environments International Magazine* 60/61 (Fall 2003): 35-36.

Winnipeg Child and Family Services (W.C.F.S) v. G (D.F.) (1997).

Wood, Evan, Patricia Spittal, Kathy Li, Thomas Kerr, Cari L. Miller, Robert S. Hogg, Julio S. G. Montaner, and Martin T. Schechter. "Inability to Access Addiction Treatment and Risk of HIV Infection Among Injection Users." *Journal of Acquired Immune Deficiency Syndrome* 36 (2) (2004): 750-754.

Canada's Indian Residential Schools and Their Impacts on Mothering

ROSALYN ING

Indian residential schools have been a part of Canada's history since the sixteenth century. Very young children, some as young as three years, were forcibly separated from their parents to attend these schools that were miles away from their communities (Ing). The purpose of this paper is to find out if there are intergenerational impacts on individuals, families, and communities for those whose parents/ancestors attended government-run Indian residential schools. The participants interviewed are all graduates or students who only learned about residential schools through their university education. Before this the children were puzzled and hurt by the lack of affection and communication of their parents' (mothers') lives. Through their university education, as the children learned about their parents' experiences, healing occurred. The children understood then that their parents did the best they could to mother under the difficult and traumatic circumstances of their own childhood in the residential school system. For those children whose ancestors or parents attended residential schools, the impacts are intergenerational. This paper explores what these impacts are and how they affect the fragile relationship between mothers and their children.

Fictitious names are used to protect the identities of the ten participants. The definition that I decided to use for those who have successful lives, despite their and their parents' legacy of residential school, was the ability to pursue and complete a university degree. Nine of the participants earned Bachelor, Master or Doctor of Philosophy (Ph.D.) degrees, and all their parents had university degrees as well. This aspect of residential schools has received little attention. I found it important and necessary to tell another side of the residential school story, focusing on those whose accomplishments include post-secondary education. It begins with a literature review on residential schools by First Nations authors, followed by examples of the intergenerational impacts. Excerpts from some of the stories of the participants will help to focus on the meaning of the results of the findings and are connected to the literature review. The conclusion will explain how going to university made healing possible and how mothering was changed for the generation that attended residential schools.

The Literature Review

There are three generations of First Nations people alive who attended residential schools; many of them attended during the 1920s. They were children separated from their parents to satisfy a goal of assimilation in Canadian Indian Policy where institutionalized racism was practiced in many forms. After separation, and away from parents and communities, First Nations languages were forbidden, and most children were punished if caught (Ing). Some had needles stuck through their tongues (Chrisjohn and Young 243) and they suffered many other atrocities and indignities. Few of the staff advocated on their behalf when "students often experienced a variety of abuses inflicted in part from the racist values of society at the time and from the people who administered the schools" (AFN 1998: 4). Church-going was routinely forced on them, and Barbara-Helen Hill refers to it as the trauma of "churchianity" because, she wrote, "it is not necessarily Christian teachings that are wrong, rather, the church's interpretation that has destroyed our people" (13). First Nations culture was branded inferior. Schools carried out a program of cultural replacement so severe that it forced some of those leaving the schools to deny their identity as First Nations people. "It took me years ... before I could admit I was an Indian even to myself. I suppose this was natural after being raised in an environment that held little or no respect for Indians" (Deiter 67). This experimentation became complete as children were also raised away from the nurturing environment of their elders and culture. Linda Bull wrote, "This naturally breaks the tie between the child and ... parents at a critical time in ... life and denies ... the affection ... so much ... desired" (25) and rightfully needed and wanted by children. Family structure and social organization were nearly destroyed and parenting was affected (Ing; Davis). The *Indian Act* was amended several times to force compliance to the goal of assimilation. For what purpose did all this manipulation serve? In the end, most of the children returned from the schools alienated from their communities and unable to fit in to the Euro-Canadian society because of the overt racism. Many of them had few resources to help them deal with this society because that important spiritual element of self-esteem was severely compromised or nearly destroyed. Others who attended these schools wrote about self-esteem to describe their plight (Willis; Bull; Ing; Knockwood). But more than self-esteem was affected. Community-based studies by Roland Chrisjohn, Charlene Belleau and others, Debbie Foxcroft, and Elaine Herbert also reveal sexual, emotional, physical, and cultural abuse. Rod McCormick discusses healing through nature for some of these residential school survivors.

In a 1994 study conducted by the Assembly of First Nations (AFN), the researchers discussed "how First Nations children were wounded during their time at residential school" (37) emotionally, physically, spiritually [culturally], and mentally.

> A child becomes wounded emotionally when the expression of feelings is suppressed, discouraged, or belittled [or when threatened]. Wounding emotionally is also affected by withholding nurturance. Finally, emotional wounding occurs through shaming and humiliation, ridiculing and "putting down" children. (AFN 1994:38)

Many children suffered indignities, either directly or indirectly. Running away was a common practice of rebellion and resistance. Most were rounded up and returned to face severe punishment in humiliating ways, such as being stripped naked and strapped, "whipped or beaten" (Jaine viii) before all the other students, to show the consequences of running away (Brass). For girls who were menstruating they were further humiliated (Bull 45; Manuel and Loyie 93). There were allegations of murders committed in which young children were forced to watch, and other deaths are mentioned (Knockwood 107; Ennamorato 134). Through these painful punishments, terrors, and humiliations, many children were unable to express feelings in any way. "Closely tied to this pain, was that experienced by not being allowed to comfort, care for and have regular contact" (AFN 41) with siblings due to separation of children. Bull and Chrisjohn both made comparisons between residential schools and Goffman's description of "total institutions." Chrisjohn took the description further in terms of the type of discipline and punishment that occurred there using Goffman's phrase "mortification of the self" (qtd. in Chrisjohn and Young 74) to describe the ways children were forced to watch others' punishment and that "such demonstrations serve as warnings" (qtd. in Chrisjohn and Young 75). He added,

> Even if a given child was personally able to avoid severe treatment [s/he] was likely to witness it being applied to other children ... there may be occasions when an individual witnesses a physical assault upon someone to whom one has ties and suffers the permanent mortification of having ... taken no action. (qtd. in Chrisjohn and Young 75)

In Chrisjohn's notes (#168) he further explains that, "The Residential School's disciplinary structure, via the Goffmanesque 'permanent mortification,' thus may have created permanent distance in the Aboriginal world between family, friends, and future spouses" (Chrisjohn and Young 138). This is liberally stretching the application, as in the notes it is used to describe how couples react in the face of terrorism. How they respond to the tactics either destroys or strengthens the "trust relationship between" them. Here it is used to give some sense or meaning as to what may have happened to children when they were "emotionally wounded" by watching their friends being treated so cruelly. Any expression of feelings was suppressed by the traumas. Expression of feelings is necessary in the nurturance of children.

Another way that children were forced into silent submission was through punishment when speaking the only language they knew (Bull; Ing; Chrisjohn and Young; Deiter; Knockwood; Atkinson; Brass). There are descriptions of one particular teacher who cuffed children on the ears saying "You silly little hussy" (Deiter 53), causing more than ear damage. For those who wet their beds at night, humiliation followed in the morning as some were forced to walk around with their sheets over their heads or wear signs (Sterling). This mistreatment caused what Bull calls "distance (social distance) placed between" the staff and the children, "and the fear—initially of the unknown, but later the fear that developed and that was instilled in their … minds as little children" for the environment was "so overwhelming … strict … militaristic" (41).

Children were always hungry (Johnson 137). There are similar stories of how they managed to survive by sneaking out and killing rabbits and cooking them (Bull 43; Deiter 74) or some other "creative means" (Chrisjohn and Young 75; Bull 41). Nearby, in the staff dining room, they could smell the roast beef, or as Shirley Sterling recalls:

> They get bacon or ham, eggs, toast and juice … We got gooey mush with powder milk … Once I found a worm in my soup. When I told Sister Theo, she told me not to be ungrateful. There were starving children in Africa. (24-25)

In some families, three generations went to residential school but most of the living generation is affected. George Littlechild wrote: "My mother and all her brothers and sisters went to these boarding schools, and so did my grandparents. They grew up without their families and never learned how to raise children of their own" (18). He was raised in a foster home. The toll has been that

> Every First Nations group has suffered a disintegration of political and social institutions of culture, language, religion and economic existence. The destruction of the personal security, liberty, health, dignity … has been felt by successive generations. (AFN 1998: 4-5)

Not only were students emotionally deprived. Another destructive outcome has been the individual attack on the culture, making children feel ashamed of who they are, persons of a proud and thriving culture before European settlement. Many children left these schools with an inferiority complex, feeling so ashamed of themselves and their families that they lived a life of denial, some never returning to their communities. Ruth Kirk, in *Wisdom of the Elders*, despairingly reflected as she was growing up,

> I felt sorry I was Indian. You keep hearing you're not much good ... I was fourteen by the time they let me go home ... it was too late. I never got close with my mother. I wanted a better life.... When my daughter came, I didn't want her to know the pain I've had.... I shielded her from being Indian *(244)*.

This has had detrimental effects on their children who feel they have been deprived of learning and knowing the positive and beautiful things about their culture. Following are the findings connecting intergenerational impacts to the literature.

The Intergenerational Impacts

In Table 1 the original 14 impacts in the first generation are carried over to the second generation; additionally 20 more categories emerge. Impacts in the third generation continue from the first and second generation, but ten others emerge, making the total of 46. It is important to understand that the impacts do not stop. One of the reasons for conducting this research is to help those who have experienced the residential schools, but it also written for their descendants. For the fourth generation, only six of the participants (who have children) were qualified to provide answers. These stories will help to focus on the meaning of the results of the findings.

Sara began her search for self and identity through her own research during her second degree at university. She recognized many symptoms and applied it personally.

> *I realized after learning about residential schools how my family ... my life was affected. I was very emotional about this; I inherited the shame from my mother and felt guilty. What I found out about residential schools made me so excited, I wanted to phone everyone [in my family] to say, "Now I know why things are the way they are, why [our] family is plagued with tragedies and why mom is the way she is!" For much of her life she had no respect for herself or being Aboriginal and was probably taken advantage of. She left that school when she was sixteen and by then had already learned that the white way was better. Her first husband was white, an important choice for her to*

Table 1. *Impacts Of Residential School*

		1st Gen	2nd Gen	3rd Gen	4th Gen
1	Denial of First Nations identity	Yes	Yes	Yes	
2	Belief in lies/myths about FN people	Yes	Yes	Yes	
3	Shame	Yes	Yes	Yes	
4	Poor self esteem	Yes	Yes	Yes	
5	Family silent about past	Yes	Yes	Yes	
6	Communication difficulties	Yes	Yes	Yes	
7	Expectation to be judged negatively	Yes	Yes		
8	Controlling father	Yes	Yes	Yes	
9	Experience of racism	Yes	Yes	Yes	
10	Violence and physical abuse in family	Yes	Yes	Yes	
11	Sexual abuse	Yes	Yes	Yes	
12	Alcoholism	Yes	Yes	Yes	
13	Parents who value education	Yes	Yes	Yes	
14	Influence of grandparent on family	Yes			
15	University education		Yes	Yes	
16	Guilt from feeling shame		Yes	Yes	
17	Anger		Yes	Yes	
18	Emotional distance		Yes	Yes	
19	Silence in relationships		Yes	Yes	
20	Lack of affection		Yes	Yes	
21	Poor interpersonal skills		Yes	Yes	
22	Parenting affected		Yes	Yes	
23	Speaking of language		Yes		
24	Non-teaching of language to children		Yes	Yes	
25	Overprotection of children through fear		Yes	Yes	Yes
26	Healing through FN intervention		Yes	Yes	
27	Western therapy		Yes	Yes	
28	Personal healing through elders		Yes	Yes	
29	Militaristic communication		Yes	Yes	Yes
30	Father away from home too much		Yes	Yes	
31	Healing through family		Yes	Yes	
32	Stopping of cycle of poor parenting		Yes	Yes	
33	Departure from abusive relationship		Yes		
34	Attendance at res sch healing workshops		Yes		
35	Inferiority complex			Yes	
36	Loyalty			Yes	
37	Incarceration			Yes	
38	Independence			Yes	
39	Language loss			Yes	
40	Lack of emotional support from family			Yes	
41	Ability to control anger toward parents			Yes	
42	Good parenting			Yes	Yes
43	Perfectionism			Yes	
44	Reclaiming of identity			Yes	
45	Learning of conflicts in school system				Yes
46	Teaching of children to be proud of culture				Yes

make, because she figured she was doing the right thing.

Olga shared when she began to learn and made connections as to why children were sent away. As a mother her reaction was one of anger, too.

> *For our parents it was mandatory or else they would have ended up in jail for not sending us and they were left with no children at home. I was angry that whole year in school. I would wake up in the morning and I would be [furious] just mad for no reason.*

Coming to terms with one's identity is a long process if denial was the norm. It affects individuals in different ways but it is still devastating until you can begin to replace the shame and guilt with facts, particularly around a family history of alcoholism. Sara realized, through her education, that:

> *The situation of my family wasn't because of who we were. It was an eye-opening, emotional experience to one day awaken and realize that there are many factors and forces outside of yourself that have affected your life and the life of your family. Until that particular point I think that I have believed the myth and the lies about our people. I did inherit the shame that my mother carried. I felt guilty and I left home at seventeen to get away because my family was plagued with alcoholism. I resented my mother because she never gave me a real father.... I never met my father.... I grew up surrounded by violence, fighting. I packed my bags, hitch-hiked across Canada....*

Running away was the only option for Sara and her unbearable home life, escaping from shame and violence. She could begin to effect some kind of resolution when she concluded there was a reason why she had no relatives. She explains that:

> *One day I was looking at* This Land is My Land *by George Littlechild, and I turned to the page that has all his ancestors and it just hit like a ton of bricks. All those things I had learned about residential schools, that was my family. I realized I have no aunties, no uncles, no grandparents, no cousins, no connection at all to my mother's family. I wept. I realized that I had no family and there was a reason for that.*

The story of Sara's family is as follows:

> *My oldest sister has struggled with alcoholism for as long as I remember. There is this [very sad] ... legacy in my family.... My mother was raped*

when she was sixteen, and had my oldest sister, who also was raped at the same age, and had a daughter as well. My oldest sister now has three daughters.... What I find quite incredible is that she [my sister] went to residential school, too; not for long but she did attend; and I just almost see it has a life of its own. She's battled with alcoholism. Her three daughters [my nieces] have had a difficult time—the youngest married somebody who has been charged with murder, the middle one has a string of bad relationships and [is] abusing her children (one child is now being raised by the grandmother); and the oldest is really a tragic story. She ... attempted suicide, and later, desperate to be loved and wanted (she is a lesbian), became involved with a new partner, a well-known addict using crack cocaine and my niece fell into the same pattern ... in a scuffle ... she stabbed an undercover policeman and is now serving sixteen years for what she did. When I think about her [my niece], her mother [my oldest sister] and her grandmother [my mother], they never resolved the issues that they had in residential school, never dealt with the shame, the unresolved trauma of that experience. I really believe that my niece being in prison right now is a part of that whole legacy, what happens when healing doesn't happen and people don't deal with that part of their lives—it is manifested and perpetuated in every generation.

Olga had important issues to overcome such as being moved so much, parenting, fear over language, and the cruelty associated with it. There was no stability. She said,

I went to three residential schools and was moved four times. I sent my son (15 years old) one year to residential school when he had behavioural problems but my daughter didn't go. I tried to give my children a good life. I never talked about my boarding school experiences, and I didn't teach them my language because I didn't want them to go through the same thing [but] I still speak my language. I had this one awful teacher who was not very kind to me. In Grade One I had ear problems, painful, both my ears were infected. I told the teacher. She didn't believe me. She hit me where I had the ache.... It really hurt—I was never able to forgive her. She would always punish me for using my language, striking me with a ruler. I had no other way of communicating, so in turn, I had a hard time communicating with my children. It was hard to explain to them why.

In her childhood, Nora had many traumas, interfering with healthy emotional development, and was further hampered by the inability to communicate in a family parented by silenced endurers of a system by saying she has "not fully dealt with my childhood." She said,

> *My grandfather also went [to residential school] and he [physically] abused my father; and my grandfather sexually abused me. I've been able to discuss this with my mother, and so I went to therapy at seventeen.*

Nora adds that her father, an alcoholic, was ashamed of the way he grew up and lived a life of deception. "He kept his Aboriginal background hidden from his previous wife [non-Aboriginal] and child; he was abusive—physically and verbally—to my mother; and when she left him, he quit." Growing up with an alcoholic and abusive father is recognized in the patterns that remain, as well as with other family members:

> *I see unhealthy patterns in my relationships with friends, family. In the past I felt I had to make a relationship chaotic to be normal. Only recently have I learned to have honest, loving relationships with people, but the chaotic urge is still there. My sister and I are not close. When conflict arises in our family, we just walk away from each other, if we're mad, silence. I feel like I missed out on so much because we are all really good people. I see it in the way we treat others and the way we can talk to others, but my brother, sister, and mother and I are not as open and honest with each other. There's still so much resentment.*

Wynn shares this about her family:

> *Dad was militant about me making my bed. White shirts or t-shirts had to be worn with a vest or sweater, never alone; and shoes, they bought me the best shoes they could afford ... they never had properly fitted shoes.*

Wynn is aware of her father's regimented or militaristic style of cleanliness and deportment. Despite these hardships on her children Wynn's mother demonstrated positive behaviours in a bad marriage, as she "was loyal to my father despite his weekend binge drinking, and instilled a strong loyalty to people ... I love ... and care [about]." But this stress has consequences. Her father's alcoholism is intergenerational but has been addressed by Wynn as she honestly declared her "alcoholism ... but I have maintained sobriety since age 25." However, other undesirable traits appeared in the family as "my brother abused me physically, emotionally and sexually; he died at 19 (still molesting me) when I was 16." A resolution is successful as "my mother turned to spirituality for healing when he died; she and I saw an elder regularly, bringing us closer as a family."

Rose adds a different slant as she recognizes some benefits and family strengths.

My mother attended residential school yet she values education. What a contradiction! I have trouble understanding her, having had such a bad experience yet highly valuing education. It was a profound realization for me that it was not the education per se that was troublesome but the school experience she had. She was able to separate her bad experiences and supported education for my brother and I. I kept my two children out of the school system [and home-schooled] until this year; they're six and eight. [As a child] I found school a struggle and had forms of identity crisis. I see the tragedy of residential schools. It should never have happened. Some families have floundered; I see darkness daily. Many did not go on to higher education, live tragic lives, and their children too. Many of my aunts and uncles [my mother's side] attended and survived. I see the strength of their spirit, the human spirit. They didn't lose sight of the value of education and have wonderful lives. We have a doctor, lawyers, social workers, a publisher, professional counselors and educators from just one family. I think our own family strength helped us through. The life shared before residential school gave us all the strength to overcome the negative aspects of the schools.

Perhaps there are more children in Earl's category that we don't hear about. Those with odds against them to survive childhood traumas can ensure their children never go through what they did by making conscious decisions such as reading and learning about positive parenting.

Well, I think I was very fortunate that both my parents made an effort to give me a solid upbringing even though they both had very difficult, emotional traumatic lives. They made a decision to stop the cycle at my generation, for me and my brother, and the following generation [his daughter]. They had to work very hard to learn good parenting skills. I remember seeing books [that my mother read] about parenting and bringing up babies on the bookshelves.

But most influential was the role by a respected elder who is also a grandfather. Earl is also able to see his elder's inspiration in his nuclear and extended family.

We were particularly lucky to have a very strong family even though all of my mother's sisters and brothers went to residential school. They had a strong early upbringing from my grandparents; my grandmother died early but my grandfather ... a very strong figure gave direction to everyone in the family. Most of ... my generation turned out well-adjusted to live and work in Canadian society, but [also maintain] ... an identity as a First Nations person. I know some cousins didn't do as well....

He admits he wasn't left unscathed as "I didn't learn my [mother's] language, and had to learn some First Nations traditions on my own" that his mother didn't practice to hand down.

Hope said "I think religion played a major support role for my mother, but my father turned away from it." She feels that the racism she experienced and "the stereotyping of the drunken and uneducated Indian" is a direct result of residential school. She is willing to say that

> *My parents had self-esteem issues. They married young and had my brother and I at an early age, and weren't prepared to have a family or a marriage. They never experienced a family, didn't know how to deal with family issues, and our family fell apart. It created self-esteem issues for me, too, thinking I came from a broken home. That's the most direct effect that it's had [on me].*

Her father went to university to study after residential school, where he met her mother,

> *then he spent 25 years on land negotiations ... doing valiant work helping the community grow and heal itself, but it was an ultimate sacrifice at the expense of time not spent with his family.... He's very respected and I admire him. My mom quit university to stay home with my brother and me, and I'm grateful. Mom later went back to complete a Bachelor and Masters degrees. We couldn't depend on each other for emotional support. There was no communication between us. I could only compare my family to TV families, and how they acted; we had no deep communication, no working out of issues as we never spoke about them. I also slept over at my girlfriend's and saw how their parents acted, communicated much more with each other, speaking about their day, nice things like that; it was comfortable to wake up and find both parents there.*

Some of these are common problems that most children of divorced/separated parents have and understandably so. But one has to question the common theme of "lack of communication" that is occurring so often in the study that is associated with silence. The intergenerational effects are the self-esteem issues, and due to father being away so much, it heightened the unspoken "silence."

Ruth recalls as a child how her mother [who has a Ph.D.] was "very distant, as though she didn't want to really be ... well, not the warm affectionate person she normally is. She needed her own space and we felt we had to keep our distance." Being distant was a coping mechanism from residential school when expression of emotions was taken away. It appears that children sense the body language and the feeling of isolation it creates, both for the parent and child. But, "in terms of my three-year old, my relationship is strong. Our family circle is really strong; yea, my child gets lots of warmth and affection." This speaks of a positive intergenerational change.

Nora may have given some insight into the silence and lack of affection in her family. In this example of *"mortification of the self,"* she describes this incident her mother shared. She

> *... told me of a time that she was with some kids at school and they [staff] let some dogs loose, who were chasing this little boy and they viciously attacked him. By the sounds of it, he tried to run away and this was his punishment, but she told me she never saw this boy again.*

Nora expresses these feelings and offers some advice.

> *When I hear those stories I'm affected on so many different levels, that pain, complete outrage. [We have] to start talking about it, but gradually because I see the pictures and it's difficult. I'm reliving it all. Mom says when she talks/ hears about residential schools she is depressed for days, so I can't get her to share or ask questions. I hate it when she's sad.*

Nora has been able to process some of her experiences in terms of its effects as she said, "residential school made people unable to communicate ... my mother found it hard even to hug us ... she wasn't always there [emotionally] for us. I remember feeling lonely and unloved." An important way to nurture children was missing; her mother was forced to watch this brutal murder as a lesson not to run away; any expression (of feelings) may have been suppressed; and carried into parenthood, making her unable to be affectionate.

Rose describes this incident of terror that her mother shared unexpectedly:

> *Once we went out for dinner together and quite out of the blue she told me about a really hard time for her at residential school where she was quite a young child and somebody from the school beat her quite badly, to the point where she was hospitalized. She had been left for dead in a boiler room, beaten with a poker. Somebody found her and took her to the school infirmary. The man came back and attempted to smother her. That was really difficult for her to share with me. To this day I don't know what possessed her to share that with me but it was a really hard story to listen to.*

Rose's story of her mother's assault speaks about her mother's fear and her own sense of:

fear ... that my mother carried.... My brother and I ... weren't given a lot of freedom ... I can only assume that she lived in fear, for her own life, friends, and family, and it's transferred to me as a parent. [Now] I regularly have an inner battle about my kids' safety. One day she called and asked how we were. I said the kids were at the local community centre. She was panic-stricken. "Are they alone? How do you know it's safe?" I had just let go of the fear myself since moving to the community and feeling it out, and saying okay, it shouldn't be a problem.

Sara began a search for the self through education and establishing a link with the First Nations community where she lives and works, and by overcoming "a sense of inferiority ... a major issue in my life, but I've tried to blend in to be part of" society.

I educated myself and that was a turning point in my life.... In my 30s ... it was unheard of for myself or anyone in my family to go to university.... I had no connection with Aboriginal people ... it was where I had an opportunity to learn anything at all about who I am as an Aboriginal person. I made a conscious effort ... to find out.... Through a residential school healing workshop I learned about the intergenerational impacts, my mother's experiences ... I know are not my fault. What motivated me to become a teacher was my mother's suffering, life of poverty, discrimination, and tragedy, because under all this is a kind, generous, and loving human being. In the classroom I faced the problems associated with residential school-drugs and alcohol abuse, poverty, family—this forced me to deal with my own issues.

It has been an ordeal to make this link, though. Similarly, Lara worked on

Reclaiming culture through the sweat lodge ceremonies with my parents. That was a good way to connect spiritually. It also helped me get through university, as it wasn't easy. I participate in sun dancing. It helps my health. Like mom's sisters, it helps them reclaim identity, and their self-esteem. I haven't had the direct experience of residential school, but it feels like I've been there in terms of the emotional expression; those who went there can't [express the emotions] because it was just so overwhelming. Internalized racism turns anger inwards, people can't articulate to know why. I've tried to recapture some of the language by taking it at university. Mom still speaks it. [Spirituality and] the different ceremonies [show] there are ways to express this that are not verbal or emotional. The value of some of the traditions developed over thousands of years is that there is an awareness of what the body needs as you are traumatized through the body, right?

Rose claims, "I was a teenager and I rediscovered my own spirituality, I feel strong in it now…. Originally education has been a tool of destroying us, but it became a tool we could use to fight with, to regain our sense of identity." In her B. Ed. studies she found her identity and gained confidence to home school her two sons; understood her roots as a child of a woman who went to residential school and what it meant for her. Nora attends "ceremonies with my mother" where "I feel safe, loved, cared for. Now I'm committed to understanding traditional knowledge as it's more spiritually valuable to me than my university [Law] degree[s]."

In conclusion, the participants resolve to move on, effecting reconciliation amongst themselves and their parents (mothers did the best they could). They interact in *a successful way* to fight the odds against them *to achieve a university degree;* deal with prejudice and discrimination in an attempt to better their own lives and their children's; and throughout, they maintain their dignity. These are essential qualities creating positive accomplishments that can be passed on to strengthen the next generation of mothers. There are many examples of harm to individuals and families (do not forget that these were very young children receiving no mothering and little guidance at the time they were at residential school). Sara (a participant who is a teacher and has three children) shared how three generations of her family were affected chaotically including drugs, child apprehensions, alcohol, and incarcerations because her mother (whom she still loves) denied being 'Indian' and did not resolve her trauma and shame associated with residential school. Other intergenerational impacts include stories of different incidents that caused trauma and shame; some of these incidents and stories are criminal as they included assault on victims, disappearance of a child, and possible homicide being witnessed by young children. As Chrisjohn wrote, "…there may be occasions when an individual witnesses a physical assault upon someone to whom one has ties and suffers the *permanent mortification* of having … taken no action" (Chrisjohn and Young 75). Any expression of feelings was suppressed by the traumas. Due to these traumas mothering for those who attended residential school was severely affected—as children they grew up not knowing how to give or show affection, necessary in the nurturance of children. Therefore, mothering became difficult and their children did not understand why mothers were unemotional and unable to show affection. Table 1 shows the fourteen impacts for first generations carried over to the second generation but additionally 20 categories emerge, and impacts from first and second generations carry to the third generation but ten more categories make the total of 46 intergenerational impacts. Education changed this group of participants—healing was affected through knowledge gained at university on the research topic of residential schools —and this inspired these mothers to gain social awareness about the injustices in this form of education and its impacts on their mothers' ability to parent. Mothering should or could have been enhanced if their mothers' experiences had been shared or resolved. This study is significant because it has consequences for all of Canadian society. All My Relations. *Ekosi, Kakinaw ni Wakomakanak.*

This article is an adaptation of Chapter Five of the author's doctoral dissertation, "Dealing with Shame and Unresolved Trauma: Residential School and Its Impact on the Second and Third Generation Adults" (University of British Columbia, 2000). The research was a winner in the 2000 Canadian Policy Research Awards for Graduate Students.

Rosalyn Ing is a Cree Elder from Manitoba. Her goal in life is seeking social justice and healing for First Nations. Although she attended residential school for eleven years of her childhood, Dr. Ing still values education as an equalizer for society's opportunities. She taught for several years at the Native Education Centre in Vancouver, moved to University of British Columbia as Coordinator of the First Nations Health Careers in 1994, and retired in 2003. She earned a Bachelor of Social Work degree, a Master of Education, and a Ph.D., all from the University of British Columbia

References

Assembly of First Nations (AFN). *Breaking the Silence: An Interpretive Study of Residential School Impact and Healing as Illustrated by the Stories of First Nations Individuals.* Ottawa: First Nations Health Commission, 1994.

Assembly of First Nations (AFN). *Residential School Update.* Ottawa: Assembly of First Nations Health Secretariat, March 1998.

Atkinson, Jim. *The Mission School Syndrome* (film). Whitehorse, Y.T. Northern Native Broadcasting, 1988.

Brass, Eleanor. *I Walk in Two Worlds.* Calgary: Glenbow Museum, 1987.

Bull, Linda. "Indian Residential Schooling: The Native Perspective." *Canadian Journal of Native Education* Supplement, 18 (1991): 1-63.

Chrisjohn, Roland and Sherri Young, with Michael Maraun. *The Circle Game: Shadows and Substance in the Indian Residential School Experience in Canada.* Penticton: Theytus Books Ltd., 1997.

Chrisjohn, Roland, Charlene Belleau, and others. "Faith Misplaced: Lasting Effects of Abuse in a First Nations Community." *Canadian Journal of Native Education* 18 (1991): 196-197.

Davis, Sarah. "The Experience of Self-Destructive Behavior in First Nations

Adolescent Girls." Unpublished Master's thesis, University of British Columbia, 2000.

Deiter, Constance. *From Our Mother's Arms: The Intergenerational Impact of Residential Schools in Saskatchewan.* Toronto: United Church Publishing House, 1999.

Ennamorato, Judith. *Sing the Brave Song.* Richmond Hill, ON: Raven Press, 1998.

Foxcroft, Debbie. *Indian Residential Schools: The Nuu-chah-nulth Experience.* Port Alberni: Nuu-chah-nulth Tribal Council, 1996.

Herbert, Elaine. "Talking Back: Six First Nations Women's Stories of Recovering From Childhood Sexual Abuse and Addiction." Unpublished Master's thesis, University of British Columbia, 1994.

Hill, Barbara-Helen. *Shaking the Rattle: Healing the Trauma of Colonization.* Penticton: Theytus Books Ltd., 1995.

Ing, N. Rosalyn. "The Effects of Residential Schools on Native Child-Rearing Practices. *Canadian Journal of Native Education* Supplement, 18 (1991): 65-118.

Jaine, Linda. *Residential Schools: The Stolen Years.* Saskatoon: University Extension Press, 1993.

Johnson, Basil. *Indian School Days.* Toronto: Key Porter Books Ltd., 1988.

Kirk, Ruth. *Wisdom of the Elders.* Vancouver: Douglas and McIntyre in association with the British Columbia Provincial Museum, 1986.

Knockwood, Isabelle. *Out of the Depths: The Experiences of Mi'Kmaw Children at the Indian Residential School at Shubenacadie, Nova Scotia.* Lockeport: Roseway Publishing, 1992.

Littlechild, George. *This Land is My Land.* Emeryville, California: Children's Book Press, 1993.

Manuel, Vera and Larry Loyie. *Two Plays About Residential School.* Vancouver: Living Traditions Writers Group, 1998.

McCormick, Rod. "The Facilitation of Healing for the First Nations People of British Columbia." *Canadian Journal of Native Education* 21 (1995):251-322.

Sterling, Shirley. *My Name is Seepeetza.* Toronto: Groundwood Books, 1992.

Willis, Jane. *Genish: An Indian Girlhood.* Toronto: New Press, 1973.

Fostering Indigeneity

The Role of Aboriginal Mothers and Aboriginal Early Child Care in Responses to Colonial Foster-Care Interventions

MARGO GREENWOOD AND SARAH DE LEEUW

This paper begins and is located in the two quite personal realms of the authors. First, the paper is focused in part on the lived realities of Aboriginal[1] mothers in Canada, an experiential place of one author who is a Cree woman and the mother of three. Secondly, the paper is located and draws from lived realities in the small communities in northern British Columbia where we (both authors) have for many years worked and made our homes. These two realms meet in the question of how, by fostering Indigenous ways of knowing and being in Aboriginal mothers and their children, one might begin to address the growing and disquieting use of child welfare discourses and programs as a means by which the state (territorial, provincial, and federal governments in Canada) intervenes into Aboriginal families. This question has particular resonance for northern and rural communities, particularly if they are reserve communities, because of the proportionally higher rates of child welfare interventions experienced in such communities as compared with their urban, southern, or primarily non-Aboriginal counterparts. Throughout the paper, then, are woven the personal (and by association, political and cultural) concerns of the authors, both of us who are concerned about ongoing colonial narratives towards Aboriginal peoples in Canada and both of us who are interested in the possibilities of changing inherently Euro-colonialist biases towards Aboriginal families, many of which are headed by single mothers. The purpose of this paper is both to document the temporal trends of child protection interventions into the lives of Aboriginal families (often headed by a lone female parent) and to propose possible women and community focused solutions for reducing such interventions.

Aboriginal families have been caring for each other and for their children since time immemorial. Euro-colonial interventions into the lands now known as Canada, however, dismissed the socio-cultural structures (including families) of Aboriginal peoples, characterizing such structures as inherently flawed when positioned against European and colonial practices and norms. The processes and practices of colonialism, while often contradictory and by no means uniform in application (Thomas), operated through means of discourse and material interventions in order to construct, reconstruct, and conceptualize Aboriginal peoples as "othered" in reference to (colonially defined) "normalcy."

As practices of discourse, colonial imaginations about Aboriginal peoples might best be conceptualized as amalgamations of singular statements or iterations that came to shape and form meanings and knowledges understood as commonly-held (Beier) toward Indigenous peoples. Discourses, as Michel Foucault reminds us, are more than "groups of signs ... but ... [are] practices that systematically *form* the objects of which they speak" (49 [our emphasis]). In Canada, colonial imaginations about Indigenous peoples were circulated and inscribed through mediums such as missionary materials, popular media, curriculum, and the arts, all of which developed and perpetuated a discourse of Aboriginal peoples being uncivilized, irrational, subordinate, and heathenistic[2] (Raibmon). As material interventions, the practices of colonialism operated through institutions such as residential schools (Milloy; Furniss; Haig-Brown), through discriminatory land and territory allocations such as "Indian" reserves (Harris 2002, 2004), and through legal policies or laws such as the Indian Act and ongoing litigation findings that deny Aboriginal histories or claims, particularly in the areas of self-government and resource allocation[3] (Armitage). What is important to remember, then, is that both through means of discursive constructions and through marital interventions, the lives of Aboriginal people in Canada were both interceded into and (re)constructed by Euro-colonial presences. These intercedings and (re)constructions were not innocent to the site of the Aboriginal family. Indeed, both the family and Aboriginal women's bodies were heavily implicated in colonial agendas, typified in Duncan Campbell Scott, the Deputy Superintendent of the Department of Indian Affairs between 1913 and 1932, statements that 1) "the happiest future for the Indian race is absorption into the general [white] population, and this is the object of the policy of our government" and that 2) "the great forces of intermarriage and education will finally overcome the lingering traces of native custom and tradition" (qtd. in Titley 34). In Campbell Scott's statements the collision of colonial agendas and Aboriginal families (via women's bodies) becomes transparent. As Julia Emberley observes, the family was the site of paramount focus in imperialist and colonialist interventions during the nineteenth and early twentieth centuries: "the [Aboriginal] family emerged as a material force in the [colonial] destruction of kinship societies and their subordination, socially and economically, to the colonial and imperial nations" (n.p.).

Through most of the nineteenth and early twentieth centuries, the Government of Canada intervened in Aboriginal families through the removal of children and the placement of those children in residential schools. These interventions were established in policy through the 1876 *Indian Act* but were consolidated in 1879 by Nicolas Flood Davin's *Report on Industrial Schools for Indians and Half-Breeds* in which he noted that the "call of the wigwam" would only be circumvented with Aboriginal children's removal from families and their placement into long-term boarding schools which would provide the "care of a mother" in the form of "circles of civilized care." By the late twentieth century, however, residential schools (as distinctly feminized spaces deigned to subordinate and substitute Aboriginal mother's parenting roles) were on the wane. The state's interest of intervening into Aboriginal families, however, had not abated; instead the means or apparatuses of intervention simply shifted from residential schools to child welfare programs. Indeed, the Government of Canada's 1996 *Royal Commission on Aboriginal Peoples* (RCAP) observed that:

> Increased activity on the part of child welfare agencies corresponded with the federal government's decision to expand its role in funding social welfare services and to phase out residential schools which, in the 1960s had increasingly assumed the role of caring for children in "social need."

In 1983, Patrick Johnston developed and employed the expression the "sixties scoop" in reference to a sustained duration during which child welfare programming intervened into Aboriginal families and apprehended their children. Specifically, Johnston reported that, in the years leading up to his publication of *Native Children and the Child Welfare System*, representation of First Nations children in British Columbia's child welfare system had increased from a 1955 low of less than one percent to a total of 34.2 percent in 1964. Johnston argued that this increase was a pattern underway across Canada, concluding that the proportion of Aboriginal children in care was significantly higher than that of non-Aboriginal children. In 1980-1981, 4.6 percent of Aboriginal children were in agency care, as opposed to under one percent of the general Canadian child population. In 1981-82, the percentage of Aboriginal children in care (as a percentage of all children in care) varied across Canada, with a low of 2.6 percent in Quebec to a high of 63 percent in Saskatchewan.

These trends have not abated. In 2005 The First Nations Child and Family Caring Society of Canada observed both that "one in ten Status Indian children in three sample provinces were in child welfare care ... compared with one in two hundred non-Aboriginal children" and that "national data suggests there are three times the number of Aboriginal children in care than there were at the height of residential schooling operations" (7). In 1999 the Canadian Coalition for the Rights of Children (CCRC) evaluated Canada's success (or lack there of) in meeting the United Nations *Convention Article 19* on the rights of the child. The CCRC concluded that, although national statistics were difficult to obtain due to provincial/territorial discrepancies in reporting, available data suggests that child neglect (as opposed to abuse) accounts for "the significant majority of child welfare

caseloads in Canada" and that "poverty and despair provide a fertile soil for child
… neglect and the social problems suffered by families across the country tend to
be even more concentrated in Aboriginal communities" (n.p.). This concentration
is due to Aboriginal peoples in Canada being far more likely to live in poverty than
members of the general Canadian population (Stout, Kipling and Stout). In other
words, Indigenous children account for a disproportionately high percentage of
children in care across Canada, their representation is not decreasing over time,
and it is very feasible to conclude that their representation is not linked to abuse
within the family but rather by a system which views impoverishment as neglectful
and thus apprehends children into the "care" of the state.

Aboriginal families are operating under a triple jeopardy in Canada. Prevailing
discourses (both historically and contemporarily) in Canada have; 1) constructed
Indigenous peoples as deficient and (consequently) in want of Euro-Canadian
intervention; 2) maligned Indigenous peoples through systematic discursive and
institutional interventions, resulting in socio-cultural and economic
marginalization; and 3) conflated poverty issues with neglectful parenting practices and thus opened Aboriginal families to the full spectrum of Canadian child
welfare policies. The child welfare system in Canada, almost by design, is
predisposed to focus on Aboriginal families. Unfortunately, the triple jeopardy is
magnified with reference to Aboriginal mothers in Canada who are the majority
of single parents, who are much more likely to be lone parents than non-Aboriginal
women, and who face increased levels of poverty.

According to Statistics Canada, in 2001 19 percent of Aboriginal women aged
15 and over were heading families on their own, compared with eight percent of
non-Aboriginal women. Furthermore, lone-parent families headed by Aboriginal
women tend to be larger than those headed by their non-Aboriginal counterparts.
In 2001, 22 percent of Aboriginal female lone parents had three or more children,
more than twice the figure for their non-Aboriginal counterparts, just ten percent
of whom had three or more children. According to Statistics Canada's Low-
Income Cut-offs (LICOs), 17.9 percent of all Canadians live in poverty. Women,
however, fare below average: whereas 16 percent of men live in poverty, 19 percent
of women do. The most disadvantaged of the populations are single, divorced,
widowed, or separated women over 65 years of age (43.4 percent of women who
live in poverty) and lone mothers under 65 years of age (57.2 percent of women
living in poverty). With specific consideration to Aboriginal women, the profile
of poverty is even more disconcerting: although the rate of unemployment for
non-Aboriginal women in Canada is 9.7 percent, 21 percent of Aboriginal women
are unemployed. Furthermore, Aboriginal women who are employed are more
likely than their non-Aboriginal counterpart to find part-time or seasonal employment, thus resulting in the simultaneous need for childcare needs while facing
economic challenges associated with paying for that childcare[4] (Stout *et al.*).

First Peoples in Canada have voiced, for some time now, significant opposition to the ongoing state initiated and sponsored efforts to intervene into Aboriginal families. In 1991, the Government of Manitoba's Aboriginal Justice Implementation Commission undertook a full review of the province's criminal justice system. The Inquiry "repeatedly heard … that any overhaul of the justice system in Manitoba must include a re-examination of the child welfare system" (n.p.) because Aboriginal peoples understood that the apprehension of their children, and the fostering of those children into (primarily) non-Aboriginal households, had detrimental effects on child development which disproportionately propelled Aboriginal children and youth toward the criminal justice system. In 1992, but published in 1998 within the Royal Commission on Aboriginal Peoples (RCAP) (Government of Canada, Indian and Northern Affairs), Josephine Sandy of the Ojibway Tribal Family Services testified that she and her community had for years been mobilizing against child welfare interventions because:

> I have watched the pain and suffering that resulted as non-Indian law came to control more and more of our lives and our traditional lands. I have watched my people struggle to survive in the face of this foreign law. Nowhere has this pain been more difficult to experience than in the area of family life. I and all other Anishnabe people of my generation have seen the pain and humiliation created by non-Indian child welfare agencies removing hundreds of our children from our communities….

What then, might be the possible solutions to Canada's (and more pronouncedly, Indigenous peoples' and mothers') challenge of apprehending Aboriginal children? In previous publications (Greenwood, Tagalik and de Leeuw; de Leeuw and Greenwood) we have advocated the need to recognize existent capacity and strength in Aboriginal communities. This is not to overlook the tremendous socio-economic hardships present in Aboriginal communities but, instead, to realize that any groups who have withstood sustained (and aggressive) efforts to assimilate them must, at some level, harbour immense resiliency and social capital. It is this resiliency and social capital, particularly in the areas of cultural capacity, Indigenous knowledges, and Aboriginal ways of knowing and being, which we will now turn to as referents for possible intervention solutions into the child welfare crisis in Canada.

Michael Chandler and Christopher Lalonde (forthcoming; see also Chandler, Lalonde and Sokol) have produced strong evidence that cultural capacity and cultural continuity are deterrents against high-risk behaviours, including youth suicide. To build and rehabilitate cultural capacity in Aboriginal communities, argue Chandler and Lalonde, requires a variety of infrastructural interventions: settlement (or addressing) of land claim issues; implementation of self-governance (at some level); development of educational, fire, health and police services; and growth of cultural facilities. Similarly, Marie Battiste has suggested that colonization has simultaneously disenfranchised First Nations peoples as Canadian citizens but disallowed and ignored citizenship in their sovereign First Nations structures. The solution to building citizenship capacity, argues Battiste, is to reclaim and rebuild Indigenous ways of knowing and being, thus producing whole and healthy First Nations citizens (Battiste and Semaganis).

Indigenous ways of knowing and being are as diverse as Indigenous peoples themselves. There do exist, however, some commonalities (Little Bear) that, when taken together, form a foundational referent from which localized or specific forms of Indigenous capacity building might begin. Indigenous philosophies are underlain by a worldview that recognizes interrelationships among the spiritual, the natural, and the self. These relationships form the beginnings of Indigenous ways of knowing, being, and relating to the world and self (Ermine). A "theology of place" (Cajete 1999) is often used as a description for Indigenous socio-cultural philosophies that anchor relationships wherein "the land has become an extension of Indian thought and being because, in the words of a Pueblo Elder, 'It is this place that holds our memories and the bones of our people.... This is the place that made us'" (qtd. in Cajete 2000: 3). Indigenous knowledges and ways of being build upon knowledges that have passed intact through generations. These knowledges sit with a context of language and orality and are evident in storytelling and ceremonies. One cannot, according to Cora Weber-Pillwax, understate the role of Indigenous languages in the preservations, restoration, and manifestation of new Indigenous knowledges and ways of being/relating with the world. For many Indigenous peoples, stories transmit and teach Indigenous knowledges and it is thus through stories that cultural teachings are passed and become imbedded within a living history. The foundations of Indigeneity are: values that privilege the interrelationships among the spiritual, the natural and the self; a sacred orientation to place and space; a fluidity of knowledge exchange between past, present, and future; and an honouring of language and orality as an important means of knowledge transmission.

The Government of Canada is increasingly recognizing the importance of building capacity in Aboriginal communities through early childhood programs which incorporate Indigenous knowledges and which are both inclusive of community members and based on bottom-up planning approaches reflective of community-driven process (such as those utilized in the *Fetal Alcohol Spectrum Disorder Framework for Action* [Government of Canada 2003]). Women continue to comprise the majority of early childhood workers in Canada[5] and, in Aboriginal communities, Indigenous women and Elders tend to be the most valuable asset of any early childhood centre or program. The links and opportunities between Aboriginal early childhood programming and efforts to diminish child apprehensions could, in some ways, not be clearer. Research demonstrates that Canada is committing a significant injustice towards Aboriginal peoples through the apprehension of children under a flawed paradigm of child welfare programming. These interventions disproportionably affect Aboriginal mothers and their children. Research also demonstrates that (re)building cultural capacity in Aboriginal communities, through a focus on fluency in areas of Indigenous knowledges and ways of being, leads to increased socio-cultural resiliency and decreased social risk factors. Structures currently exist, in the form of early childhood development and education programs, which have imbedded within them curricular frameworks to promote Indigeneity and which inherently support and draw upon Aboriginal women and mothers. If, then, a solution is to be at hand to the state's increasing incursion into Aboriginal mothers' families, it seems eminently possible that the solution might exist in bridging Aboriginal early childhood education and development programming with programming that supports and fosters Indigeneity in Aboriginal mothers.

We began our discussion by locating ourselves in questions surrounding child welfare interventions into the lives and families of Aboriginal mothers in Canada. In rural and northern British Columbia, we witness on a daily basis these incursions and their socio-cultural ramifications in Aboriginal communities. In our work in and with First Nations communities and with fellow Aboriginal mothers, we hear stories of pain surrounding child apprehensions and of the ensuing bureaucratic confusion which mothers face in efforts to have their children returned. We have also witnessed, in our ongoing relationship with an Aboriginal Head Start Program located in a northern community, examples of inspiring successes during which Aboriginal mothers, because of their involvement in their children's programs, achieve life goals previously thought unattainable. Over a decade, eight Aboriginal mothers involved in this northern early childhood program achieved their undergraduate degrees; other mothers became involved in boards of directors, in research projects, and in participatory program evaluation processes. Ultimately these skills led to increased competency levels and senses of self.

Canada has a very problematic legacy when it comes to the treatment of the county's First Peoples. This legacy has not abated in the realm of child apprehensions. If the nation has an interest in stemming this legacy, resources and attention should likely converge both in redressing problematic discursive conceptualizations of Aboriginal peoples and in supporting existing Aboriginal early childhood programs as means through which to foster Indigeneity in Aboriginal mothers. This latter will surely increase existing socio-cultural capital and capacity in Aboriginal communities and families, thus facilitating Aboriginal mothers' abilities to exercise strength and control in advocating for themselves and their children. Through fostering Indigeneity in Aboriginal mothers, then, there exists the potential to counteract the state's ongoing child welfare intervention into Aboriginal mothers' families. The final outcome might well be healthier Aboriginal mothers and children of tomorrow

Margo Greenwood, an Indigenous scholar, is an Assistant Professor in the Department of Education at the University of Northern British Columbia, the Director of the National Collaborating Centre on Aboriginal Health and the Site Director of the Centre of Excellence for Children and Adolescents with Special Needs, the UNBC Task Force on Substance Abuse.

Sarah de Leeuw is a Ph.D. candidate in the Department of Geography at Queen's University and the Research Coordinator of the Centre of Excellence for Children and Adolescents with Special Needs, the University of Northern British Columbia Task Force on Substance Abuse.

[1]Throughout this paper we use the terms Aboriginal and Indigenous interchangeably to denote Canada's First Peoples, including First Nations and Inuit peoples, and to denote Métis people in Canada. Where applicable, we use the names of specific First Nations (i.e. Nisga'a) or we make specific reference to Inuit, Métis, or First Nations.

[2]For historic materials that demonstrate such language, see for instance: Tate; Welcome; Government of Canada and Davin.

[3]For further information on the means through which Canada's legal system systematically negates Aboriginality, see for instance: Bell and Michael Asch; Green.

[4]The links between 1) state intervention into lone-parent Aboriginal mother led families; and 2) menial employment are neither well researched nor well established. If, however, Aboriginal children are apprehended principally on grounds of neglect, and if their mothers (when employed) are both ineligible for social service supports for child care and unable to pay for child care independently, it follows that moments arise when children are likely come under the gaze of child welfare programs as a result of their mothers seeking and/or finding employment.

[5]For more information on the recruitment and retention of early childcare workers in Canada, and their demographics, see Ferguson and Miller.

References

Armitage, Andrew. *Comparing the Policy of Aboriginal Assimilation: Australia, Canada and New Zealand.* Vancouver: University of British Columbia Press, 1995.

Battiste, Marie and Semaganis, H. "First Thoughts on First Citizenship: Issues in Education." *Citizenship and the Transformation of Canada.* Ed. Y. M. Herbert. Toronto: University of Toronto Press, 2002. 93-111.

Beier, J. Marshall. "Of Cupboards and Shelves: Imperialism, Objectification, and the Fixing of Parameters on Native North Americans In Popular Culture." In *Indigeneity: Constructing and Re/Presentation.* Eds. James N. Brown and Patricia M. Scant. Commack, NY: Nova Science Publishers, 1999. 35-57.

Bell, Catherine and Michael Asch. "Challenging Assumptions" The Impact of Precedent in Aboriginal Rights Litigation." *Aboriginal and Treaty Rights in Canada: Essays on Lay, Equality, and Respect for Difference.* Ed. Michael Asch. Vancouver: University of British Columbia Press, 1997. 38-74.

Cajete, G. "Look to the Mountain: An Ecology of Indigenous Education." *A People's Ecology.* Ed. G. Cajete. Santa Fe, NM: Clear Light Publishers, 1999. 6-19.

Cajete, G. "Indigenous Knowledge: The Pueblo Metaphor of Indigenous Education." *Reclaiming Indigenous Voice and Vision.* Ed. M. Battiste. Vancouver: University of British Columbia Press, 2000. 181-191.

Canadian Coalition for the Rights of Children. "The UN Convention of the Right of the Child: How Does Canada Measure Up?" Online: http://www.rightsof children.ca/reports.htm Accessed: April 18, 2006.

Chandler, Michael J. and Christopher Lalonde. "Cultural Continuity as a Hedge Against Suicide in Canada's First Nations." *Transcultural Psychiatry* (forthcoming).

Chandler, Michael J., Christopher E. Lalonde, and Bryan W. Sokol. "Personal Persistence, Identity Development, and Suicide: A Study of Native and Non-Native North American Adolescents." *Monographs of the Society for Research in Child Development.* 68 (2) (2003): 1-128.

Davin, Nicolas Flood. *Report on Industrial Schools for Indians and Half-Breeds.* Ottawa: Government of Canada, March 14th, 1879.

de Leeuw, Sarah and Margo Greenwood. *A Qualitative Inquiry in Existing Strengths and Capacities in the Gitxsan Communities of Northwestern British Columbia.* Health Canada and the Centre of Excellence for Children and Adolescents with Special Needs. Prince George: British Columbia, May 2003.

Emberley, Julia. "Genealogies of Difference: Fundamentalisms, Families, and Fantasies." Paper presented at *TransCanada – Literature, Institutions, and Citizenship: An Interdisciplinary Conference.* Vancouver, BC, June 23-26, 2005.

Ermine, Willie. "Aboriginal Epistemology." *The Circle Unfolds: First Nations' Education in Canada.* Eds. Marie Battiste and Jean Barmen. Vancouver: University of British Columbia Press, 1995. 101-112.

Ferguson, Elaine, and Connie Miller. *Recruitment and Retention of Qualified Early Childhood Care Staff in Early Childhood Centres: Recommendations.* Halifax:

Child Care Connection-Nova Scotia, 2000.

First Nations Child and Family Caring Society of Canada. *Wen:de – The Journey Continues: The National Policy Review of First Nations Child and Family Services Research Projects, Phase Three*. Ottawa: First Nations Child and Family Caring Society of Canada, 2005.

Foucault, Michel. *The Archaeology of Knowledge*. Trans. A. M. Sheridan. New York: Pantheon Books, 1972.

Furniss, Elizabeth. *Victims of Benevolence: Discipline and Death at the Williams Lake Indian Residential School, 1891-1920*. Williams Lake, BC: The Cariboo Tribal Council, 1992.

Government of Canada and the Public Health Agency of Canada. *Fetal Alcohol Spectrum Disorder (FASD): A Framework for Action*. Ottawa, 2003. Online: http://www.phac-aspc.gc.ca/publicat/fasd-fw-etcaf-ca/appendix_e_html. Accessed: September 19, 2006.

Government of Canada, Indian and Northern Affairs. "Volume 3, Chapter 2 – The Family." *Royal Commission on Aboriginal Peoples*. Ottawa, 1996. Online: http://www.ainc-inac.gc.ca/ch/rcap/sg/sim2_e.html. Accessed: May 1, 2006.

Government of Manitoba. (June 29, 2001). "Chapter 15 – Child Welfare." *Aboriginal Justice Implementation Commission Final Report*. Online: http://www.ajic.mb.ca/reports/final_toc.html. Accessed: April 10, 2006.

Green, Joyce. "Canaries in the Minces of Citizenship: Indian Women in Canada." *Canadian Journal of Political Science* 34 (4) (December 2001): 715-738.

Greenwood, Margo, Shirley Tagalik and Sarah de Leeuw. "Beyond Deficit: Exploring Capacity Building in Northern and Indigenous Youth Communities Through Strength-Based Approaches." Eds. R. Tonkin and L. Foster. *The Youth of British Columbia: Their Past and Their Future*. Victoria: Western Geographical Press, University of Victoria, 2005. 175-188.

Haig-Brown, Celia. *Resistance and Renewal: Surviving the Indian Residential Schools*. Vancouver: Arsenal Pulp Press, 1988.

Harris, Cole. *Making Native Space: Colonialism, Resistance, and Reserves in British Columbia*. Vancouver: University of British Columbia Press, 2002.

Harris, Cole. "How Did Colonialism Dispossess? Comments from an Edge of Empire." *Annals of the Association of American Geographers* 94 (1) (March 2004): 165-182.

Johnston, Patrick. *Native Children and the Child Welfare System*. Toronto: Canadian Council of Social Development in association with James Lorimer and Company Publishing, 1983.

Little Bear, Leory. "Jagged Worlds Colliding." *Reclaiming Indigenous Voice and Vision*. Ed. Marie Battiste. Vancouver: University of British Columbia Press, 2000. 77-85.

Milloy, John. *A National Crime. The Canadian Government and the Residential*

School System, 1879-1986. Winnipeg: University of Manitoba Press, 1999.

Raibmon, Paige. *Authentic Indians: Episodes of Encounter from the Late-Nineteenth Century Northwest Coast.* Durham and London: Duke University Press, 2005.

Statistics Canada. *Women in Canada: A Gender-Based Statistical Report. Ottawa, Ontario.* Online: http://www.statcan.ca/english/freepub/89-503-XIE/0010589-503-XIE.pdf. Accessed: April 2, 2006.

Stout, Madeline Dion, Gregory D. Kipling, and Robert Stout. *Aboriginal Women's Health Research Synthesis Project: A Final Report. Ottawa.* Ontario: Centres of Excellence for Women's Health, Women's Health Bureau, Health Canada, May 2001.

Tate, Rev. C. M. *Our Indian Missions in British Columbia.* Toronto: The Methodist Young Peoples Forward Movement for Missions, Methodist Mission Rooms, c1830.

Thomas, Nicholas. *Colonialism's Culture: Anthropology, Travel and the Government.* New Jersey: Princeton University Press, 1994.

Titley, Brian E. *A Narrow Vision: Duncan Campbell Scott and the Administration of Indian Affairs in Canada.* Vancouver: University of British Columbia Press, 1986.

Weber-Pillwax, C. "Orality in Northern Cree Indigenous Worlds." *Canadian Journal of Native Education* 25 (2001): 149-165.

Welcome, Henry S. *The Story of Metlakatla.* London: Saxon and Co., 1887.

Aboriginal Women vs Canada

The Struggle for Our Mothers to Remain Aboriginal

D. MEMEE HARVARD-LAVELL AND JEANNETTE CORBIERE LAVELL

> *A nation is not conquered until the hearts of its women are on the ground. Then it is done, no matter how brave its warriors nor how strong their weapons.*
>
> —Cheyenne Proverb

Many of those present in Kelowna for the First Ministers Meeting in November 2005 noted the historic importance of this gathering. Not just because it was the first time that both Aboriginal and non-aboriginal governments had come together in an effort to address the deplorable living conditions of our nation's Aboriginal peoples, but perhaps more importantly because it was the first time that Aboriginal women had been granted an official seat at the table. Indeed, as we sat at the head table, a quick look around at the various Premieres, National Aboriginal leaders, and even the Prime Minister himself, brought home the realization that, as Aboriginal women, we were distinctly out of place. This was the first time (at least in the last few centuries) that we, as Aboriginal women, have had a voice in the decisions that affect our lives as Aboriginal people, and hopefully a sign that those present were finally ready to hear what we had to say.

Despite the power and respect accorded to women our pre-contact societies, or perhaps because of it, since the first days of settlement the Europeans colonizers have not only ignored the voices and concerns of our Aboriginal grandmothers, but have in fact worked hard to silence them. Whether their actions were simply an unconscious reflection of their own patriarchal social structures, or a deliberate attempt to disrupt the strength and social organization of our nations, the colonial imposition of male-centric ideologies and institutions have caused significant damage in our communities. Sadly, the resulting

social and economic marginalization of Indigenous women, along with a history of government policies that have torn apart Indigenous families and communities, have pushed a disproportionate number Indigenous women into dangerous situations that include extreme poverty, homelessness and prostitution. (Amnesty International 5)

Aboriginal women experience spousal violence at a rate twice that found for Aboriginal men, and in comparison to non-aboriginal women, according to police reporting statistics, they are three times more likely to experience spousal abuse, and eight times more likely to be killed by their spouse (Mann 2).[1] In fact, Aboriginal women in the 25-44 age range are five times more likely than non-aboriginal women to die of violence (Amnesty International). Clearly, as both Amnesty International and the Royal Commission on Aboriginal Peoples conclude, the contemporary violence against Aboriginal women and children specifically, and the overall myriad of social problems generally, are to be understood as a direct result of various government policies imposed without consent upon our peoples. While such policies may have been imposed without our consent, as a direct result of the courage of women like Jeannette Corbiere Lavell, Mary Two Axe-Early, and subsequently Sandra Lovelace, they did not continue unchallenged.

It is important to acknowledge at this point that although *we* currently recognize the extraordinary diversity that exists not only between specific Aboriginal groups, but also within these communities, this fact has largely been ignored (by those in power) throughout the history of our nation which has in effect created a commonality of experience in contemporary society that crosses all tribal, linguistic and geographic barriers. Indeed, through a variety of legislative acts, beginning with, but certainly not limited to, the provisions of the Indian Act, Aboriginal women as a group have historically and continually been denied many of the rights that others take for granted in this country, with a range of often devastating results for many of these women on an individual level.

Although quality of life is difficult to measure quantitatively, figures from Statistics Canada indicated alarming levels of poverty among Aboriginal women, with over 70 percent of Aboriginal women generally, and over 80 percent of on-reserve Aboriginal women specifically, earning less than $20,000 annually (Hull 6-1). In 2000, the average income of Aboriginal women generally was only $16,519, with Registered Indian women living on-reserves earning only $14,000, compared to $23,065 for non-aboriginal women (INAC). Unfortunately, not only do Aboriginal women have lower incomes and lower rates of employment than all other women in Canada, they also have lower incomes than Aboriginal men, despite having higher levels of education and lower rates of unemployment (CLC). Indeed, a study conducted in Saskatchewan indicated that without a high school education an Aboriginal woman can expect, on average, a mere $89,502 in earnings for her entire lifetime, while an Aboriginal man of the same qualifications can expect $344,781 (Petten). Although this gender gap lessens with increased education, as a university degree brings in $1,249,246 for Aboriginal women as compared to $1,386,434 for Aboriginal men, relatively few Aboriginal people attain such levels of education. Indeed according to the 2001 census, the proportion of Aboriginal people with university degrees, approximately eight percent, remains significantly lower than the non-aboriginal population, at approximately 20 percent (Statistics Canada).

Clearly many Aboriginal women are living below the poverty line, over 40 percent in fact, which is significantly more than the number of Aboriginal men, and double the percentage of non-aboriginal women (UNPAC). This situation is compounded by a higher than average birth rate among Aboriginal women, and a higher than average percentage of female headed single parent families. Indeed, according to Hull's 2001 report, one in three (33 percent) Aboriginal mothers was a single mother, compared to one in six (16 percent) of non-aboriginal mothers in Canada. Furthermore, Aboriginal families generally, and Aboriginal single-mother families specifically, tended to be larger than those of non-aboriginal Canadians: 33 percent of Aboriginal single mother families had three or more children as compared to only 16 percent of non-aboriginal single mothers (Hull, 2001). Unfortunately, a report of the National Anti-Poverty Organization (Neal) indicates that 80-90 percent of Aboriginal single mothers in urban areas exist below the poverty line without adequate housing. Given our apparent tendency to have more babies, more "deadbeat dads," and less economic opportunity, it is not surprising that we find Aboriginal women have a lower life expectancy than non-aboriginal women, and higher incidences of diabetes, HIV/AIDS, tobacco addiction, suicide (up to eight times the rate for other women) (Mann 6), and homelessness.

Contrary to popular meritocratic ideologies (founded upon colonial amnesia) the appalling situation of contemporary Aboriginal mothers can, and must be, understood as a direct result of centuries of ill-advised (if not outright ill-intentioned) government policies that have been imposed upon the First Peoples. For most our nation's history Aboriginal people generally, and Aboriginal women specifically, had absolutely no say in what happened in their own communities much less the rest of our (supposedly democratic) country. While the year 1920 was a milestone in the historic struggle for the recognition of gender equality and the rights of women here in Canada—and most women were jubilant in their celebrations of the official recognition of their legal right to vote—Aboriginal women had little cause for celebration. Although it held the promise of universal suffrage, as it recognized that "every eligible Canadian over 21, male or female" was entitled to vote in federal elections, the 1920 *Dominion Elections Act* still included a number of exceptions based explicitly on "reasons of race." Indeed Aboriginals (who were known as Indians during this period), the Inuit, and Asians (a category that included Chinese, Japanese and Hindus) were still excluded. Apparently, at this point in Canada's history the basic rights guaranteed to the citizens of a democratic nation applied only to its Caucasian members. Although gender was no longer an acceptable criteria for exclusion, clearly race still was (CBC 2004c). Chinese- and Indo-Canadians were subsequently granted the right to vote in 1947, and Japanese-Canadians obtained the same a year later in 1948, yet Aboriginal peoples were not granted this privilege until over a decade later (CBC 2004a).[2]

Today in 2006, Aboriginal people generally, and Aboriginal women specifically still do not enjoy equality with the non-aboriginal population in Canada, not just in terms of economic standing, employment, health and education standards, and overall quality of life, but also in terms of basic human rights. Aboriginal people, Aboriginal women specifically, have been specifically excluded from the basic human rights protections that other Canadians take for granted. In a country like Canada this may be hard to imagine. Indeed, we prefer to envision events of this nature occurring over the ocean, in some distant foreign land. Surprisingly though, as a result of a frequently overlooked section of the *Human Rights Act*, section 67 to be exact, which states clearly that "nothing in this Act affects any provision of the *Indian Act* or any provision made under or pursuant to that Act" our government has allowed for the existence, in effect of human rights free zones on reserves all across the nation. An Aboriginal person who is experiencing discrimination in his or her First Nation with regard to band member registration, use or occupation of reserve lands, wills and estates, education, housing, etc., has no recourse, they cannot appeal to the usual human rights commissions or tribunals. This lack of basic human rights protections for Aboriginal people is of particular concern for Aboriginal women generally, and Aboriginal mothers specifically.

One of the key areas of legislated discrimination against Aboriginal women was found in the *Indian Act* itself. For well over a hundred years, beginning in the 1870s and continuing until as recently as 1985, under the provisions of section 12(1)(b), upon their entrance into marriage with a man not possessing Indian Status,[3] the Canadian government stripped tens of thousands of Aboriginal women (and any subsequent children) of their Indian Status, and all the rights such status entailed including access to health care, education, and perhaps most importantly the right to live in their own homes and communities. Conversely, under the Act, not only did Indian men not lose status upon marriage to a non-aboriginal, their spouses gained status as did their children. As a result of being forcibly uprooted and disconnected from their communities many of these women were subsequently dependant both economically and socially upon their spouses for support (Amnesty International 6). Furthermore, since the extinguishment of Indian Status was irrevocable many Aboriginal women were left without recourse in the event of domestic violence, divorce, or widowhood.

D. Memee Harvard-Lavell and Jeannette Corbiere Lavell

Jeannette Corbiere Lavell, an Ojibway woman from the Wikwemikong First Nation, and the first Aboriginal woman in Canada to challenge this discriminatory section of the *Act*, describes her experience:

> Several months after my marriage to David Lavell in April 1970, I received a letter from Indian Affairs, advising me that I was no longer a member of my community. With this letter came a cheque, made out to me, for around $35, described as my share of the capital and revenue monies held by the Queen on behalf of the Wikwemikong Band. Although I had been aware of the provisions of section 12(1)(b) of the *Indian Act* before my marriage, the letter from Indian Affairs caused me to reflect on my situation. I was very close to my own community, and I knew a lot of women who were in the same situation as I. Through my work with the Friendship Centre and the Company of Young Canadians, I had become aware of my human rights, and I decided to challenge the confiscation of my Indian status. I did not cash the cheque, and I retained Clayton Ruby to act for me. On December 17, 1970 he sent to the Indian Registrar my protest against the deletion of my name from the Register and Band list. I argued in my protest that since Indian men did not also lose status upon marriage, that section 12(1)(b) of the *Indian Act*, under which I had lost status, violated the guarantee of equality before the law given by s. 1(b) of the *Canadian Bill of Rights*. (Eberts)

It is important at this point to clarify that it was not the loss of the right to own or inherit property on the reserve, or the right to have a share in treaty monies, or the right to not pay taxes that was of greatest concern for these women, but rather it was this loss of community support that was the hardest to bear. According to Lavell,

> My own family was supportive of my decision to challenge the removal of my status. The Chief at Wikwemikong at that time, John Wakegijig, was also supportive; his own daughter had lost her status when she married a non-status man. However, some members of my community put pressure on me or on my parents to get me to stop my protest. Among them was a teacher at the local school, originally from Quebec, who had become a status Indian upon her marriage to a Band member. She was very public in her criticism of me, including writing to the local newspaper, the Manitoulin Expositor. Sadly Mr. Wakegijig lost his life in a traffic accident in 1970, and the two chiefs who succeeded him were not supportive of my challenge. However, the birth of my son, Michael Forest Nimke Lavell, on August 29, 1970, had strengthened my resolve

to persist in my challenge. I could not register him as a status Indian, and he was not a member of my community. It concerned me that he was so excluded from my community. (Eberts)

Thus, at least for Lavell, it was the loss of her ability as a mother to pass on all rights and privileges to her children that was of the greatest concern. Neither she nor her children would be able to live among her people. Even in its contemporary manifestation, as opposed to the more historical notions of communal tribal living, for most members of the Aboriginal community everyday survival is still dependant upon extensive networks of family and friends who support and reinforce each other. Unlike the non-aboriginal middle-class whose adult members can generally afford to pay others to assume their familial responsibilities, such as child and elder care, those who have almost no economic opportunity, much less actual economic security, must rely heavily upon the help of others. For those so-called "primitive peoples" who still not only believe in the cliché that "it takes a village to raise a child" but in fact still actively practice it, the loss of community is especially hard on the women as they become mothers and caregivers. Lavell explains,

> The provisions of s.12(1)(b) caused me, and many other Indian women, great hardships. They separated us from our communities, and also made it difficult, if not impossible, for us to raise our own children in our communities where they would have the benefit of close contact with our parents and extended family, and our traditional culture. Under s. 11 of the *Indian Act*, white women marrying status Indian men could obtain Indian status, and thus live on reserve and experience life in our communities, and enjoy the other benefits of Indian status, whereas s. 12(1)(b) banned us from our own communities if we married a non-status male. I know from my own experience that the harm done by this discrimination against Aboriginal women and by s.12 (1)(b) continues to this day, and is reinforced by the provisions of the second generation cut-off. (Eberts)

Although this was a clear case of gender discrimination, (a carry over from the not so distant past when those who drafted such laws believed that all women, Aboriginal or not, were the property of men, either their fathers or subsequently their husbands) Lavell lost at the County Court level. It was argued that she had not experienced discrimination based her gender since she was not being treated any differently than any other Canadian woman, and her marriage had in fact given her the status and the rights enjoyed by all other Canadian women. Judge Grossberg suggested that it was actually to her benefit that she was no longer an

Indian, as she could now enjoy the same rights and freedoms as other Canadians.

Not so easily deterred, Lavell appealed Judge Grossberg's decision to the Federal Court of Appeal, which ruled unanimously in her favour finding that Section 12(1)(b) was in fact plainly discriminatory since Indian women were not being treated the same as Indian men. Unfortunately, but not surprisingly, under pressure from the federal government and several (federally government funded) Native organizations Lavell's case was then appealed to the Supreme Court of Canada by the Attorney General of Canada. Interestingly, while Lavell and her supporters were conducting bake sales in order to raise sufficient funds to travel to Ottawa to take part in the proceedings, the Government of Canada was known to have paid significant amounts of money to the National Indian Brotherhood (the precursor of the Assembly of First Nations) among others to cover the expenses of coming to speak out against Lavell specifically, and the rights of Indian women generally. According to Lavell's recollection,

> The Government of Canada funding was used for at least two purposes. One was to finance opposition to my position in court. The other was to finance conferences, organized by the Chiefs, to discuss the issue of section 12(1)(b). I attended such conferences in both Saskatchewan and Alberta. Women participated in such conferences, but received funding only if their position was in favour of s.12(1)(b). The Saskatchewan Chiefs, for example, financed a women's workshop, but one of the conditions of such funding was that the women in attendance take a position opposed to mine. The Alberta Indian Association hired Vicki Crowchild to speak against my position, using funding obtained from Indian Affairs. I and my supporters raised our own funds to attend these meetings. Once, on a train to Ottawa, I sat next to Ms. Crowchild, who warned me that "white men are going to have our lands" because of the position I was taking in the courts. The Government of Canada even financed a conference in Ottawa, organized by the Chiefs, during the period when my court case was being heard by the Supreme Court of Canada. An MP, Jim Manley, raised in the House of Commons his objection to the Government financing of those opposing my case. As a result, I believe that the Government agreed to provide some funding to my counsel, Mr. Ruby. (Eberts)

Such actions taken on the part of the government against the very people it has the duty to protect, is by all accounts not only deplorable, but incomprehensible in a nation that supposedly guarantees fair treatment under the law for all its members. Sadly, while such actions were indeed reprehensible they were not surprising given our centuries long history of systemic governmental abuse of

Aboriginal women in Canada.

Ultimately, Lavell lost by one vote. Justice Ritchie claimed that the Bill of Rights guarantees only the equal application of the law to both genders, not that the content nor the outcome of such laws were to be free of discrimination. The case was eventually taken to the United Nations by Sandra Lovelace and the resulting international embarrassment for Canada lead to what we now call Bill C-31, a rare amendment to the historic *Indian Act*, that in 1985 allowed for the return of well over 100,000 Aboriginal people who had lost their status, or perhaps more correctly those who had their Indian status taken away. Although many women and their children have been re-registered, Bill C-31 has simply created several new categories of Indian and only postponed the extinguishment of Indian status a couple of generations. While Lavell, and many other women like her, were reinstated as 6(1) Indians, her three children were classified as 6(2) Indians, which means their children, her grandchildren, will only be considered Indians should her children marry status Indians. Should her children marry non-Indians, her grandchildren will automatically be considered non-Indian. In a sad twist of fate, or perhaps a particularly ingenious governmental trick, Lavell's struggle for the right to marry whomever she pleases and still remain an Indian person is currently being relived by her children.

> While my three children received status pursuant to Bill C-31 and they all have full membership in Wikwemikong, some of their children do not. My daughter has two daughters, Autumn Sky and Eva. Only Autumn Sky has status; her sister does not. My grandson Neeganwhedung, Nimke's son, has full status, but Nimke's daughter Kyana has no status. This is because of the legal effect of what is now 6(2) of the *Indian Act*, the "second generation cut-off." A person who derives Indian status from only one parent, like my daughter and son, must have children with a status Indian in order for those children to have status. Autumn Sky and Neeganwhedung are both members of Wikwemikong, while their siblings living under the same roof, are not. This discrepancy in status between my grandchildren, depending on whether their other parent is a status Indian or not, will affect their ability to live with me, or perhaps even to visit me, on reserve when they are older. (Eberts)

One current strategy to circumvent this exclusion of our children has been for grandparents to adopt the grandchildren in question. Thus, contemporary Aboriginal mothers are faced with giving up all their legal rights to their own children in order to give those children the rights and security of becoming a member of their First Nation community. Clearly, the basic right of Aboriginal mothers to have Aboriginal children and grandchildren is not so basic after all. In her address to the Standing Committee on Indian Affairs and Northern Development Lavell made the following point about her experience,

> I know who I am. When the combined forces of the government and the courts of this country tell me that I am not and legally separate me forever from my community, it is they who are wrong. I pointed out to the Committee that the massive amount of public money spent on my court battle (which I believe was over ten million dollars in public funds) could have been much better spent finding a way to achieve a positive result for native people. (Eberts)

Interestingly, although the act of entering into marriage no longer results in hardship for Aboriginal women, currently the dissolution of a marriage still does. As a result of persistent failure of the federal government to afford Aboriginal women the same protection guaranteed to all other women in Canada, First Nations women living on-reserve do not have the right in law to an automatic 50/50 division of matrimonial property upon divorce (Mann). According to subsection 91 (24) of the *Constitution Act* of 1867, which gives the federal government exclusive authority over the "Indians and Lands reserved for the Indians," the provincial or territorial laws that govern the division of assets upon marital breakdown are deemed inapplicable with regard to matrimonial real property (lands) on reserves. Thus, many Aboriginal mothers find they have no legal claim to their own home and are either forced to leave, which can jeopardize any claims for custody of minor children, or worse yet, remain in an abusive situation for lack of viable alternatives (Mann). This is a choice no woman should ever have to make, much less a woman living here in Canada, a nation that supposedly values and protects equality for all regardless of race, or gender, unless you happen to be Aboriginal, or worse yet, an Aboriginal woman.

When we begin to understand the current situation of Aboriginal women in Canada as the logical outcome of centuries of inequity and discrimination, will we stop blaming the victims and begin the necessary process of envisioning real solutions to the persistent socio-economic disparity? Given the increased risk of poverty, homelessness, domestic violence/abuse, food shortage, gestational diabetes, HIV/AIDS, and drug and alcohol addictions, it would seem that comparison to many other occupations, being an Aboriginal mother is possibly one of the most dangerous jobs in contemporary Canadian society. Furthermore, given the fact that the job tends to require raising larger numbers of children on significantly less funds in poorer environmental conditions, it is arguably also one of the most difficult jobs. While many of us would shudder at the thought of raising children without the luxury of electricity, clean water, and indoor plumbing, in many remote northern communities such conditions are not only found in the memories of our grandmothers, or in the pages of pioneer stories, they are the day-to-day reality for many Aboriginal mothers. However, the fact that the Aboriginal population is increasing faster than the non-aboriginal population, despite all the aforementioned barriers and risks, is a testament to the strength, creativity, resilience and perseverance of our Aboriginal mothers. They have struggled to hold our families and communities together facing assault from both Church and State. They have chopped wood, hauled water, or lead demonstrations and organized protests; they did whatever was necessary to ensure that we would continue as a people for generations to come. The future of our nation rests in the arms of these women and it is for that reason that they have earned our respect, admiration and love. Their hearts are strong and therefore so too are our people.

Dawn Memee Lavell-Harvard, Wikwemikong First Nation, Manitoulin Island, Ontario, is currently President of the Ontario Native Women's Association, a full-time student currently completing her Ph.D. in Education at University of Western Ontario, and is the first Aboriginal person ever to receive a Trudeau Scholarship. Perhaps more importantly, she is also a full-time mother of two little girls, Autumn Sky (eight years) and Eva Lillie (two years). Her research addresses the epidemic of low academic achievement and high drop-out rates among Aboriginal populations in Canada. In examining the experiences of those few Aboriginal people who have successfully completed post-secondary education, she seeks to help define appropriate directions for educational restructuring. She is also the President of the Southern Ontario Aboriginal Diabetes Initiative; Vice-President of the Ontario Aboriginal HIV/AIDS Strategy; and on the Board of Directors of the Native Women's Association of Canada.

Jeannette Corbiere Lavell, is Ojibway First Nation, and member of the Wikwemikong Unceded Indian Reserve on Manitoulin Island, Northern Ontario. Educated on the Reserve and fluent in her own language, Ojibway, she left her community at twelve years of age to complete high school at St. Joseph's Convent, North Bay, Ontario. She received her Ontario Teacher's Certificate from McMaster University, Hamilton, Ontario in 1976 after spending many years in the social services field working with her own people in the city of Toronto. In August 1973, Jeannette's case, now known as the Lavell case, was lost at the Supreme Court of Canada, by one vote. In April 1985, after the Canadian Charter of Human Rights and Equality was enacted in the new Canadian Constitution, Jeannette regained her Indian Status and was re-instated to the Band List of the Wikwemikong Unceded Indian Reserve along with her three children. Jeannette has been teaching Fine Arts, and Parenting to Secondary Students at Wasse-Abin Wikwemikong High School. She and her 91-year-old mother, Rita L. Corbiere, are still active in community, band council, and Aboriginal Women's Organizations.

[1]Given a historical mistrust of police, justice systems, and the social services, in fact many Aboriginal women are less likely to report spousal abuse and therefore we can assume that the actual rates of family violence are even higher than reported.

[2]While Aboriginal people had been granted the right to vote back at Confederation in 1867 it was conditional. Until 1960 when the federal government finally removed the restrictions against Native peoples with regard to voting, the only way for an Aboriginal person to obtain basic democratic rights in Canada was to first renounce their status as an Aboriginal person of Canada (CBC 2004b). To renounce their Aboriginal rights, heritage, culture, communities, and ultimately their families, was often deemed a price too high to pay, even for democratic rights, and not surprisingly very few Aboriginal people actually exercised this option. While the 1960 change in legislation was a huge step toward recognizing the Aboriginal people as legitimate and equal members of Canadian society, with all the rights and privileges that membership entails, it was not enough.

[3]In order for an Aboriginal woman to maintain her status she had to marry a "status Indian" man; if she married a Métis, Inuit, non-status Aboriginal, or non-Aboriginal she would lose her right to be an Indian under the *Act*.

References

Amnesty International *Stolen sisters: Discrimination and Violence Against Indigenous Women in Canada*. 2004. Online: www.amnesty.org. Retrieved May 29, 2006.

Canadian Broadcasting Corporation (CBC). "Correcting a Racial Injustice." *The CBC Digital Archives Website*. 2004a. Online: http://archives.cbc.ca/IDC-1-73-1450-9555/politics_economy/voting_rights/clip1. Retrieved May 29, 2006.

Canadian Broadcasting Corporation (CBC). "Diefenbaker and the Native Vote." *The CBC Digital Archives Website*. 2004b. Online: http://archives.cbc.ca/IDC-1-73-1450-9556/politics_economy/voting_rights/clip1. Retrieved May 29, 2006.

Canadian Broadcasting Corporation (CBC). "McClung's 'Mock Parliament'." *The CBC Digital Archives Website*. 2004c. Online: http://archives.cbc.ca/IDC-1-73-1450-9553/politics_economy/voting_rights/clip1 Retrieved May 29, 2006.

Canadian Labour Congress (CLC). "Statement on June 21, 2004 'Aboriginal Peoples Day'." 2004. Online: http://canadianlabour.ca/index.php/Aboriginal-Workers/464. Retrieved May 29, 2006.

Eberts, Mary. Personal interview with Jeannette Corbiere Lavell. Thunder Bay, Ontario, Spring 2006.

Hull, J. *Aboriginal Single Mothers in Canada, 1996: A Statistical Profile*. Ottawa: Minister of Public Works and Government Services Canada, 2001.

Indian and Northern Affairs Canada (INAC). *Aboriginal Women: A Profile From the 1996 Census.* Ottawa: Minister of Public Works and Government Services Canada, 2001.

Mann, M. *Aboriginal Women: An Issues Backgrounder.* Ottawa: Status of Women Canada, 2005. Online: http://www.swc-cfc.gc.ca/resources/consultations/ges09-2005/aboriginal_e.pdf. Retrieved May 29, 2006.

Neal, R. *Voices: Women, Poverty and Homelessness in Canada.* Ottawa: National Anti-Poverty Organization, 2004. Online: http://www.napo-onap.ca/en/resources/Voices_English_04232004.pdf#search=percent22voicespercent 20women percent20poverty percent20and percent20homelessness percent22 Retrieved May 29, 2006.

Petten, C. "Huge Earnings for Educated Aboriginals: University of Saskatchewan Study Education and Lifetime Income for Aboriginal People in Saskatchewan." *Windspeaker* 20 (2002): 12.

Royal Commission of Aboriginal People. *Aboriginal Peoples in Urban Centres: Report of the National Round Table on Aboriginal Urban Issues.* Ottawa: Minister of Supply and Services Canada, 1993.

Statistics Canada. *2001 Census: Education in Canada, Raising the Standard.* Ottawa: Government of Canada, 2001.

United Nations Platform for Action Committee (UNPAC). *Women and the Economy: Aboriginal Women and the Economy.* 2003. Online: http://www. unpac.ca/economy/awe.html. Retrieved May 29, 2006.

"They Let Their Kids Run Wild"

The Policing of Aboriginal Mothering in Quebec

CHERYL GOSSELIN

This essay explores the discrimination experienced by an Aboriginal mother and her fight to attain retribution for the violations of her human rights. Specifically, I develop a critical analysis of the regulation strategies of the Quebec state, conveyed through its youth protection services, court system and language legislation, and its treatment of Joann-May Cunday and her children. These strategies rely on colonial, neo-colonial, and nationalist processes to produce an identity that marks her as an unfit parent, non-Quebecoise, and her mothering practices subject to policing. I argue that the dominant ideology of motherhood was used to cast Cunday's mothering practices as antithetical to normalized versions of good mothers, thereby, enabling the policing of her Aboriginal maternal identity.

This chapter is arranged by three interrelated themes: First, the policing of First Nations mothering practices by state institutions through the upholding of the dominant version of patriarchal motherhood; second, the nationalist constructions of certain women as the biological and cultural reproducers of the nation. The combined processes of nationalism and colonialism, historically and today, work to ascribe to white women (Catholic, French-speaking) the label of mothers of the nation and Aboriginals as outside this configuration. Lastly, Quebec language laws, specifically the Charter of the French Language, a piece of nationalist legislation which is designed to protect French and uphold the collective rights of the French culture and society over the rights of the individual.

In her book, *Mother Outlaws*, Andrea O'Reilly reveals how patriarchal motherhood as a dominant ideology and institution in our western society is the standard by which all women are judged and regulated. Women who adhere to this version of motherhood are deemed to be good mothers. Those who mother outside or against this institution are seen as bad. These women are then subjected to the policing of their mothering practices by individuals and state institutions that have a stake in maintaining the values of the patriarchal family and proper gender codes of feminine conduct. Aboriginal mothers and their mothering practices are viewed by patriarchal, white society as external to the institution of motherhood because of their heritage, culture and familial values. A number of colonial and neo-colonial practices define First Nations mothering as inconsistent with governing modes of motherhood that have resulted in the policing of Aboriginal women and their families. Examples of this policing include the old residential school system which separated generations of First Nations children from parents and the current practice of removing children from their homes after labeling Aboriginal mothers as "bad" through either neglect, physical abuse, drug or alcohol addiction. Alternatively, First Nations women imagine for themselves mothering identities based on their cultural origins that allow them to resist and unsettle familiar notions of what a good mother is.

One Aboriginal woman who was judged to be a "bad" mother and punished for it is Joann-May Cunday, a member of the Opaskwayak band of the Cree Nation in Manitoba. I met Cunday in the spring of 2005 as she was trying to attain retribution for violations of her human rights from a provincial court Tribunal. Her ordeal began in 1999 when she moved her family from Manitoba to Sherbrooke, Quebec to live with her then boyfriend. After an incident of spousal abuse and the temporary seizure of her two young children by state authorities, Cunday fought a rigid bureaucratic youth protection system that denied her access to documentation and services in the language of her choice as well as an unsympathetic social worker who repeatedly chastised her "bad parenting skills." I relate here Cunday's six-year ordeal with particular focus on the Human Rights Tribunal that I witnessed. During this process, the lawyer for the social worker constructed a narrative in which she juxtaposed the ideal of motherhood versus Aboriginal mothering. She accomplished this by framing the social worker as the epitome of good mothering while Cunday was cast as a mentally unstable parent who, by virtue of her heritage, was permissive with her kids and "let [them] run wild."

Methodological Concerns

This research is guided by my feminist principles of giving voice and agency to my subject. I struggle with the idea of how best to approach this topic. My conversations and emails with Joann-May Cunday over the past year have convinced me that her story must be told. But I am not a First Nations mother nor do I want to appropriate Cunday's experiences. I am a white academic who has the privilege of embarking on the political project of seeking social justice in a society that differentiates and subordinates people on the basis of race, ethnicity, and gender classifications. I saw for myself the injustice done to Cunday and all Aboriginal women; an injustice endorsed by the Quebec courts.

In addition to my position as a white academic, I am an anglophone minority living in a French province. While I cannot compare my situation with Cunday's,

I have experienced marginalization on the basis of my language and heritage even though my origin is bi-cultural and I was born, raised, and still live in Quebec. As an insider and outsider, I am attempting "to decolonize my mind and divest my identity and body of power and domination," as Gabriel Bedard says we must do (41). I am also engaged in trying to comprehend and resist all forms of oppression and develop anti-racist ways of thinking and doing. As George Sefa Dei claims "we must not only acknowledge the reality of racism in society, we must also question how our white powers and privileges operate" (28). My work then supports the notion of "relational accountability" (Wilson and Sarson qtd. in Wilson) whereby I am not "directly in control of the contributions [Cunday] makes, but instead am accountable for creating and preserving a space in which [she] can share knowledge" (Wilson 7).

Literature Review

The dominant model of patriarchal motherhood today is, according to Andrea O'Reilly, intensive mothering. As an ideological construction with a set of accompanying discourses it evolved "in response to women's increased social and economic independence" (O'Reilly 10). Intensive mothering is characterized by the following demands: only biological mothers can properly care for children; mothering is a 24 hour a day, seven days a week commitment; a child's needs come before the mother's; mothers must rely on the experts for advice; a woman must be totally "satisfied, fulfilled, completed and composed in motherhood"; and "mothers must lavish excessive amounts of time, energy, and money in rearing their children" (11). As O'Reilly argues, this type of motherhood is oppressive because it negates a woman's selfhood and denies her power and authority (11). As a culturally specific ideal it is unattainable for most white, middle-class, heterosexual women, and for those mothers whose identities fall outside these parameters, their attempts at mothering are constantly questioned, challenged, and regulated. Although First Nations women are not discussed in *Mother Outlaws*, several authors in the text show how lesbian (Radbord; Comeau) and African-American (Lawson; Wane) mothers are rendered powerless through the policing of their identities and their commitment to seeking alternative modes of mothering that destabilize dominant discourses of patriarchal motherhood.

The experiences of Aboriginal mothers today must be analyzed against the backdrop of colonial and current neo-colonial practices and discourses. Kim Anderson, in her work on reconstructing Native women's identities, reveals how Aboriginal motherhood was respected and revered among family, community and nation. "Motherhood was an affirmation of a woman's power and defined her central role in traditional Aboriginal societies" (Anderson 83). Colonization by European Whites shattered the social fabric of indigenous familial and community life through the imposition of patriarchal domestic values. This destroyed traditional admiration and authority for Native motherhood that led to family breakdown, abuse, poverty and an internalized, negative Native female identity (Anderson).

One of the most destructive colonial practices was the residential school system. From 1879 to 1986 Native children were taken from their parents by the Canadian government and Anglican Church to be placed in residential schools where they were "civilized" and assimilated into white society (Milloy). The consequences to Native motherhood was the severing of daughters from their mothers' and extended kin's maternal knowledge, the loss of their cultural heritage and the teaching of gender and marital roles that conformed to dominant western conceptions of femininity as subservient and passive. The residential school system can be viewed as the policing of Aboriginal mothers as it dislodged the centrality of women from the family and labeled their parenting skills as abnormal.

The legacy of residential schooling continues as the trauma suffered by these children impacts on successive generations of mothers and their abilities to nurture (Ing). These intergenerational wounds are used by current neo-colonial discourses as justification to mark indigenous parents as neglectful and abusive as well as the removal of children from their home environments.

Several researchers have explored the processes of reclaiming Native womanhood (Anderson, K.; Maracle). Much of this involves constructing a maternal identity that is again a source of power and affirmation of Native women's selfhood. Part of this reclamation is about building "identities that are inseparable from their connections to family, history, community, place and spirituality" (Wilson 9). The recovering of Native motherhood supplants dominant versions of patriarchal motherhood and is, as O'Reilly argues, a source of empowered motherhood (12).

Joann-May Cunday's Story

Before I give my analysis of the tribunal, let me provide some background events to Joann-May's experiences in court. Cunday's French-Canadian boyfriend starting abusing her shortly after arriving in Sherbrooke, Quebec with her two children. On the night of November 14th, 1999, she tried to escape his violence, drugs and alcohol. Living in Sherbrooke only a short time, she did not know anyone except a Francophone neighbour who spoke English. She was isolated from family and other social supports and did not speak French. So that night, after her boyfriend came home drunk and threatened to harm her, she fled in a panic and sought the help of the police. They returned to the home with her and kicked the boyfriend out for the night. The next day, in retaliation, he accused her of being an unfit mother to youth protection services so they took custody of her children.

The youth protection agency assigned her a Francophone social worker that spoke only a bit of English when she was forced to. She also refused to translate her working notes or provide Cunday with documentation in English so she could understand the assessment of her case. During her interviews the social worker made it obvious to Cunday that she did not approve of her or the way she was raising her kids. At one home visit the social worker said to Cunday that she was not being cooperative. This was because she refused to stay with her boyfriend and keep the family unit intact while working on his behaviour together. At another interview the social worker believed the kids to be "misbehaving." When Cunday tried to explain that raising children was done differently in Indigenous cultures, the social worker told her, "that [her lifestyle] was not the way people lived in Quebec and that discipline was important…" and "[i]f you were happier where you were before, you can go back if you like" (Human Rights Tribunal 4). At a later court proceeding in Youth Division, the social worker said to Cunday in front of her lawyer that, "if she wanted to adopt the Indian way of life she could go and live in the North where they have no rules or regulations and let their kids run wild" (Human Rights Tribunal 3).

Outraged and frustrated by this treatment she went to Quebec's Human Rights Commission in 2000 with the complaint that the social worker and the Centre jeunesse de l'Estrie, through vexatious acts and remarks, interfered with her rights to the safeguard of her dignity, without distinction or exclusion based on language and ethnic origin, the whole in violation of sections 4, 10, 12 and 23 of Quebec's Charter of Human Rights and Freedoms (Human Rights Tribunal 1). The Commission ruled in Cunday's favor noting her rights had been violated and ordered the agency to pay her $8,000 in moral damages. It also ruled that in certain circumstances where the rights of parents or children may be adversely affected, the agency must take measures to provide services and documents in a language comprehensible to them. But the agency refused to obey the ruling by appealing the decision.

Meantime, fearing that her children would be taken away again, she sent her kids back to live with their grandmother in Manitoba where she joined them a short while after. It wasn't until five years later, in May of 2005, that the case was held before a Human Rights Tribunal. The Tribunal overturned the earlier decision and argued the agency did not have to produce services nor documents in English and that the social worker had not discriminated against Cunday on the basis of cultural or ethnic origins. Cunday was also ordered to pay the court costs. It is the proceedings of the Human Right Tribunal that I analyze next.

The Policing of First Nations Motherhood

Joann-May Cunday's mothering practices and lifestyle choices were constantly questioned by the social worker before the tribunal. Her dislike of the way Cunday was raising her children was clear. She asked Cunday why she was living with an abusive partner and why she fled her apartment on the night of November 14th, 1999, leaving her kids at home with the abuser. The subsequent taking away of her kids, more questions about sending her kids back to Manitoba to stay with her mother without telling youth protection; about why the kids had different fathers (one son is bi-racial); and about why one son was always sick are indicative of the policing of First Nations motherhood.

During the tribunal, the lawyer for the defendant tried to show Cunday was mentally unstable by suggesting her panic attacks and weight loss problems always existed and were not the result of her ordeal with youth protection services and personnel. On the stand, Cunday was visibly upset and uncomfortable with a justice system that was foreign to her culture. To ease the pain, she connected to the powers of her ancestors through the sweet grass and bear-claw that she brought for strength. At one point during her testimony, all eyes were on her as she ceremoniously held these sacred objects. The curious stares of the three commissioners, two lawyers, and social worker appeared to me as evidence of their incomprehension of Indigenous culture and the important role of spirituality.

In the final decision the tribunal stated, "she was overwhelmed by events and could not understand what was happening to her" and "her anxiety was such that she had panic attacks, with the result that it is not surprising she misinterpreted the social worker's remarks" (Human Rights Tribunal 8). Cunday's lifestyle and mothering practices destabilized the social worker's, the lawyers', and the court's views of what normal motherhood should be. With no understanding of the connections between individual Native womanhood, culture and spirituality, the participants perceived her to be unstable, overwhelmed, and full of anxiety and thus not a good mother. The result was the policing of her Aboriginal mothering practices by the Tribunal whose decision punished her for these customs.

Nationalist Constructions of Women as the Biological and Cultural Reproducers of the Nation

Nationalism as an ideology of group affirmation and self-identification is concerned with the construction and maintenance of the nation and its boundaries (Anderson, B.). These boundaries are crafted through different cultural, national and gendered identities belonging to the nation while excluding others from it. It is the interplay of these identities that create an imagined community and a narration to go along with it (Anderson, B.). Many feminists have argued that the imagined community and the nation in narratives of national belonging are differentiated by gender (West; Walby; Yuval-Davis and Anthias). While men are the nation, women are symbolic of it and are usually scripted as mothers of the nation (Sharpe). Depending on the colonial relations of the past and nationalist concerns of the day only certain women are thought to embody the ideals of the imagined community and have public and private support to bear and raise children. Other women are either policed or punished for reproducing. Quebec, as a white-settler society with its own history of colonization and imperial rule, has symbolically encoded white, Catholic and French-speaking women (the "*pur laine*") as bearers of the nation.

This nationalist configuration was explicitly evident during the tribunal proceedings. It played out in the juxtaposition between the ideals of virtuous patriarchal motherhood performed by the defense lawyer and the social worker and the framing of Cunday's Aboriginal motherhood as suspect. The defense lawyer, through her questions and style of examining Cunday, and the social worker produced the tensions among these two versions of motherhood. Joann-May Cunday was cast as the mentally unstable mother who was so upset by the social worker's remarks that "[she lost] considerable weight, [developed] sleeping problems and an unhealthy fear of losing her children" (Human Rights Tribunal 5).

Cunday was also cast as an unreliable witness. The defense lawyer kept after Cunday while on the stand to remember dates, names of people etc. as if she was deliberately trying to confuse her, "the complainant was reticent throughout her testimony and evasive in her answers. She could not remember important facts" (Human Rights Tribunal 8). She was again a permissive mother who "let her kids run wild." "She did not want a government body to intervene in her situation and was not open to recommendations from the youth division or the social worker" (Human Rights Tribunal 8). And Cunday was perceived to be so unstable that she could not choose her friends rationally. "The tribunal heard the testimony of [Cunday's neighbor] who said she was present at the meetings between Cunday and the social worker and testified that the social worker 'affirmed that the lifestyle valued by Cunday was not acceptable in Quebec and that she would have to return to Manitoba if she wanted to live as an Amerindian.' The tribunal was perplexed by that testimony because the social worker herself testified that she had never met [the neighbor] prior to the day of the tribunal" (Human Rights Tribunal 5).

The defense lawyer herself upheld the dominant version of good motherhood. She is a white, middle-class, professional woman from the high-powered, Montreal law firm of Heenan, Blaikie. She was also visibly pregnant at the time. In one exchange between herself and the judge, the judge called a ten-minute recess saying, "enough time to go for a cigarette." The lawyer remarked, lovingly patting her round belly, "not with the little one here."

During her questioning of the social worker, the lawyer constructed a narrative in which the youth protection agency worker represented the highest standards of motherhood through her professionalism and dedication to her clients. She is middle-aged, middle-class, a mother herself and Francophone, a true Quebecoise. From testimony by co-workers, her career is spotless. On the stand, she could remember specific dates, times, places of meetings and names of people involved. "The tribunal preferred the testimony of [the social worker], who was clear and precise on all points about which she testified, and who showed she was experienced in such situations, that [she] made her remarks respectfully and not aggressively, whereas the complainant was agitated and in the grip of intense anxiety" (Human Rights Tribunal 8). In yet another comparison between good and bad motherhood, the social worker had access to her case notes during her testimony while Cunday came with her sacred objects. The professional notes were regarded as an approved tool for use in court opposed to the spiritual aids that seemed to be only a curiosity at the tribunal.

Clearly, as reflected in the final report of the tribunal, the proceedings constructed Cunday as the bad mother because of her cultural customs, lifestyle choices, mental state, friends and mothering practices. Her identity as a First Nations woman, a mother and her mothering knowledge were undermined and viewed as suspect. Reinforcing this identity as "bad" were the lawyer and her client both of whom represented the epitome of "good" Quebecoise motherhood; a position and ideology ascribed meaning through the historical practices of colonialism and contemporary forces of nationalism.

Quebec Nationalist Politics and Language Laws

Much emphasis was placed on the fact that Joann-May Cunday neither spoke nor understood French. She was cast as an outsider in every situation. She was an Aboriginal, English-speaker from Manitoba living in Sherbrooke in her dealings with youth protection, the social worker, the court system and the law. The province's language policies were used to justify the racist and discriminatory treatment Joann-May and her family received.

The Charter of the French Language was instituted in 1977 by the Quebec government to protect and preserve the French language and identity. In the area of health and social services the charter allows for documents filed in clinical records to be drafted in French and English, as deemed necessary by the person generating them. However, according to the law each health or social service has the right to draft such documents in French alone. According to the Tribunal, "[the social worker's] report was in French because that is her mother tongue, and she is more comfortable in it than in English…. Professionals who are required to draft an assessment report have a strict right to do so in French, and the absence of a translation of the report [and services] does not constitute unfair treatment or distinction based on race, language or ethnic origin" (7).

Clearly, the French language was protected over Cunday's individual and cultural rights. In this case, it was the collective rights of Quebec as expressed by the social worker's desire to conduct herself in French only that overrode the individual rights of Cunday to safeguard her human rights and dignity. Following the letter of the law, the commissioners precluded the idea of a compromise and where an exception be made in Cunday's case which would have allowed her to comprehend what was going on and give her the power to make her own choices.

The final decision of the Tribunal recognized that "the remarks made [by the social worker] are a reminder to the complainant that she is not from here and does not understand the practices of the Centre jeunesse de l'Estrie, but they do not constitute distinction, or exclusion for that matter, on the basis of her race or ethnic origin" (9). The court interpreted Cunday's Aboriginal identity as the occasion to construct her as the outsider and used this to endorse discrimination and racism.

Conclusion

In conclusion, motherhood was very evident in the tribunal proceedings and at times seemed to be a major focus. The process reveals how women who practice mothering outside the institution of patriarchal motherhood are judged and policed. Joann-May Cunday was discriminated against in three ways. Firstly, by the youth protection agency and its refusal to provide English services and documents for her. Secondly, the social worker perceived her to be a "bad" mother because of her Native heritage and customs. Lastly, the Tribunal framed her as an inferior mother on the basis of her lifestyle choices and mothering practices which are rooted in her Aboriginal identity, culture, and nationhood. None of the Tribunal participants understood the cultural frameworks or worldviews from which Cunday gained her power as an Aboriginal mother.

The Tribunal proceedings were about motherhood; the exemplary mother versus the punishable mother. The historical and contemporary relations of colonialism and nationalism weighed heavily in defining how the plaintiff and defendant would be positioned. It was no accident that the lawyer compared the social worker as benevolent mother with Cunday as the bad mother. She, herself a conscientious mother-to-be, was able to draw on these two constructions because the colonial, neo-colonial, and nationalist relations were readily available to her as a privileged, white woman. I argue that when the three male commissioners sat down to deliver their judgement, the fact that Cunday was cast as a bad mother affected their decision to dismiss her charges. They ended up policing her in their findings and, to add insult to injury, made her pay the court costs.

I hope my readers feel that I have created a space for Cunday to share her experiences. I thank Joann-May Cunday and her family for allowing me to tell her story to as many people as possible, for her courage in coming forward and speaking out against this injustice, and for being an empowered mother.

References

Anderson, Benedict. *Imagined Communities: Reflections on the Origin and Spread of Nationalism.*2nd Edition. New York: Verso, 1991.

Anderson, Kim. *A Recognition of Being: Reconstructing Native Womanhood.* Toronto: Sumach Press, 2000.

Bedard, Gabriel. "Deconstructing Whiteness: Pedagogical Implications for Anti-Racism Education." *Power, Knowledge and Anti-Racism Education.* Eds. George Sefa Dei and Agnes Calliste. Halifax: Fernwood Publishing, 2000.41-49.

Comeau, Dawn, "Lesbian Non-Biological Mothering: Negotiating an (Un)familiar Existence." *Mother Outlaws: Theories and Practices of Empowered Mothering.* Ed. Andrea O'Reilly. Toronto: Women's Press, 2004. 155-167.

Human Rights Tribunal. Judgement #450-53-000003-026, District of Saint-Francois, Quebec, May, 24 2005.

Ing, Rosalyn. "Canada's Indian Residential Schools and its Impacts on Mothering." Paper delivered at the Association for Research on Mothering, 9th Annual Conference: "Mothering: Race, Culture, Ethnicity and Class," Toronto, October 20-24, 2005.

Lawson, Erica, "Black Women's Mothering in a Historical and Contemporary Perspective: Understanding the Past, Forging the Future." *Mother Outlaws: Theories and Practices of Empowered Mothering.* Ed. Andrea O'Reilly. Toronto: Women's Press, 2004. 193-201.

Maracle, Lee. *I Am Woman.* Vancouver: Press Gang Publishers, 1996.

Milloy, John S. *A National Crime. The Canadian Government and the Residential School System 1879 to 1986.* Winnipeg: The University of Manitoba Press, 1999.

O'Reilly, Andrea, ed. *Mother Outlaws: Theories and Practices of Empowered Mothering.* Toronto: Women's Press, 2004.

Radbord, Joanna, "Lesbian Mothers and the Law of Custody, Access, and Child Support." *Mother Outlaws: Theories and Practices of Empowered Mothering.* Ed. Andrea O'Reilly. Toronto: Women's Press, 2004. 145-154.

Sefa Dei, George. "Towards an Anti-Racism Discursive Framework." *Power, Knowledge and Anti-Racism Education.* Eds. George Sefa Dei and Agnes Calliste. Halifax: Fernwood Publishing, 2000. 23-39.

Sharpe, Joanne P. "Gendering Nationhood: A Feminist Engagement with National Identity." *Body Space.* Ed. Nancy Duncan. London: Routledge, 1996. 97-108.

Walby, Sylvia. "Women and Nation." *International Journal of Comparative Sociology* 23, 1 (2) (1992): 81-100.

Wane, Njoki Nathani, "Reflections on the Mutuality of Mothering: Women, Children, and Other-mothering." *Mother Outlaws: Theories and Practices of*

Empowered Mothering: Ed. Andrea O'Reilly. Toronto: Women's Press, 2004. 229-239.

West, Lois, ed. *Feminist Nationalism*. London: Routledge, 1997.

Wilson, Alex, *Living Well: Aboriginal Women, Cultural Identity and Wellness*. Winnipeg: The Prairie Women's Health Centre of Excellence, March 2004.

Wilson, Alex and Janet Sarson, *Focus Groups for Social Change: A User's Handbook*. Duluth, MN: Praxis International, 2003.

Yuval-Davis, Nira and Flora Anthias, eds, *Women-Nation-State*, New York: St. Martin's Press, 1989.

LITERARY REPRESENTATIONS OF ABORIGINAL MOTHERING

Woman Dreaming

An Exploration of the Australian Aborigine's Return to Heritage

DEBRA BRUCH

Since the 1970s, Australian Aborigine authors have been motivated to promote an understanding of their culture to their generation and the generations that followed for the purpose of restoring self-identity to their people. Led by Sally Morgan in literature and Jack Davis in theatre, Aboriginal authors see a return to culture as a return to heritage, and that their heritage, culture, and self-identity are centered on what is known as Dreamtime, or The Dreaming.

According to this understanding, to know Dreamtime is for an Australian Aborigine to know oneself and reconnect with a heritage and culture in which to thrive. Since Dreamtime is associated with heritage, to understand it also means to acknowledge that their generation has lost its connection to the distant past. This acknowledgement requires an examination of history to discover the factors that led to the suppression of the Australian Aboriginal culture by the wider (white) Australian society.

Three woman authors who share this common goal of promoting an awareness of Australian Aboriginal heritage are Hyllus Maris and Sonia Borg, co-authors of *Women of the Sun*[1] and Sally Morgan, author of *My Place*.[2] Their writings merge, separate, and dance Dreamtime, culture, history, heritage, and self-identity to create powerful and meaningful stories. Basing their stories on historical events, the authors create woman mother figures who carry the Dreaming and pass the cultural and belief system on to their children and youth in the face of tremendous opposition.

In writing *Women of the Sun* and *My Place*, Hyllus Maris, Sonia Borg and Sally Morgan express the reasons why the Australian Aborigines are distanced from their heritage as they write strong Aboriginal women mother characters who see their main role as nurturing children and youth and teaching their heritage. The authors create white societies within their fictive worlds as having tremendous impact on their characters. The authors endow their stories with events, attitudes, and values that parallel their view of historical events, attitudes, and values. In their writings, Maris, Borg, and Morgan portray women who represent a significant threat to a society dominated by white laws and attitudes. Paralleling history, the white societies in the literature act under the convenient umbrella that describes their purpose as civilizing the Australian Aborigine. Aboriginal mothering, in this context, means that older Aboriginal women characters teach The Dreaming and nurture younger characters for the purposes of maintaining or restoring their Aboriginal heritage and culture under extremely difficult and debilitating circumstances.

The Aboriginal Woman as Teacher

The story in *Women of the Sun* historically begins before *My Place* and portrays the tribe living in peace before their encounter with white men, and where Aboriginal women have an equal role with men in the tribe. While the Aboriginal men are primarily concerned with hunting, the main role of Aboriginal women is to teach. Not only do they teach younger women herbal medicine (Maris and Borg 12), but Dreamtime.

Dreamtime is the Australian Aborigine's belief system that forges their culture and gives them a strong sense of belonging. When Conara teaches the girls a dance and Towradgi teaches their ancestral history in *Women of the Sun*, the women are carrying Dreamtime, passing on their culture, strengthening the girls' sense of belonging, and merging past and future with the present. Unlike other indigenous tribal communities, the Australian Aborigine experience of Dreamtime does not mean living in the moment to the exclusion of past and future; it is an awareness of the past and future as part of the present. They do not see any difference. The past not only influences the present, it *is* the present. Everything created in the present was also created in the past.

By teaching Dreamtime, Aboriginal women characters strengthen the bonds of belonging and teach children and youth acceptable ways to relate to the earth and the clan. For youth to learn acceptable social relationships, Aboriginal women characters teach them to follow the Law of The Dreaming. According to Elder, these injunctions, referred to as "the Law," are fundamental in understanding Aboriginal interpersonal relations and every aspect of their way of life (214). Law forms customs, beliefs, norms, and values. According to Gillian Oxford, the ancestors created all of the social laws and rituals that "ensured the increase of nature, a process in which they play an essential part even to this day" (Oxford 88). For children, this is the beginning of Dreamtime awareness. Knowledge of Law gives characters a sense of self-worth. For children to become men and women, however, this awareness of Dreamtime must transcend knowledge. As Murra points out in Episode One of *Women of the Sun*, a man must act like a man. "He must not only know our customs, but how to *live* the Law" (31).

In Law also reside acceptable relationships with the earth. In *Women of the Sun*,

Towradgi nurtures youth by securing where they belong, not merely as a member of the community or tribe, but in relationship with the earth. Everyone and everything exists together in its place. If an Aboriginal child kicks a stone or twig, he or she is instructed by a tribal elder to replace is exactly as it was (Lawlor 42). In *My Place,* Daisy teaches Sally to return living creatures unharmed to the swamp (Morgan 59).

Because ancestors created Dreamtime Law, it is important for the Aboriginal women in *Women of the Sun* to teach about the ancestors and past happenings. One of the tribal names for Dreamtime is "altjeringa," which means "In the Beginning." It's the time when ancestral beings appeared and peopled the earth. They walked across the land and created all the geographical landmarks, and gave birth to all living things, including people (Oxford 88). Everywhere they went, they left something of their spiritual essence. Sometimes their travels were short, and they were spatially confined (Elder 214). While the stories differ from region to region, the fundamental beliefs and worldviews seem to be common amongst all Australian Aborigine people. In *Women of the Sun*'s Episode One, Towradgi explains their ancestral beings to Wonda and Alinta:

> Long ago the sun hadn't risen yet. And it was here that our ancestors were made by Pund-jel and Pal-ly-an. Pund-jel, he made the men; Pal-ly-an, he made the women. Women like you and me . . .
> *She suddenly stoops and picks up a handful of black earth.*
> Put out your hands.
> *The two girls open their hands and TOWRADGI gives each of them some of the earth, then closes her hands around the girls', so that they hold the earth in their fists.*
> This is your mother . . . this is your body . . . your flesh, your blood, your sinews . . . our ancestors were made from this earth. . . . (Maris and Borg 13)

These ancestral beings were larger than life, and were often more cruel and primitive than their human descendants, whose laws they themselves established. At the end of their walking, they disappeared into the ground, sea, and sky, but their bodies were recognized by representative trees, rocks, and sacred stones (Oxford 88). Some left their images in paint on the rock walls of shelters (Elder 214). One way that Aborigines recognize this ancestral action to prepare for the sacred, spiritual experience of renewal is by painting the body. Details of the routes taken by these beings are the physical features they left along the way and are the basis of Aboriginal topographical knowledge. "The location of these tracks and specific sites and accounts of these journeys were communicated from one generation to the next through songs, dances and other rituals that were begun at the time of the first initiation" (Oxford 88).

When Conara teaches the dance in *Women of the Sun*, the younger women not only remember, but they interact with the ancestors through their intricate rituals of song and dance. The legends and rituals help the youth not only understand his or her true self and gain self-identity, they offer the vocabulary of experience and action that connects them to their heritage.

Aboriginal women as nurturing teachers in the literature parallel the earth as nurturer. Indeed, Towradgi is an earth mother character. While characters do not call the earth an "earth mother," their connection to the earth is vital for self-identity and a sense of belonging. The actions of ancestors in sculpting the earth tied earth to its people. In *My Place*, Arthur recognizes a relationship with the earth. (212) The earth contains the energy of ancestors' actions, and through Dreaming humanity receives that energy. As Robert Lawlor points out:

> For them, as for perhaps no other culture, the earth is the center of the intelligence of creation; a symbol and memory of the primordial Dreaming; a receptacle of all seeds cosmic, metaphysical, and biological; the nurturer of all life, both visible and invisible. By listening to the songs and energies of the earth the Aborigines hear the voices of the universal Dreaming. (48)

The earth is vital and alive, "saturated with significations" (Stanner 227). Created in the past before human living, the earth is the living ancestor of men and women. This way, via the ancestors, the earth nurtures characters in the literature, but the degree of nurturing depends on the Aboriginal woman's degree of Dreamtime awareness. Once an older Aboriginal woman character effectively teaches a younger woman, this connection to ancestors and the earth is established. But it is more than connection: it is a one-ness, an inseparable spirit. As Oxford points out, "Man and nature are indivisible" (90). If the connection is successful, the Aboriginal youth begin to gain identity and a keen sense of belonging. In *My Place*, this phenomenon happens when Daisy sets aside her fear and shame and tells her story to Sally. Sally then gains a strong sense of self-worth and identity.

The Australian Aborigines acknowledge people not only as direct descendants from the earth, however, but see their bodies as the same earth element. An Aboriginal woman interviewed on television said, "With your vision you see me sitting on a rock, but I am sitting on the body of my ancestor. The earth, his body, and my body are identical." ("Blackout"). The earth as element and the human body as element are one and the same. The purpose of the walkabout is to help a person become renewed in their one-ness with the earth, and, therefore, with each other. Visions of the dead come through the energy of the earth. Some Aborigines, as in *My Place*, believe they are able to communicate through the spirit of the earth to other people.

Characters are also committed to protect the land; that is part of their Law. In Episode One of *Women of the Sun*, Goodman (a white European) comes to purchase the land, but the Aborigines have no concept of "purchase" or word for it in their language. Turuga tries to explain to Goodman that "This is the land of the Nyari people, this is their heart and their spirit; it is the breath of their body. From eternal time it has been handed down to us: from generation to generation. Now we who are here are its keepers for all the days of our lives. We are the land. And the land is us." (Maris and Borg 46)

In *Women of the Sun*, the first violence by white men targets Aboriginal women. When McNab explains to Goodman that a particular tract of land is for the women only to walk upon and that it is against their Law for a man to walk on it, he replies: "Stuff and nonsense!... You can't stop the march of progress. This virgin country's waiting for the plough—for sheep, for cattle. These are exciting times. If we don't take the land, others will!" (Maris and Borg 47) Despite knowing the section of land is sacred to women, McNab later allows white men to camp on it. His disrespect results in the first violent clash between white men and the Aborigine (52-54). That white men first fire on Aboriginal women in *Women of the Sun* is significant, for the heart of culture resides in the women in this drama, specifically in Towradgi. Fearful of her, the white men call her a witch (54). White society's idea of progress concerning land does not matter, however. In Episode Four, Alice comments on this process of "progress" and how it has changed the landscape when she maintains that the earth is still sacred regardless of what is built on the land, or how tall the buildings (197).

There is nothing romantic or sentimental about the Aborigines' connection to the earth. Indeed, the primary relationship between earth and person is Law and Law requires self-discipline. The ancestors established patterns of human behavior thereby creating culture and shaping the Aborigines' values and actions toward others and the earth.

The Law demands self-discipline and centers on protection. Protection provides a healthy foundation for Aboriginal women to relate to youth in *Women of the Sun*. Not only does the drama portray the natural protection between mother and child as between Maydina and Biri, but nurturing transcends this natural sense of protection. Older women attempt to forge bonds with characters outside their clan through Dreamtime connections and, once established, the Law of protection opens avenues to restore heritage. Most of the visions in *My Place* connect to the Law of protection. The reason most of the visions come to Gladys, Daisy, and Sally is to protect them. Gladys knows that the Aborigines' purpose in the swamp was to protect her (Morgan 244) long before Daisy reveals it (347). The Law seems to be flexible enough for Daisy to give Gladys an initiation scar as protection (252). Gladys was a baby at the time, but it was necessary for Daisy to give that protection before the government took Gladys away from her.

Debra Bruch

Aboriginal Women Carry The Dreaming

When the white invaders kill Towradgi in *Women of the Sun*, her death does not represent the end of Dreamtime but represents an end of a connection to the earth as mother. Not only do characters separate from their clan, but because they disconnect from the earth, characters lose their sense of self-identity. But as *Women of the Sun* and *My Place* strongly assert, Aboriginal women continue to carry The Dreaming and continue to teach and nurture youth amidst fear and degradation imposed by white society.

Historically, the Australian government attempted to destroy the Aboriginal culture either by assimilating Aboriginal culture into its own white Australian society or by eliminating it. The following, more overtly racist sentiment expressed in 1892 by G.T. Simpson, the Member of Parliament for Geraldton, was sufficiently widespread amongst the settlers to sanction ongoing political atrocities. He writes, "It will be a happy day for Western Australia and Australia at large when the natives and kangaroos disappear..." (Hasluck 192). The *Bulletin* newspaper stated in 1892 that "unconnected with any feeling of duty or humanity, there is no valid reason why the nigger should not be wiped out by—let us say— natural decay." All too often during the nineteenth century, the white man was content to hurry nature and eliminate the Aborigine themselves. They "became vermin which must be exterminated" (Clark 106). Arthur confirms that white men shot blacks for sport (Morgan 181). Daisy expresses her bitterness when she says that people "like us'd all be dead and gone now if it was up to this country" (Morgan 105).

When extermination was not thorough, white society attempted to destroy the Aboriginal culture by separating Aborigines from their family and their belief system. For the Australian Aborigine to become separated from Dreamtime means to shatter self-identity and relationships with the earth, with others, with ancestors, Law, and the rituals associated with The Dreaming. Because Dreamtime is associated with heritage, to understand it means also to understand why today's Aboriginal generation has nearly lost its connection to their distant past.

Here *My Place* differentiates between Aboriginal men and Aboriginal women. Arthur does not seem to teach others about Dreamtime but is portrayed as a victim separated from family and heritage and his living is concerned with survival and trying to attain a sense of status in white society. Daisy, on the other hand, is not as concerned with survival because she is placed in servitude nearly all of her life until she is able to move in with her daughter, Gladys. Slyly, Daisy teaches Sally until Dreamtime becomes a part of her granddaughter even though Sally does not seem to recognize it. A turning point in Sally's relationship with her mother, Gladys, happens when Sally sees her dead relatives in a dream, and during the same night, Gladys also sees Sally with them in her own dream (Morgan 227), for in

Dreamtime, the living and dead meet through visions and physical manifestations. The dead seen in visions do not necessarily need to be immediate relatives, however. After Daisy and Gladys move into a house with a swamp near the back, Daisy complains about the Aborigines living in the swamp and having corroborees every night (Morgan 292). While Daisy knows that these Aborigines in the swamp were people from long ago who used to live there before the white man came (347), their corroborees were loud. Gladys also hears them (244). The word, "corroboree," is often used to refer to sacred rituals (Balme 407); however, "corroboree" is also used to describe non-sacred song and dance. The different meanings are distinguished by the context in which the word, "corroboree" is used.

Until late in the stories, Aboriginal women do not have the freedom to live their lives unfettered, for their life choices are determined by others having the power to punish and kill. In *Women of the Sun*'s Episode Two, Maydina has little choice if she and Biri are to survive. Once Maydina follows Muller to the mission she becomes trapped, she loses her identity, and she loses her ability to protect.

Episode Two of *Women of the Sun* portrays an Aboriginal woman as teacher and nurturer in Maydina as it recounts the Aborigine's experiences in Christian missions. Historically, the more "enlightened" white people of the mid-to-late nineteenth century tried to "save" the Aborigines from themselves, but their attempts were motivated less by concern than by self-salvation. White society placed Aborigines in missions in order to bring them to their idea of Christ and therefore to a better life here on earth—imposing their idea of civilization—that meant a destruction of the Aborigine culture by assimilation (Clark 105-106). Maris and Borg describe a corrupted Christianity as law in contrast to Dreamtime Law to portray how white society attempted to assimilate the Aborigine into their culture as well as its justification for doing so. Aboriginal characters must change their names, wear white people's clothing, be taught Christian religion, and attend church (Maris 78, 80). In *My Place,* Arthur recounts that when he arrived at the mission, the people of authority Christened him by changing his Aboriginal name, Jilly-yung, to Arthur (183). Contrasting with Dreamtime Law, Mrs. McPhee's regulations in *Women of the Sun* employ fear in order to control behavior. To eat, they must work (Maris and Borg 80).

The heart of white society's belief system is control in *Women of the Sun*; that is, control is the power under which white people live and motivates how they treat the Aboriginal women. The way for the women to live under this controlling mechanism is obedience. Mrs. McPhee in Episode Two is expected to obey her superiors and in turn the Aboriginal women are expected to obey her. She says, "Let us tell May [Maydina] and Emily [Biri] of the life hereafter that will be theirs if they are good and obedient" (Maris and Borg 86). However, she does not mean obedience to God, but obedience to her. *My Place* tells us that as children in orphanages and as young adults, Daisy, Gladys, and Arthur consistently experienced the misuse of power under the supervision of white people. All were beaten when disobedient. Arthur was beaten so badly, he kept the scars for the rest of his life. Under their pretext of "being a part of the family," Daisy worked as a servant to a white household most of her life.

Under fear of punishment and death, Aboriginal women in the literature continue to carry The Dreaming and their role as teacher and nurturer, but instead of restricting their teaching to members of the clan, women recognize all Aborigines as family, and the role of older Aboriginal women is reestablished. In Episode Four, Granny supports her granddaughter, Alice, and, like Towradgi, represents the earth as mother. Granny undauntedly keeps Alice and the rest of the family connected to heritage.

In the literature, Aboriginal women find ways to connect with younger women, sometimes by recognizing totems, for totems help form bonds between characters. In Dreamtime, each ancestor was responsible for a particular totem, to which all his descendants, animal and man, belonged. Traditionally-oriented Aborigines believe that they have a special affinity to or a "totemic" relationship with various species and to various places in the landscape associated with them. Cowan points out that "Totemic identity signifies a spiritual link with ancestral activity at the time of the Dreaming. Furthermore, it extends his [the Aborigine's] persona far beyond that of the conventional ego into a realm which partakes of the divine" (Cowan 51). Members

> of a "totemic" group have a set of obligations which may include the carrying out of rituals at a particular site in order to ensure season propagation. The spirits of unborn children are believed to be located in various natural features such as pools or rocks, and after death the spirit returns to the same place. Any place that is directly related to the concept of the Dreaming, or owes its origin or inspiration to the ancestors is regarded as a sacred site. (Elder 214)

In *Women of the Sun*, when Maydina comes to Balambook, she encounters an old Aboriginal woman named Maggie. By recognizing Dreamtime via the totem, they form a bond of friendship (Maris and Borg 81-82).

The Australian Aboriginal Woman Must Be Silenced

The stories of *Women of the Sun* and *My Place* assert that extermination and the attempt to change the Aboriginal belief system did not succeed in destroying the Aboriginal culture. Aboriginal women characters pose a significant threat to the fictive white society when they carry and attempt to promote Dreamtime by teaching their children. For white society, the answer, historically as well as in the literature, lay in separating mothers from their children as well as institutionalizing living conditions. In Episode Three of *Women of the Sun* living conditions are terrible, freedom is severely restricted, education does not exist, work is dictated by the white manager, fear of white control dominate lives, Aborigines are seen as alien (not citizens of Australia), and young women are in constant danger of rape by Felton. Children are taken away to distant towns, for Aboriginal mothers are thought to be a degrading influence on their children. In this episode, Nerida speaks against the government that denies Aboriginal rights and says that the government's main objective is to "give up our language, our culture" (Maris and Borg 161).

Separating mother and child combined with diminished living conditions nearly succeeded in destroying the Aboriginal culture. Aboriginal people were so significantly oppressed and dehumanized that The Dreaming was nearly lost. Other concerns dominated women's lives, and separating mothers from their children meant that teaching no longer continued. Pointedly in the literature, Aboriginal women are not allowed to teach their beliefs. When Maydina teaches her daughter Biri, and thereby breaks white regulations, authorities take Biri away in order to separate the child from her mother's influence (Maris and Borg 112-113). In Episode Three, the police take two children away from their mother, Alma (144). Generations of Aborigines consequently did not know their heritage, the Dreamtime. In Episode Three of *Women of the Sun*, no Dreamtime is acknowledged except when Bill, Nerida's father, dies of tuberculosis, and the messenger bird announces his death (168). The curlew bird is the messenger of death, and when he calls, death is eminent (Maris and Borg 55). Aboriginal women were silenced.

Besides separating mothers from children, a way to silence Aboriginal women was by the practice of white men having sexual intercourse with Aboriginal women. In *My Place*, Daisy's mother was forced to have sexual intercourse with the station's white owner, and while Daisy never admits it, she alludes to also being raped by her white father that resulted in giving birth to Gladys. Historically and in the literature, children were called half-castes. For the Australian Aborigine, the black skin pigment gene is recessive while the white is dominant. Consequently, for each generation of mixed race, the child becomes more white in appearance.

This physical change in appearance from one generation to the next spurred A.O. Neville, the Commissioner of Native Affairs for Western Australia from 1915 to 1940, to focus on the Aboriginal child. Not only did rape further dehumanize Aboriginal women, the physical appearance of their children gave the government a reason to separate Aboriginal mothers from their children. The practice was to separate mother and half-caste child, place the child in government reserves or orphanages to be "properly" raised in white society, and, depending on how white the skin, determine if the child was suitable to continue in servitude to white society. In *My Place*, Arthur tells of Governor Bedford coming to the mission and separating "lighter kids from darker kids" (184). As Arlene Elder points out, since British officials believed Aborigines to have no recognizable culture, and therefore no historical integrity, Aborigines were to be either forcefully assimilated, their women raped and *their* children taken from them to be westernized in orphanages and Reserve dormitories, or annihilated (Elder 205). A.O. Neville both denied the atrocities and revealed the reason behind the violence toward Aborigines when he wrote in 1948:

> Indigenous primitive peoples seem to reach a zero hour from which point they are faced either with extinction or their acceptance of new methods which may save them. Our Aborigines have surely reached that stage, and we must see to it that their acceptance of our way of life raises them to new standards of usefulness, health and happiness and the abandonment of all that is evil in a culture which is outworn and often repugnant. (13)

While in *Women of the Sun* Maydina's child is taken away from her as a form of punishment and to "protect" the child from Maydina's influence, Morgan writes more accurately about child separation from their mothers as a way for white society to destroy the Aboriginal culture. *My Place* examines the consequences of rape and the practice of separating half-caste child from mother. As children, Daisy, Arthur, and Gladys as well as the rest of the half-caste children were separated and placed in orphanages under the "protection" of the government. They became wards of the state. As Gladys states, "Aboriginal women weren't allowed to keep children fathered by a white man" (301). Girls seemed to have been taken as early as a few months old while boys were taken once they reached adolescence (Morgan 184). Arthur was taken to the Swan Native and Half-Caste Mission when he was eleven or twelve years old under the pretext that he was to be educated and returned to the station. However, he never saw his mother again (181). Daisy was taken to serve a white family while Gladys was taken to Parkerville Orphanage, both with the promise of education.

My Place tells us that silencing the Aboriginal woman via separation resulted in a loss of self-identity and fear. Characters did not know where they belonged. A morbid fear of authority, especially government authority, was a part of Daisy's existence all of her life and impacted her relationships with her family members. Sally points out that her mother and grandmother approached people in authority as if they were frightened (96). Daisy's fear never abated. Furthermore, both *My Place* and *Women of the Sun* portray historical attitudes, for in Australian society to be Aborigine was considered demeaning, even well into the 1980s. In *Women of the Sun*, Joy Cutler, Ann's adopted white mother, moans "It's all so ugly, ugly, ugly!" when Cutler tells Ann she is Aboriginal (213).

Aboriginal mothering is reduced to shame. *Women of the Sun* parallels *My Place* when Ann feels as ashamed for her Aboriginal heritage as do Sally's immediate relatives during her youth. In *My Place*, during the 1950s, Sally's classmates insist she is not Australian because of her dark (but not typically) Aboriginal appearance (38). Out of fear, Gladys tells Sally and the rest of her children to tell people they are Eastern Indian (39). In *Women of the Sun*, Ann believes that she is Polynesian (Maris and Borg 200). In *My Place*, Daisy always hides whenever people come to the house for fear of showing herself black enough to be Aboriginal. Both Gladys and Daisy are afraid that the government would take Sally and her siblings away after Sally's white father died. Jill, Sally's sister, makes it clear to her that to be Aboriginal is a terrible thing. Nobody wants to know an Aborigine; he or she is simply a social outcast (Morgan 98). When Sally discovers that her grandmother is black, and that she is, indeed, Aboriginal (97-98), it strikes a very deep chord within her that she could not ignore.

Aboriginal Women Restore Their Heritage

Despite the stigma of shame and once the Australian government relaxed its restrictions, some Aboriginal women are strong enough to restore their heritage. Episode Four of *Women of the Sun* recounts the struggle of an older woman, Alice, to meet her child, Ann (Lo-Arna), and the resulting clash between Alice's need to reconnect and her daughter's shame. Alice has close connections with The Dreaming (Maris and Borg 180) and restores the Aboriginal mother as teacher. She states that "My job's working with the children, that's what I'm best at: teaching the culture" (183). Once she discovers that her daughter is alive, she needs to connect her daughter to her heritage, to land, and to Dreamtime. Alice expresses the need for the mother's role to be reestablished as teacher and nurturer when she says, "This is our land, we've got to help her understand it. This is where we come from…. She is Pund-jel's daughter—a sun woman … Lo-Arna…" (221). Later, Alice becomes angry when Cutler, the white father, asserts that their daughter, Ann, is not really Aboriginal. Alice replies, "Oh yes, she is. Her mother is…. And my mother is, and my mother's mother, and her mother before that. That makes her Aboriginal right back to the time of the ancestors" (228).

In *My Place*, Sally Morgan adopts the role of mother when she decides to write the stories of her life and those of her mother and grandmother. Near the end of Daisy's life, Jill, Sally's sister, hears the bird call, the messenger of death. Jill says that the bird call was "something spiritual" and believes that Daisy will die soon (356). Daisy dies in peace. The death of her grandmother solidifies Sally's need to help restore the Aboriginal heritage. At first she denies hearing the call, but when Daisy dies, she acknowledges with certainty that she heard the bird call (358).

Women of the Sun ends by acknowledging that the culture of the Australian

Aborigine has not yet died. In Episode Four, while white society still dictates living conditions for Aborigines, we find that it has not destroyed their culture completely. As a daughter of the sun, Alice Wilson teaches those of her people who will listen. Her lost daughter, Ann, is restored to her, and we are left with the hope that their culture and their Dreamtime will again be strong. In *My Place*, Gladys sums up her hope for the future when she says, "I like to think that, no matter what we become, our spiritual tie with the land and the other unique qualities we possess will somehow weave their way through to future generations of Australians" (Morgan 306). While the Australian Aborigine will never return to their distant past, their self-identity could return through their heritage of Dreamtime. The task to teach and nurture is placed on Aboriginal mothers.

Debra Bruch is an Associate Professor of Theatre at Michigan Technological University. Besides teaching and directing, Debra has been active in the Association for Theatre in Higher Education, the national theatre association in the U.S. for the academe, especially with the Religion and Theatre Focus Group of which she has held a leadership role for years, has chaired, and now is the immediate past chair. Debra is currently the general editor for the peer-reviewed journal, The Journal of Religion and Theatre. *She is interested in the relationship between Australian culture and Australian drama and theatre, and has published and presented papers which explore Australian Aboriginal drama. She is now deep in research for a book manuscript,* A Cultural History of Australian Theatre.

[1] *Women of the Sun* is an award-winning four-episode television drama which portrays the history of Australia's Aboriginal people from the time white civilization encountered Aborigines to the 1980s. This epic drama follows the struggles of the Aboriginal people from being forcefully separated to being reunited with their spirituality and their identity in the hope that they will regain what they have lost. Each episode follows the life of an Aboriginal woman, and each episode's title corresponds to the name of the woman whose story takes center stage.

Episode One, titled "Alinta—'The Flame'" is set in South-eastern Australia from 1824 to 1834. In this episode, two white men are found by an Aboriginal tribe that has never before seen the white race. They accept one of the men, named McNab, teach him their beliefs and values, and make him a member of the tribe. Eventually, more white men come to take the land, and McNab betrays the Aborigines. The white settlers end up massacring the entire tribe except Alinta and her child, who escape alone into the bush.

Episode Two, titled "Maydina —'The Shadow'" is set in south-eastern Australia during the 1890s, mainly at the Balambool Homestead which is a mission run by Christian people. Maydina and her young daughter, Biri, escape from vicious sealers, confront a kindly rover, and end up living at the mission. Eventually, Biri is taken away, and Maydina never sees her daughter again.

Episode Three, titled "Nerida Anderson," is set in 1939 at a government reserve in Victoria. The episode begins as Nerida returns home from a fruitless search for work in the city. As in the Balambool Homestead, the Aborigines at the government reserve are unwillingly dependant on officials for food and housing. Unhealthy conditions and a misuse of authority cause unrest among the Aborigines and they try to fight the government system. Eventually, most of the Aborigines break the law and leave the reserve to fend for themselves.

Episode Four, titled "Lo-Arna," is set in a Victorian country town and in Melbourne during 1981. Lo-Arna is the Aboriginal name of a young woman named Ann Cutler. Her father, a successful white businessman, took Ann away from her Aboriginal mother and raised her. However, Ann grew up to believe that she was Polynesian and adopted by the Cutlers. She also grew up to hate Aborigines. Alice Wilson, Ann's Aborigine mother, discovers Ann as her daughter and Ann discovers her true heritage. With great difficulty, Ann accepts her heritage.

[2]Sally Morgan's *My Place* is a moving autobiographical novel about the discovery of her heritage which artfully evokes Aboriginal culture and Dreamtime. Curious about her ancestry, Morgan visits her grandmother's birthplace at Corunna Downs Station in Western Australia and in doing so confronts a painful mystery that initiates her journey of self-identity. Morgan begins by examining her own life experiences growing up in Perth during the 1950s and 1960s. But her story becomes more devastatingly moving when her search releases the stories of her mother, Gladys, her great-uncle, Arthur, and her grandmother, Daisy.

References

Balme, Christopher B. "The Aboriginal Theatre of Jack Davis: Prolegomena to a Theory of Syncretic Theatre." *Crisis and Creativity in the New Literatures in English.* Eds. Geoffrey V. Davis and Hena Maes-Jelinek. Atlanta, GA: Rodopi, 1990. 401-417.

"Blackout." ABC Documentary Series. Aboriginal Production Unit, 1990.

Bulletin, June 11, 1892.

Clark, C. M. H. *A History of Australia: Vol. V: The People Make Laws 1888—1915.* Victoria: Melbourne University Press, 1981.

Cowan, James G. *The Elements of the Aborigine Tradition.* Rockport, MA: Element Books Ltd., 1992.

Elder, Arlene A. "Self, Other, and Post-Historical Identity in Three Plays by Jack Davis." *Journal of Commonwealth Literature* 25(1) (1990): 204-215.

Hasluck, Paul. *Black Australians, A Survey of Native Policy in Western Australia,*

1829-1897. Melbourne: Melbourne University Press, 1942.

Lawlor, Robert. *Voices of the First Day: Awakenings in the Aboriginal Dreamtime.* Rochester, VT: Inner Traditions, 1991.

Maris, Hyllus and Sonia Borg. *Women of the Sun.* Sydney: Currency Press, 1983.

Morgan, Sally. *My Place.* New York: Arcade Publishing, 1990.

Neville, A. O. "Contributory Causes of Aboriginal Depopulation in Western Australia." *Mankind, Official Journal of the Anthropological Societies of Australia* 4 (1) (September 1948): 3-13.

Oxford, Gillian. "The Purple Everlasting: The Aboriginal Cultural Heritage in Australia" *Theatre Quarterly* 7 (Summer 1977): 88-100.

Stanner, W. E. H. "Religion, Totemism and Symbolism" *Aboriginal Man in Australia: Essays in Honour of A.P. Elkins.* Eds. R.M. Berndt and C.H. Berndt. Sydney: Angus and Robertson, 1965. 207-237.

"Confused with the Sorrow"

Aboriginal Mothering in *The Antelope Wife* and *Gardens in the Dunes*

ROXANNE HARDE

> In any society a mother is unavoidably powerless. Nature's indifference—illness, death, and damage to the child or its closest loved ones—can frustrate the best maternal efforts. To unavoidable powerlessness is added avoidable social powerlessness. Almost everywhere the practices of mothering take place in societies in which women of all classes are less able than men of their class to determine the conditions in which their children grow. (Ruddick 1980: 343)

Near the center of Louise Erdrich's 1998 novel *The Antelope Wife*, an Ojibwa woman, Rozin, grieving over the death of one of her twin daughters, which was caused by her husband during his botched and drunken attempt at suicide, nearly loses the other twin to a virulent influenza. In a chapter narrated by the dog Almost Soup, Rozin, herself a twin who has lost her sister, moves into the reservation home of her twin mothers to mourn the loss of her child; Almost Soup observes the depth of Rozin's grief alongside her disregard for mothering her remaining daughter, as he points out that she has been "confused with the sorrow over her one twin into lack of care for her other one" (86). Similarly, near the beginning of Leslie Marmon Silko's 1999 novel *Gardens in the Dunes*, Grandma Fleet, one of the few remaining people of the Sand Lizard tribe, tells her granddaughters the story of their mother's birth. Grandma Fleet sets this story in the midst of her tribe's history—a tribe and history nearly destroyed by repeated assaults from settlers, miners and the military—and she explains why she almost chose bleeding to death over mothering her baby: "To go on living when your body is pierced by pain, to go on breathing when every breath reminds you of your lost loved ones—to go on living is far more painful than death" (51). In my epigraph above, from her germinal essay, "Maternal Thinking," Sara Ruddick (1980) argues that mothers are rendered powerless and maternal efforts negated because of unavoidable conditions, those caused by nature, and avoidable conditions, those caused by society. Erdrich and Silko write both types of powerlessness into these novels. Their Aboriginal mothers become unavoidably powerless through nature's indifference: a child's illness in *The Antelope Wife*, and complications from childbirth in *Gardens in the Dunes*. Avoidable powerlessness, caused by a dominant white colonial and patriarchal society, works against effective mothering in both novels. Confused with sorrow caused by their many losses and by their own powerlessness, these mothers are often strengthened by their own cultural traditions and able to engage with the practice of mothering.

Following Ruddick, this essay examines the discussion of Aboriginal mothering in *The Antelope Wife* and *Gardens in the Dunes*, novels that tell stories of mothers confused by sorrows caused by a dominant culture. I consider how some of the protagonists in these novels continue to mother in spite of being rendered powerless and how that mothering honors and regenerates Indigenous traditions. I also consider those mothers who cannot continue to care for their children, who become the absence at the novel's center, an absence that refutes pervasive North American cultural stereotypes of Indigenous mothers even as it evokes pity for mothers rendered powerless under the assault of their own cultures. Specifically, I offer a dual argument: in depicting dysfunctional Aboriginal mothering, Erdrich and Silko explicitly criticize dominant social ideologies that work to destroy Aboriginal people and their cultures; in writing empowered Aboriginal mothering, they deny those attitudes and reinstate traditional cultures. Where Ruddick uses her theories to open a feminist critique of social institutions that negatively effect mothering, I contend that Erdrich and Silko embed in these novels a feminist Indigenous critique of the ways in which the dominant society works against effective Aboriginal mothering. However, Erdrich and Silko also write women who resist social oppressions and satisfy the demands of mothering in stories that are profoundly positive, like Grandma Fleet responding to the demands of tradition to mother her infant. Even as these texts contain multiple narratives in which mothers are hopelessly "confused with the sorrow," and mothering breaks down under various social interferences and persecutions through the American nineteenth and twentieth centuries, they offer insight into Aboriginal approaches to mothering.

"Daashkikaa. Daashkikaa": Mothering Cracked Apart

In the first chapter of *The Antelope Wife*, Aboriginal mothers are disempowered, murdered and displaced. Titled "Father's Milk," the chapter tells the story of a young Cavalry soldier during a U.S. military raid on an isolated Ojibwa village. Faced with "the death yells of old men … the feral quiet of the children," the soldier, Scranton Roy, feels a "sudden contempt" for them all, as he takes "pleasure in raising, aiming. They ran fleet as their mothers" (4). As he looks for more targets, an old woman tries to hit him with a stone, and he stabs her with his bayonet: "but her body closed fast around the instrument. He braced himself against her to pull free, set his boot between her legs to tug the blade from her stomach" (4). From the mention of children and their mothers, the narrative moves to the violation of a grandmother, and if she is violated with a mechanical "instrument," the terms are explicitly sexual and reproductive as Roy plants part of his body on her vagina to remove his blade from her belly. Erdrich further connects this violation to mothering as the grandmother dies: "his gaze was drawn into hers and he sank with it into the dark unaccompanied moment before his birth. There was a word she uttered in her language. Daashkikaa. Daashkikaa. A groan of heat and blood. He saw his mother, yanked the bayonet out with a huge cry, and began to run" (4). The moment of the grandmother's death seems to take Roy through the processes of his own birth, through the dark, heat and blood, to face his own mother, and his next actions might be seen as redemptive. Roy drops his gun and begins to follow a village dog who flees the massacre with a baby strapped to its back. Roy rescues the child then puts her to his breast to stop her cries. After days of suckling, his body responds by producing milk. Awakening "to a huge burp from the baby … who looked, impossibly, well fed" (7), he thinks of the Christian text, "ask and ye shall receive," as he "tasted a thin blue drop of his own watery, appalling, God-given milk" (8).

The death of the elder, the great-grandmother of the baby girl Roy adopts, introduces the idea of disempowered mothers and mothering that is, in the word used by the old woman, daashkikaa or cracked-apart. Roy cracks apart Aboriginal mothering as he adopts this child, thereby displacing her mother, family and Ojibwa culture with the presence of a lone white Christian male, even as he cracks apart biological mothering by nursing the girl on father's milk. In a study of eating and windigo behavior in *The Antelope Wife*, Julie Tharp argues that in the character of Roy, "a nurturing male," Erdrich defies "the stereotype of female nurturance" (119, 123). While I understand the merits of Tharp's argument, I do not see Roy's behavior in such a positive light. Because he connects his milk to the Christian text, I suggest that from the start Roy's ministrations to the Ojibwa baby should be understood as compromised and complex as those of any missionary. True, he saves the child, but he steals her birthright and displaces her mother for his own redemption. In contending that "women have mothered in conditions of military and social violence, as well as economic deprivation, governed by men whose policies they could neither shape nor control," Ruddick points out that mothers may be aided or assaulted by individuals in power "who have an interest in fostering and shaping the growth of her child" (1980: 343, 348). Following Ruddick, I see Roy's behavior as an assault on traditional Ojibwa mothering and culture, behavior that haunts him through his long life, until he journeys back to make reparations to the community he attempted to destroy. In "Maternal Work and the Practice of Peace," Ruddick argues that "the oppressions of poverty, racism, tyranny, and war are not abstractions in maternal lives, but acute daily sufferings which affect a mother's most fundamental hopes, fears, abilities" (1985: 99). In *The Antelope Wife*, the narrative thread that takes the reader from Roy's assault on the child's family to his replacement of her mother reveals the suffering he causes and insists that Roy's actions, any of them, cannot be seen as benign.

Pointing out that "no woman's birthgiving is ever more than a beginning" Ruddick describes the fundamental questions about sexuality and death in which responsible mothering is enmeshed (1994: 44). The ferocity of Blue Prairie Woman's mourning for her firstborn makes clear that she considers giving birth to be only the beginning of mothering, and she sexually devours her husband on his return from the traplines as they create twins from their excess. Roy's theft of the child seems especially malignant during the narrative of her mother's grief. Faced with continuing enormity of Blue Prairie Woman's grief, the remaining elders arrange for a new name, Other Side of the Earth, which allows her to survive while her spirit wanders after the lost girl. Eventually, her spirit locates the child, and she leaves her twin girls with her mother Midass to "raise them as her own" (15). When she nears the home of Scranton Roy, her child rejoins her just as Roy's wife dies in childbirth, leaving him another child, a son, to nurse. In a study of fiction about the "mother without child," Elaine Hansen argues that when "the relational aspect of motherhood is disrupted or thwarted," we can better examine the practice of motherhood and the figure of the mother (15). As a mother without a child, Blue Prairie Woman/Other Side of the Earth offers insight into Aboriginal mothering and its ties to cultural traditions: the expectation that other community members will help raise children and the renaming ceremony. As a mother with her daughter restored, she does the same. She quickly contracts a European disease, "her body is an eager receptacle for the virus," which her daughter resists because of the antibodies in Roy's milk (19). In her dying, this mother sacrifices her dog, turns it into food for the child, then reenacts childbirth in a singing, painful struggle that ends with her death and a child able to survive: "her song is wistful, peculiar, soft, questing. It doesn't sound like a death song" (19). As a young woman, Blue Prairie Woman ran with a herd of deer, learned to call them to her with a song that "was peculiar, soft, questing," and married a deer husband before rejoining her village and marrying a Shawano (56). This unnamed daughter sings her mother's questing song, calling to her a herd of antelope; she joins them and becomes an Antelope Wife. Given her situation and the imperatives of her mothering, Blue Prairie Woman seems to labour again in childbirth that this child might survive after her death. The girl is reborn as one of the deer people, a survivor.

Erdrich continues the story with this girl's descendant, another Antelope Wife with three beautiful daughters. She is stolen by Klaus Shawano, separated from her children, and taken to Minneapolis. Klaus's various careers as a seller of Indian artifacts and a seller of waste management on tribal land define him as exploitative if not fully oppressive. Named Sweetheart Calico after the fabric Klaus used to bind her, this mother goes insane, escapes from Klaus for periods of time in which she is a drunk, prostitute and/or street person. Tharp sees Blue Prairie Woman's mothering in the Ojibwa tradition as a "tribal protectiveness toward her descendants, Sweetheart Calico and her daughters," and she links "Sweetheart Calico's complete inability to understand or adapt to urban life [to] her and her daughters' connection to traditional Native culture" (118). Sweetheart Calico's degeneration in the face of urban life should also be seen as a reaction to the loss of her children. While they are described only by Klaus, who emphasizes their beauty and blames it for his actions, he at least makes clear that the youngest is an adolescent who still needs her mother. Published a year before *The Antelope Wife*, Hansen's study considers in Erdrich's first four novels the "significant numbers of abandoned children and dead or maimed mothers" (120). Hansen's work is relevant also to the story of Sweetheart Calico, in its argument that in spite of the power of traditional Aboriginal mothering and women's involvement in tribal affairs, generations of these mothers "have had their children taken from them.... Native American mothers have lost children to disease, to boarding school, and to adoption ... the figure of the mother without child is more likely to represent the historical norm rather than the exception" (118). Klaus's obsession with the Antelope Wife functions to her as oppression; taken from her children and home, she is a mute broken woman.

In *The Antelope Wife*, Erdrich offers both the stolen child and the stolen mother, and in each case of disempowered mothering, she writes mothers who simply will not let go of the discipline of mothering, the children they love, and the traditions to which they belong. Ruddick argues that while a mother's power begins with the capacity to bear children, her "unique and extraordinary physical intimacy with them" affords her continued power (Ruddick 1980: 343). At one point, alone in a homeless shelter and away from Klaus's killing love, Sweetheart Calico "remembered running beside her mother. Her daughters danced out of black mist in the shimmering caves of their hair. When she touched their faces, they poured all their love through their eyes at her. Klaus, she never dreamed about or remembered. He was just the one she was tied to" (52). In her absence, her daughters' unhappiness brings trouble to their community, and an elder repeatedly tells Klaus to stop being foolish and return her; he eventually does and seems shocked when she immediately makes her way home to her children. For all the passion of Klaus's obsession, he means nothing more to her than maternal powerlessness.

"When Jesus Would Let Their Mother Come Home": Mothering, Oppression and Inauthenticity

Like *The Antelope Wife*, *Gardens in the Dunes* is a novel of disempowered and resilient mothering. Set in the American Southwest after the turn of the nineteenth century, it is remarkably bare of fathers; they are replaced by the military, the police, and the residential school system. However, where Erdrich offers mothers who are able to mother effectively but are prevented, temporarily, from doing so, Silko writes one of those mothers who are, in Ruddick's terms, "unable to respond because they themselves are victims of violence" (Ruddick 1980: 34). Silko narrates the story of the remaining members of the Sand Lizard tribe, a desert people who live in close relationship with the natural world. The family—Grandma Fleet, her daughter, and granddaughters Sister Salt and Indigo—face a variety of challenges from Euro-Americans. The girls' mother is an important absence at the center of the narrative; she exists in the past instead of their present and remains nameless. She is one of those mothers Ruddick describes, whose "powerful maternal presence," is displaced as she becomes "the powerless woman in front of the father, the teacher, the doctor, the judge, the landlord—the world," and her history of oppression represents the history of her people (1980: 343). She is captured and imprisoned at Fort Yuma as a young woman, taken to work for a minister, impregnated by him, and cast out by his wife. She journeys back to the family's desert gardens in time to give birth to Sister Salt. When her daughter is four, this mother is again kidnapped and returned four years later, pregnant with Indigo, whose darkness suggests other than another white lover. Finally, she disappears at the end of a Ghost Dance, when the ritual is interrupted by the military and Indian police, the dancers scattered or arrested. Her family sees her run away and later hears reports that she was not arrested, but followed the Messiah across the Colorado river.

Silko embeds the history of the Ghost Dance in her narrative, and while the Sand Lizard family and other tribes take strength from following Wovoka and participating in the rituals, the Ghost Dance becomes another means of jeopardizing Aboriginal mothering and traditional ways. Noting that Silko's work connects Native cultures to broader historics and political questions, Jeff Karem argues that "Silko launches her most sophisticated assaults on the assumptions of Western culture" regarding issues that are not fully Native American. There is an underlying uneasiness concerning the Ghost Dance in the novel, brought to the surface when Grandma Fleet brings news that her daughter escaped, following the Messiah rather than the Paiute Wovoka and his people, but her granddaughters care only about the absence of their mother. The narrative makes clear the connection between Euro-American culture and thwarted Aboriginal mothering: "Indigo wanted to know when Jesus would let their mother come home" (44). Hertha Wong argues that in light of colonial oppressions, a mother abandoning her children is not always "an act of selfishness"; it may be "an act of despair or an act of desperate mercy" (186). Neither Sister Salt nor Indigo blame their mother for her absence, which lasts for the duration of the novel; as Hansen notes, in the newly heard story of the Aboriginal mother without child, "forgiveness is possible in part because the mother herself is construed as a victim … and in part because the community has a well-established tradition of providing alternatives when the biological mother cannot or will not care for her child" (134). With their mother gone, confused by the promise of a Christian salvation, Grandma Fleet provides alternative mothering.

Shortly after the raid on Wovoka and his followers, Grandma Fleet dies, and the girls are captured: Sister Salt is imprisoned and Indigo is sent to a residential school. She escapes and is taken in by a wealthy childless couple, Hattie and Edward. Her time with them, traveling across America and Europe, offers a juxtaposition of Aboriginal and Western mothering amidst repeated cultural clashes that set white Americans against Native Americans and all ancient cultures. Hattie sees it as her "duty to educate the child to enable her to survive in the white man's world," but Indigo offers only resistance (309). Hattie's approaches to mothering fit well with Ruddick's theory of "inauthenticity" in maternal thought, in which a mother endorses "the values of the dominant culture" and thereby negates her own and her children's values, privileges obedience to the dominant people, denies the value of nature, supernature and humanity, and trains children for powerlessness (Ruddick 1980: 354-55). Herself an early feminist whose radical work on women in the Gnostic gospels resulted in her dismissal from graduate school, Hattie practices inauthentic mothering. Although she finds Indigo's traditional beliefs and habits appealing and even sensible, Hattie works very hard to change the child into the model of an upper class white child and remove the effects of traditional Aboriginal mothering.

"This Baby Needs You": Mothering and Tradition in *Gardens in the Dunes*

In a study of disenfranchised Native men in fiction, Judith Antell relies on Paula Gunn Allen's "feminine principle," which delineates the traditional power of women in tribal life, and she follows Allen in arguing that maternity in Native culture reaches far beyond biology: "'Who is your mother?' Is a serious question in Indian Country, and the answer enables the questioner to place the respondent correctly with the web of life, in each of its dimensions: cultural, spiritual, personal, historical. Failure to know one's mother is failure to know one's significance, one's reality, one's relationship to earth and society" (213-15). The traditional mothering Indigo received from her mother, grandmother, and even her sister, gives her a solid sense of her identity, her culture and its history. Ruddick suggests that one interest governing maternal practice is to produce a child appreciable by its society, and Silko privileges Aboriginal society over attempted appropriations of the Sand Lizard girls by the dominant society (1980: 354). Early in the novel, a white woman tries to steal Indigo from Grandma Fleet who screams until the child is returned. At the end, after reuniting Indigo with her sister, Hattie is shocked at Indigo's lack of response to Edward's death, and at the awkwardness between them after a short absence; as she realizes "Indigo returned to the life and sister she had before she was taken away to boarding school," Hattie understands that, like the woman on the train, she cannot appropriately mother the Sand Lizard girl (439). Indigo knows who her mother is.

In defining mothering as a discipline, Ruddick points out mothering's emotional investments and argues that while economic and social conditions may "make that love frantic, they do not kill that love.... Mothers typically find it not only natural but compelling to protect and foster the growth of their children" (1980: 344). In *Gardens in the Dunes*, as Grandma Fleet nears her own death, she tells her granddaughters why mothering is important, natural and compelling: "After my first baby, your mother, was born, the bleeding would not stop"; when Indigo asks how she survived, Grandma explains that, while she wanted to die and join her loved ones, the medicine woman gave her juniper berry tea and told her, "You are needed here. We need you. This baby needs you" (51). Grandma Fleet's recovery comes from her love for her baby and the medicine given her by nature. She maintains a deep connection to the natural world, the earth mother revered by the novel's Sand Lizard women, throughout her life: "Grandma Fleet walked, with only the aid of her cane, at an energetic pace; she seemed to be her old self again. Sister smiled; she had been worried about Grandma's health, but all the old woman needed was a good rain" (48). Grandma Fleet uses what she knows of nature both to survive and to ensure the survival of her descendants. Her teachings enable Indigo and Sister Salt to live and thrive in the old Sand Lizard gardens as they follow the old ways. Her grand-mothering is traditional, disciplined and effective, and its ties to mother earth, as Peter Beidler points out in his study of Silko and Erdrich's approaches to the environment, go far beyond stereotype to offer complex depictions of the natural world and human responses to it.

Grandma Fleet's mothering ensures the survival of her great grandson as well. When Sister Salt becomes sexually active, she follows the practice of sex in the manner of the Sand Lizard people: "Sand Lizard mothers gave birth to Sand Lizard babies no matter which man they lay with; the Sand Lizard mother's body changed everything to Sand Lizard insider her. Little Sand Lizards had different markings, and some were lighter or darker, but they were all Sand Lizards. Sex with strangers was valued for alliances and friendships that might be made" (202). Sister Salt reacts to her pregnancy as taught by her mother and grandmother: "at first she had difficulty understanding the language her baby spoke to her from the womb, but then she recognized the Sand Lizard words pronounced in baby talk. She had not heard the Sand Lizard language spoken for a long time, except in dreams" (333). While she listens to her baby, Sister Salt does not always follow his advice; he tells her to stop eating the greasy meat her lover brings her and to return to the desert gardens. When she does not listen to her body or her baby, he is born too early. She recognizes him as a Sand Lizard ancestor, returned to help the survival of his people: "he was a serious baby who didn't smile often but who cried only when he was angry; wet or hungry, he remained silent because he was a grandfather and not someone new" (432). Her attention to the child and her reliance on the old teachings ensure his survival. When his father refuses to believe the baby will live and focuses solely on western expansionism and the accumulation of wealth, Sister Salt leaves with the "little grandfather" and builds a community of women. Eventually she reunites with Indigo, and they all return to their traditional home.

"The Old Name, the Original": Mothering and Tradition in *The Antelope Wife*

Tradition and history also enrich and ensure the success of Aboriginal mothering in *The Antelope Wife*. A novel also concerned with environmental issues and the effects of a dominant culture on Indigenous life, it clearly connects the old ways to successful mothering. The novel is divided into four parts, numbered in both English and Ojibwa; each part begins with an epigraph about nameless women beading, the first two discuss twins who bead the pattern of the world, the third a woman who colors her quill beads blue and green in the old way, with "a mixture of her own piss boiled with shavings of copper," and the fourth a woman who hungers for the cranberry red whiteheart beads brought by traders and made "by the addition, to the liquid glass, of twenty-four-carat gold" (98, 183). In the case of the blue beads, the woman making them finds that after a day of abusing her family, she both felt badly for her conduct and created the most beautiful dark blue beads. In the case of the red whiteheart beads, the woman traded everything for the gold-laden beads so clearly a part of the colonial enterprise, then when her children, hungry because of her neglect, eat them, she picks up a knife and hunts them to retrieve her beads. Erdrich thus aligns traditional ways with appropriate mothering, and Euro-American influences with Aboriginal mothering that breaks down.

The narrative further aligns each set of beads with characters who represent effective and compromised mothering: Blue Prairie Woman's blue beads are with the stolen baby girl, who wears them as she runs naked with the antelope people, then passes them to her descendants. They show up at the end when Zosie relates her dream of them to Cally, the dream that gave Cally and her sister their Ojibwa names; they are the second Blue Prairie Woman and Other Side of the Earth. Hearing of the beads, Cally, herself a namer and interpreter of dreams, hungers for them and finds them in the mouth of Sweetheart Calico; they are the reason she has remained silent since her capture. The Antelope Wife trades them to Cally for her freedom; Cally works for her release from Klaus that she may rejoin her daughters. The red beads show up at the end; they are the beads Augustus Roy traded to Midass for her granddaughter Zosie, and thus married a woman "who had every reason on this earth to hate his grandfather. From whose cabin he would disappear" (239). Tharp argues that in Scranton Roy's journey back to the village where he had killed the elderly woman and taken the baby, "the balance is shifting in the right direction," as his grandson stays to marry Zosie: "compensation need not be an eye for an eye, but rather may follow the tribal tradition of taking a new family member to replace the one killed" (128). She concludes that Erdrich offers an approach "that will resist the devouring presence of mainstream excess and help people not only to refrain from devouring one another, but to learn to nurture one another as well" (129). However, Augustus Roy is devoured by his wife and her twin, after he becomes lover to both and mutilates Zosie's ear that he may tell them apart. His disappearance is not linked, I suggest, to his infidelity and the confusion loving him causes both women, but to Zosie's pregnancy. When she tells Cally the story of the names, she reveals that she is the birth mother to Rozin and Aurora, that she had the dream of the name when pregnant, and in the dream she thinks of the nights and mornings she "woke wishing for Augustus" (217). A home with a man trying to possess two women may have been no place for a baby; the twin mothers of the twin babies removes him from their home. Late in the novel, family members tease the twins about Augustus's fate, about the rumor that they ate him; when asked who took the first bite, one of them responds by referring to Zosie's bitten ear: "he did" (202). The beads traded for Zosie and, in fact, Mary too, were sewn into a blanket for a baby who loves their color. The beads become that child's family name, Whiteheart Beads, which comes down to Richard Whiteheart Beads, a red man with a white heart, whose selfish desires and obsessions, whose "deep clawed, hungry" love for Rozin, destroy everything he touches, including one of his own twins (58).

In Almost Soup's chapter, the dog narrates the story of Cally's illness after her twin's death. He points out that the twin grandmothers notice Rozin's lack of care for her child, and he attributes part of her reaction to grief to the effects of nontraditional medicine, in this case antidepressants; he sees her "shrinking into the wall of grief, becoming tiny and bird-boned" (85). In calling her confused *with*, instead of the more regular *by*, sorrow, Almost Soup suggests the depth of Rozin's grief; her mourning radiates out from her center. Confused with a sorrow whose depth comes from her love for her child but which originates in interference from the dominant society, Rozin engages in disempowered mothering. However, faced with a seriously ill living child, Rozin sets aside mourning the lost one and nurses Cally back to health; like Blue Prairie Woman's insistence on setting aside her infants to mother her lost daughter, Rozin focuses on the child that needs her most. Later in the novel, she enacts the Ojibwa rituals that ensure Deanna, whose

Ojibwa name is Other Side of the Earth, is safe and happy on the other side. Rozin's mothering, rooted in tradition as was her own mother's, nurtures Cally (who is given the name Blue Prairie Woman), and ensures the flourishing of her child and her culture. Empowered by traditional mother, from her mother and twin grandmothers, and by "the old name, the original," this Blue Prairie Woman is strong in her culture, strong enough to free the Antelope Wife and return her to her daughters.

Conclusion: "Back Together in New Patterns"

After freeing the Antelope Wife/Sweetheart Calico from Klaus, Cally has a vision of her grandmothers digging in the garden, finding her lost *indis mashkimondenz*, the birth holder she dropped when she became ill. This act of mothering by her grandmothers causes her to "know that part of my life where I have to wander and pray is done," and she remembers a dream vision of her mother's that she can now interpret as "the shape of the world itself.... Gakahbekong. The city. Where we are scattered like beads off a necklace and put back together in new patterns" (220). Cally, like Sister Salt and Indigo, represents in these novels a third generation of young women who can see new patterns, who demonstrate a rootedness, including their understanding of the discipline of mothering, in Aboriginal traditions that does not preclude their ability to thrive in the Euro-American world. The first and second generation of mothers written by Silko and Erdrich, while often rendered powerless by the dominant society, demonstrate a continuous resistance to that disempowerment. While the cases of Sweetheart Calico and the mother of the Sand Lizard girls are tragic moments in which Aboriginal women are prevented from mothering responsibly, in the main these characters represent successful, most often relying on traditional, approaches to Aboriginal mothering, as they refuse to be confused with the sorrow.

Roxanne Harde is an assistant professor of American literature at the University of Alberta-Augustana. She researches American women,s writing and children's litera-ture using approaches from feminist cultural studies. Her work has appeared in several journals, including Christianity and Literature, Legacy, Studies in Puritan Ameri-can Spirituality, The Journal of the Association for Research on Mothering, *and* Mosaic, *and in collections such as* Things of the Spirit: Women Writers Construct-ing Spirituality *(Notre Dame 2004).*

References

Antell, Judith A. "Momaday, Welch, and Silko: Expressing the Feminine Principle Through Male Alienation." *American Indian Quarterly* 12 (3) (1988): 213-20.

Beidler, Peter G. "'The Earth Itself Was Sobbing': Madness and the Environment in Novels by Leslie Marmon Silko and Louise Erdrich." *American Indian Culture and Research Journal* 26 (3) (2002): 113-24.

Erdrich, Louise. *The Antelope Wife*. New York: HarperCollins, 1998.

Hansen, Elaine Tuttle. *Mother Without Child: Contemporary Fiction and the Crisis of Motherhood*. Berkeley: University of California Press, 1997.

Karem, Jeff. *The Romance of Authenticity: The Cultural Politics of Regional and Ethnic Literatures*. Charlottesville: University of Virginia Press, 2004.

Ruddick, Sara. "Maternal Thinking." *Feminist Studies* 6 (2) (1980): 342-67.

Ruddick, Sara. "Maternal Work and the Practice of Peace." *Journal of Education* 167 (3) (1985): 97-111.

Ruddick, Sara. "Thinking Mothers / Conceiving Birth." *Representations of Motherhood*. Ed. Donna Bassin et al. New Haven: Yale University Press, 1994. 29-45.

Silko, Leslie Marmon. *Gardens in the Dunes*. New York: Scribner, 1999.

Tharp, Julie. "Windigo Ways: Eating and Excess in Louise Erdrich's *The Antelope Wife*." *American Indian Culture and Research Journal* 27 (4) (2003): 117-31.

Wong, Hertha D. "Adoptive Mothers and Thrown-Away Children in the Novels of Louise Erdrich." *Narrating Mothers: Theorizing Maternal Subjectivities*. Eds. Brenda O. Daly and Maureen T. Reddy. Knoxville: University of Tennessee Press, 1991. 174-92.

Lost Mothers and "Stolen Generations"

Representations of Family in Contemporary Aboriginal Writing

HILARY EMMETT

> In their grief the women asked why their children should be taken from them. Their anguished cries echoed across the flats, carried by the wind. But no one listened to them, no one heard them.
> —Nugi Garimara (Doris Pilkington), *Follow the Rabbit Proof Fence*.

In 1995 the Australian Human Rights and Equal Opportunities Commission (HREOC) was charged with the massive task of conducting a National Inquiry into the past laws, practices and policies which had resulted in the separation of Aboriginal and Torres Strait Islander children from their families. The Inquiry conducted an extensive program of hearings in all Australian States and Territories. During this time 535 individual oral and written testimonies were collected from Indigenous people affected by removal. Evidence was also heard from adoptive or foster parents and written submissions were solicited from Indigenous organizations, State and Territory Governments, church and other non-government agencies, and former mission and government employees. In the resultant monumental report, entitled *Bringing Them Home*, the Inquiry found that in the period 1910-1970 no fewer than one in ten Aboriginal children had been separated from their families and at certain times in certain places the figure was as high as one in three. Such children, and their descendants, have come to be known as the "Stolen Generations." The Inquiry also noted significant breaches in the duty of care owed to these children by the institutions and foster homes in which they were placed. Over one in four of those interviewed by the Inquiry reported the experience of severe physical abuse while one in six reported instances of sexual abuse and exploitation (HREOC 194). In conclusion, the Inquiry made 54 recommendations to the Federal Government, including an extensive plan for reparation that emphasised the need for acknowledgement and apology from all government and non-government agencies involved in the practice of child removal.

This document, encyclopaedic in scope and emphatically liberal and benign in intent, sought to produce the kind of redemptive and coherent family romance implied by its title. However, in highlighting the destruction of Aboriginal capacities for mothering and caring enacted by state-sanctioned child removal, *Bringing Them Home* simultaneously testified to the impossibility of such a project. While the report undoubtedly performed significant cultural work— particularly in drawing the attention of white Australia to the history of child removal over the past century—it also, like the 1967 Moynihan report on African-American family networks (Moynihan 76), emphasised the fractures in Aboriginal family structures. I propose that alongside the picture of absent-mothering *Bringing Them Home* produces, we should examine the ways in which writing by Indigenous people since its publication mourns these fractures and fissures while also insisting on the resilience and adaptiveness of Aboriginal family structures. These "post-Stolen Generations" narratives are significant not only as individuals' accounts of the devastating effects of child removal, but also when considered in relation to one another: as part of a group of texts that insists on stories as a proud mark of membership. That is, all the novels considered here imagine stories as an inheritance which, although it can never make up for the fact of dispossession, displacement, and loss, nevertheless contests the intended effects of policies and actions that sought to remove Indigenous peoples from their families, communities, and lands. Kim Scott's *Benang*, Vivienne Cleven's *Her Sister's Eye*, and Larissa Behrendt's *Home* all insist upon the passing of stories across and between generations, producing complex and rhizomatic webs of relations between characters whose family trees have been pruned and poisoned almost beyond recognition.

The HREOC narrative begins at the turn of the century with the anxiety generated by the emergence of a substantial "half-caste" population in Central, Western and Northern Australia. This anxiety gave rise to probably the most pernicious period of decision-making in relation to Indigenous peoples in Australian history. Originating in the western and northern reaches of Australia, policy and practice in this period (1910-1937) was characterised by its emphasis on the "biological absorption" of Aboriginal peoples into the white population. Absorption was to be achieved by removing mixed-race children from their traditional communities and socialising them as "white" at boarding schools such as the one located at the Moore River (Mogumber) Native Settlement that provides the backdrop for two of the texts under discussion here. These children would then be "merged" with white settler society as domestic servants, and ultimately, marriage partners for settler Australians. The term "absorption" was coined in 1929 by A. O. Neville, Western Australia's Chief Protector of Aborigines and enthusiastically employed by administrators in other states. The absorption theory was not officially tabled at a Federal level until the Commonwealth-State Native Welfare Conference of 1937. Strongly influenced by Neville, the delegates to the conference resolved that:

the destiny of the natives of Aboriginal origin, but not of the full blood, lies in their ultimate absorption by the people of the Commonwealth, and it therefore recommends that all efforts be directed to that end. (qtd in HREOC 32)

The drive to "biologically" absorb (and later, culturally assimilate) bi-racial children originated in the belief that "full-blooded" Aboriginal Australians were doomed to imminent extinction as members of a dying race. Only children of mixed descent were to be rescued from this fate; the death sentence imposed on Aboriginal peoples was commuted in those who might have "passed" as white. The effects of "whiteness" were not simply limited to skin-tone, but were also thought to be higher intelligence, a better developed moral sensibility, the capacity to adapt to change, and the possession of a capitalist work ethic. Under these assumptions it was the duty of the State to ensure that partially-white children had the opportunity to become productive members of the newly Federated Australian nation. Hence, documents regarding Aboriginal children were littered with references to "weeding out" light-skinned children,[1] to identifying those children of "non-tribal" character,[2] and to the need for vigilance in ensuring that those children who had been separated from the "vicious" influence of the native camp remained so.[3] Even on reaching the age of majority, such children were prevented by law from associating with their parents and extended families. Their "privileged" status of citizenship in the nation then, was predicated on their absolute scission from their Aboriginality.

In his comparative study of slavery, *Slavery and Social Death*, Orlando Patterson terms this mode of enforced cultural apostasy "natal alienation:"

> …Slaves differed from other human beings in that they were not allowed freely to integrate the experience of their ancestors into their lives, to inform their understanding of social reality with the inherited meanings of their natural forbears, or to anchor the living present in any conscious community of memory. (5)

While the policies of absorption and assimilation differ from those of enslavement in a number of ways, I propose that the concept of natal alienation may be fruitfully mobilised in order to name the effect of absorptionist policies. For example, the intent to alienate Indigenous children from their heritage as early (and hence as completely) as possible is evident in the debates that raged as to the age at which it was best to remove children. In Federally administrated territories during the post-war years removal was universally considered to be in the children's best interests, but, due to the traumatic nature of the separation, it was prohibited before the age of four years old. This limitation was subse-

quently revised to three months old on the basis of evidence that the psychological trauma enacted on the child as a result of separation from its mother was
proportional to the age of the child at the time of removal (Macdonald 55). The
younger the child, the less severe the trauma and, conveniently, the less chance
there was that the *tabula rasa* that was the child would remember anything of
his/her familial and cultural origins. If the mother was hospitalised at the time
of birth, the process was expedited further. Mothers were simply refused access
to their children who were then placed in institutions or with white families
immediately, and in this way literally alienated from their children from the
moment of parturition (Parry 149).[4]

These measures to prevent mothers bonding with their babies, and vice versa,
were supplemented by the systematic denigration and denial of Aboriginal
mothers' very capacity to bond with their children. It was not simply that children
should have no memory of their families, but a myth was circulated that mothers
soon lost their memory of their children. In 1908 James Isdell penned a now
infamous report to the Department of Aboriginal affairs. His chillingly dismissive
words became the lore that governed removal practice well into the 1940s:

> I do not hesitate for one moment to separate any half-caste from its
> Aboriginal mother, not matter how frantic her momentary grief may be
> at the time. They soon forget their offspring.[5]

With the discrediting of social Darwinism in the 1950s, attacks on the
Aboriginal capacity for motherhood shifted in focus to their failure to adhere to
the white Australian familial norm. Maternal inadequacy due to race and culture
became maternal incapacity because of poverty. In 1953 the "colour-blind"
"Ordinance to Provide of the Care and Assistance of Certain Persons" ruled that
the children of any persons found wanting in their "manner of living," their
"perceived standards of social habit and behaviour," their "personal associations,"
and their "ability to manage their own affairs" were to be automatically declared
wards of state (Parry 146-147). Indubitably numerous cases existed where
Indigenous children were at serious risk of disease and malnutrition; however, in
legal terms, dispossession and poverty were also synonymous with "neglect" and
thus many Aboriginal families had little chance of measuring up to the standard
set by white Australia. As "Penny" recounts,

> a regimented existence replaced our childhood innocence and frolics—
> the sheer ... togetherness, safety and comfort of four of us sleeping in one
> bed. Strange how the bureaucracy adopts a materialist yardstick when
> measuring deprivation. (HREOC 86)

The silence and powerlessness of Aboriginal mothers in the face of child removal has often been interpreted as compliance or the kind of unfeeling forgetfulness with which Isdell justified his own unsentimentality (Parry 148). Indeed, the testimonies of relinquishing mothers are glaringly absent from *Bringing Them Home*—an absence for it has been criticised (Brunton 3-8). I can only speculate that this absence is due in great part to the shame and guilt suffered by women who gave their children up for adoption, or sent them away to school, only to lose contact with them completely or to hear in much later years stories of the abuse and privation many children suffered at the hands of their "rescuers." The words of a woman named "Fiona," removed in 1936 from Ernabella mission in South Australia, testify to the resistance to attempts to attenuate family bonds enacted by Aboriginal mothers:

> our mothers weren't treated as people having feelings. Naturally a mother's got a heart for her children and for them to be taken away, no-one can ever know the heartache. She was still grieving when I met her in 1968.... She said that because my name had been changed she had heard about the other children but she'd never heard about me. And every sun, every morning as the sun came up the whole family would wail. They did that for 32 years until they saw me again. Who can imagine what a mother went through? (HREOC 130)

While government officials like Isdell and Gale had obvious reasons for imagining that Aboriginal mothers felt little on being separated from their children, Fiona's testimony, like with the words of Nugi Garimara (which I have quoted as the epigraph for this essay), speak to a far more complicated barrier to "imagin[ing] what a mother went through." It was not that their pain was not expressed, but that nobody cared to hear it.

Nugi Garimara's *Follow the Rabbit Proof Fence* is a memoir of her mother's experience of the absorption policy and her extraordinary escape from the Moore River Native Settlement. First published in 1996, a year before *Bringing Them Home*, Garimara's account was one of the earliest to draw public attention to the history of child removal. For more than sixty years prior to this the insistent threnody of these mourning mothers had been met with the now infamous "Great Australian Silence."[6] On the publication of *Bringing Them Home* this silence might have been brought resoundingly to an end, but far from prompting acknowledgement from the conservative Liberal-National coalition government on behalf of the nation, the report and its authors were publicly attacked, their narrative dismissed as an example *par excellence* of the kind of "black armband" approach to Australian history that the Coalition government and its academic supporters so deplore.[7] Following the release of the report the landscape of Australian history became the terrain of a full-scale "history war" as critics and defenders alike rushed to comment on the alternative narrative of the past it proposed.[8] While this outpouring of words certainly calls for analysis, my intention here is to isolate one particular response that calls for a different kind of silence. Indigenous novelist and activist Melissa Lucashenko has suggested that the most appropriate action white Australia can take is to "just shut up" (16). She quotes words spoken by a friend of hers at the funeral of a mutual friend, a victim of the removal policy:

> "They just won't shut up about it will they?" she asked in some anguish, meaning the mainstream commentators. Despairingly she added, "I don't want an apology from that prick, I don't want to hear them going on and on and on about it.... I just want them to shut up." (16)

This woman's frustration points to one obvious inadequacy of the kind of governmental acknowledgement the report sought to bring about: that all the words in the world cannot undo the losses of family, language and culture the absorption policies inaugurated. Still, while those such as Lucashenko's friend are worn out by the semantic gymnastics of bureaucrats and public intellectuals, an alternative source of words may be found in recent novels by Indigenous writers. There can be no complete reparation of the losses caused by removal, but a national narrative committed to the *presence* of such absence may open up an ethical space of listening in its silence. This kind of ethics of listening has been propounded by literary scholar John Frow (367), but is linked in his work to the politics of Australian historiography (Olubas and Greenwell). My purpose here is not historiographical—as the all-too-brief historical outline above indicates. Rather, I seek to open my own ears, and the ears of others, to the ways in which Indigenous writers and speakers have put their experiences and responses into words and, just as significantly, on what counts they remain silent.

In his 1999 novel, *Benang: From the Heart*, Kim Scott's narrator, Harley, notes that the mothers in his narrative, "exit the story too quickly. You wonder how we can continue" (139). In the place of actual contact between the generations of women in the novel Scott employs magical realism in order to recoup the voice of Fanny Benang, the matriarch of the extended Nyoongar family to which Harley discovers he belongs. *Benang* encompasses the history of the five generations of a Nyoongar family—a history marked at every turn by the insistent attempt of one white man, Ernest Scat (Ern),[9] to engender "the first white man born" (10).[10] The novel is written from the point of view of Ern's grandson, Harley, who seeks to break free from his grandfather's stranglehold on the family's past and its future. Not only did Ern embark on a mission single-handedly to "whiten" the population of South-Western Australia by forcing himself on a series of Nyoongar women employed as domestics in his home, he carefully selected one son, Tommy (the son of his "wife," Topsy, who is in fact his legal wife's half-sister) on whom to bestow the title of first white man born. Unfortunately for Ern, Tommy resists his father's project by "re-mixing" blood in fathering a son with Ellen—a woman of mixed descent who was to be part of Ern's own personal crusade. The honorific passes to their child, Harley, who similarly frustrates his grandfather's attempts, not by remixing blood, but by telling stories.

Following an invocation of sorts, in which Harley announces his intention "speak it from the heart," to sing the stories of his great-great-grandparents, to write "a simple family history, the most local of histories" (Scott 1999: 8, 10) the novel opens with an image of blinding whiteness, "a whiteness which was surface only, with no depth and very little variation" (11). This whiteness turns out to be the ceiling of a hospital. Following a car accident, in which Harley's father Tommy is killed, Harley discovers that he has a "propensity for elevation" (12). He realizes that this "uplift" occurs when he relaxes and "lets [his] mind go blank," a *terra nullius*, we might say. Whiteness is thus associated with blankness, erasure, deracination. Harley's bizarre elevation both satirises and laments the success of Ern's attempt to "breed out the colour" and wipe out the history of Western Australia's indigenous people (Slater 2005: 150). That this kind of "breeding up" is not what Ern had in mind is clear from his "terror—and later, *indignation*" at Harley's "propensity to drift" (Scott 1999: 162; original emphasis). For this reason he indulges his newfound capacity, a human kite floating on the land breezes and ocean currents out to the horizon (162). But he is roughly hauled back to earth by his Uncle Jack Chatalong and taken on the literal and metaphorical journey that will ultimately ground him—for Harley also discovers that it is writing, storytelling that counters the effects of his rootlessness. By producing a narrative that challenges and disrupts the "notes, references and immaculate indexes" (36) compiled by his grandfather, Harley devises the means to "knot and tie" himself down (147). Much to his grandfather's fury he begins to write "pages and pages;" however, he finds that the work he produces "was still [Ern's] story, his language, his notes and rough drafts, his clear diagrams and slippery fractions which had uplifted and diminished me" (36-37). Trapped within Ern's archive, shaped and marked by his words, Harley turns his rage and despair against his now-paralysed grandfather: "I soon turned to my grandfather's flesh. I wanted to mark him, to show my resentment at how his words had shaped me" (37). White (re)marks on black skin become black marks on white skin.

> …Full of frustration and anger at my place in Grandad's story, I wrote
> END, CRASH, FINISH into his skin. I poured black ink and ash into
> the wounds and tended them carefully so that the skin would heal and
> seal the letters stark and proud. (445)

Harley and Ern are rescued from their cycle of violent symbiosis by the intervention of Uncles Will and Jack who guide the two of them through Nyoongar territory and its associated history. In the process, Harley learns to hear and pass on his ancestors' stories—as Lisa Slater succinctly describes it: Harley becomes *marban* (a magical shapeshifter) able to "enter different temporal zones … [and] not only hear the stories of his great, great grandmother Fanny, but [also] witness the events of her life and write them into his history" (Slater 2006: 53). It is Fanny who gives her Nyoongar name to the novel: "Pinyan or Benang…. There is a Nyoongar word, sometimes spelt, benang, which means tomorrow. Benang is tomorrow" (Scott 1999: 464). *Benang* thus simultaneously signifies both past and future. It is the name given to the text which will reverse the history that "carried on one heritage and ignored another," a reversal which Harley enacts "not only for the sake of [his] own children, but for [his] ancestors, and their children in turn" (19). Such a reversal is no mean feat for the narrator or, indeed, his audience. The effect produced by the first several chapters of the novel is one of genealogical bewilderment, *natal alienation*. In reflection of the experience of countless Indigenous children removed to homes and settlements characters' names are changed and questioned. Names simultaneously denote both a kinship link and a specific individual (Halbwachs 71); the erasure of a proper name bestowed by a child's family or community is therefore one of the simplest ways to alienate that individual from the group. Anna Haebich writes of the Moore River settlement (which makes repeated appearances in this novel) that children were deliberately arbitrarily assigned names on their arrival so that many grew up never knowing their family name (1988: 208).[11] More often than they are changed, names in this novel are repeated—witness Sandy One and Sandy Two Mason, or the tantalising, haunting women named Ellen, the name of Tommy Scat's lost sister, and also the name of the absent mother of his son. The reader's position therefore comes to mimic Harley's in that neither party can pinpoint exactly where he fits into his family tree.

Yet it is precisely from the unruliness of his genealogy that Harley comes to draw strength. Rejecting the "sharply ruled diagrams" by which his grandfather plotted out the generations of his eugenicist project (Scott 1999: 27), Harley's narrative creates a family "tree" that is more rhizomatic than rigidly arboreal.[12] It ceases to matter that relationships are not strictly defined along white, nuclear lines; rather what matters is that all the descendants of Fanny Benang are brought into relation with one another for the first time. Slippages in family position that are intolerable to Ern are incorporated into Harley's narrative as evidence of the endurance of the Benang "blood-and-land-line" (49). Ern scoffs at Kathleen's appellation of her Aunty Harriette as "mother" after her own mother, Dinah, disappears (later to be found at the Mogumber settlement). The Indigenous tradition of designating all maternal aunts "mother" (and all cousins thus "sister") has no place in Ern's rigidly perpendicular system.[13] Similarly, the collapsing of generational distinctions that occurs when Dinah, "accepted what her mother had bequeathed her" and took on the name, Benang (103), cannot be countenanced by the white authorities. In their thinking, since she bears the same name, she must *be* Fanny Benang. For Harley, this is entirely possible, although not in the way the authorities insist:

> it may have been…that the two of them had come together so close to their home to make yet another effort to keep the spirit they represented alive in the face of continuing betrayal. (Scott 1999: 103)

In this passage the name, "Benang, Pinyan" is the means by which Fanny's spirit is passed on to her children and children's children. "It is the same people. We are of the same people" (103). It is the storyteller Fanny who enables Harley to "fill in the gaps" of his grandfathers notes and diagrams, and who "add[s] body to the yarns" (244):

> Later in the night Fanny and the fire spoke to all the sleeping, slumped bodies. She mumbled and sang softly to herself, often with words they might not know. Sometimes of the children she had lost, the father and mother that were taken. Her brothers, sisters.
>
> Wondering, always, how to say it softly enough so that they might remember (Scott 1999: 245).

Vivienne Cleven's *Her Sister's Eye*, published in 2002, evinces a similar insistence on matrilineal or matrilocal memory. Yet like *Benang*, it does not simply replace patrilineage with matrilineage, but depicts a matriarch who is the repository of an entire community's history and memory. The novel thus shows that identity is not an individual *creation-ex-nihilo*, but rather the result of a complex and necessary web of relationships. While not explicitly a story of child removal, *Her Sister's Eye* dramatises a persistent theme in Stolen Generations discourse. One testimonial cited in *Bringing Them Home* noted in terms that echo both Scott's and Cleven's: "[i]t's like you're the first human being at times. You know, you've just come out of nowhere; there you are" (HREOC 13). Link-Up, an organization founded in 1980 by historians Peter Read and Coral Edwards in order to reunite stolen children with their families, told the inquiry "you have to know where you come from before you can know where you are going" (HREOC 234). These sentiments are expressed in Cleven's novel by Archie Corella, a "no one," a man without memory, without history: "he has no past. History is the backbone of all life, that much he knows, and if ya don't have history, ya don't have life" (Cleven 87). Archie's memory is eventually returned to him by the agency of Nana Vida, the Aboriginal matriarch who has seen three generations pass through the town of

Mundra—a town with its own history of bloody conflict between its Indigenous inhabitants and the settlers who sought to drive them violently from this outpost of shabby-genteel, white "civilisation." In both black and white English "Nan" or "Nanna" is an affectionate diminutive of Grandma; it is fitting that a woman named to evoke both matriarchy and life should be the means of situating Archie in history and thus returning him to life. Like Fanny Benang, Nana Vida is the repository of stories from the past that must be brought to light. "People need to know their history," she remarks, "otherwise there's this terrible feeling of being lost. There's things I know that may hurt ya real bad…. But the time has come" (140). As Harley discovers in channelling his great, great grandmother's experiences there is immense pain and trauma bound up in history that is released with every re-telling. But despite and, indeed, because of this Nana Vida insists the story must be passed on:

> What I told you, pass on, girl. Keep this alive, tell em all. Funny thing, is history. If you remember what others went through to get ya here then all is not lost. Some died for you, others fought for you. Always remember where you're from. There's hope. Always hope. (Cleven 229)

Larissa Behrendt's 2004 novel, *Home*, is also anchored by a matriarch who is the sole direct link to the history of the extended family network:

> [Granny] is the eldest member of my Aboriginal family and the last to speak the old language fluently. [She] is the cousin of my grandmother, Elizabeth, and one of the few people living who remember her as a little girl before she was taken away by the Aborigines Protection Board. Granny has been the link to our heritage for me, my father, and every member of our now scattered clan. (17)

But although the novel begins with the narrator's visit to her ancestors' lands and focuses initially on the story of her grandmother, Garibooli (or Elizabeth as she is known in white circles), the primary relationships emphasised in her narrative are, in fact, the lateral bonds between siblings. As in Scott's text, mothers pass all too quickly out of the narrative. Garibooli's mother, Guadgee, dies shortly after her removal, and it is her brother, Euroke, (Sonny) who continues the family's search for their lost kinswoman. The two are never reunited, but are connected spiritually. On the night Garibooli passes away "she could see his face … clearly in the stars. As she looked into the sky, his hand reached down and beckoned her to join him, telling her not to be afraid" (Behrendt 124). Euroke, in turn, feels "a presence drawing close to him, a warm embrace, and he [thinks] of his sister, hovering near but just out of reach" (125). On Garibooli's death, her six children are scattered across the globe. Her two eldest sons take "advantage" of the outbreak of the Second World War to leave Australia all together, her daughter takes up a dressmaking apprenticeship, and the three younger children are sent to an orphanage when their white father fails to take responsibility for their upbringing. The final two thirds of the novel tell the story of these siblings—the attempts of Patricia and Bob to maintain the bonds of family, and the struggles of the other children to overcome the shame and pain that their Aboriginality marked them out for at the hands of predatory adults and racist peers. Behrendt's narrative does not shy away from the devastating effects of institutionalisation on these children— Danny falls victim to substance abuse while Daisy conflates sexuality with love and in the process destroys relationships of those closest to her.

Nevertheless, *Home* ends redemptively. Like her grandmother, Candice too has a spiritual bond with her brother, Kingsley, "her dark, moody, counterpart" whom she loves "most in all the world" (Behrendt 14), but unlike Garibooli, she has been lucky enough to maintain this relationship, even entering into a legal practice together in order to pursue Indigenous rights through the medium of the law. Her father, Bob, is also reunited with his mother's family who are still based on what is traditionally Eualeyai/ Kamilaroi nations territory in north-western New South Wales. A key player in Bob's reintegration into the community is his cousin, Henry, known as "Uncle" to Bob's daughter, Candice, the narrator of the story. At the time of telling, Henry "has several nieces and nephews staying with him. At the moment they number five. Some are blood, others he just loves and feels responsible for" (16-17). As in Scott's novel, Indigenous kinship networks are depicted as rhizomes—complex, "grass-like" systems that move beyond nuclear, or even blood, relationships to draw formerly disconnected people into relation with one another.

All of these novels entail a return to a specific location that is designated "home." However, this space cannot be recognised or claimed as such (as it is literally unrecognisable to the amnesiac Archie Corella) until a set of stories has been told about it. Homecoming, then, may be brought about by narrative: an effect not lost on the authors of *Bringing Them Home* whose primary recommendation was the establishment of an archive of testimonies of Indigenous peoples affected by removal policies (HREOC 651). Yet these novels insist that such stories must also have a life outside the archive. This is not to say that they have not been concretised in narrative in the form of the published book itself, but rather that in being so, they are portable, accessible, exchangeable. In all these novels home is both a specific area or region and, at the same time, a set of stories that may be carried, like a book, from place to place. This conception of home obviously also has great significance for Australian land rights legislation which requires evidence of an ongoing, unbroken connection to land, but is equally central to the claims of the Stolen Generations. Over and against white Australia's attempts to imagine

Aboriginality as a purely biological affair, that could be "bred out," these novels construct a model of Indigenous kinship which certainly values blood-ties, but not as the be-all and end-all of what makes people into brothers, sisters, aunts, uncles, fathers, and even mothers. In *Benang*, *Her Sister's Eye*, and *Home*, stories provide a lodging-place, a "home" from which to set out to explore so much of what it might mean to claim an Indigenous identity.

Hilary Emmett is a graduate student at Cornell University. Although her doctoral dissertation focuses primarily on the literatures of the United States, her position as an Australian scholar living and teaching in the U.S. has heightened her awareness of both Australia and North America as post/colonial regions in relation to how they deal with issues of race, indigeneity and multiculturalism. She aims to promote further comparison of the nations that exist within these geographical areas.

[1]A. O. Neville to H. W. Wright, the Director of the Gnowangerup Mission, 1939: "I feel that it would be wrong to allow light-coloured children to grow up as white natives.... We must go on weeding out the light coloured children" (qtd. in Beresford and Omaji 54).

[2]F. I. Bray, Commissioner in the Western Australian Department of Aboriginal Affairs, to the Victorian department, 1943: "Although some half-castes are tribal in character, we usually endeavour to treat them as non-tribal...we usually segregate them into institutions or missions" (qtd. in Beresford and Omaji, 55).

[3]James Isdell, travelling inspector for the Western Australian Department of Aboriginal Affairs (qtd. in Haebich 2000: 451).

[4]This practice was not limited to Aboriginal mothers of bi-racial children, but was also rigorously utilised in the case of young, white, single mothers resulting in the 1999 NSW State Inquiry into Adoption Practices.

[5]This brief quotation is one of the most oft-cited in all the source material on the removal policy. In *Broken Circles,* Anna Haebich gives a detailed account of Isdell's travels in Western Australia and his resultant recommendations to the Western Australian Department of Aborigines (2000: 234-249). Isdell's attitude became known as "Gale's Lore" due to the diligence with which Charles Gale, the Chief Protector of Aborigines at the time, ordered separations to be enacted.

[6]In his 1968 Boyer Lectures (a year after Indigenous people were granted Australian citizenship) the anthropologist W. E. H. Stanner addressed the exclusion of Indigenous experiences from national narratives of Australian history. Their absence, he argued, was the result of an institutionalised forgetting designed to relegate their existence to a "melancholy footnote" to an otherwise glorious history (214).

[7]Coined by historian Geoffrey Blainey in his 1993 Sir John Latham Memorial

Lecture the term "black armband history" has come to function as a shibboleth denoting any narrative that takes as its object the violent and less-than-heroic aspects of Australian history.

[8]See, for example, Stuart Macintyre and Anna Clark's *The History Wars*, and Bain Attwood's *Telling the Truth About Aboriginal History*.

[9]The close etymological connection of Scat with scatology, combined with the fact that Ern is employed to dispose of the town's nightsoil, ironises Ern's (in fact the historical Neville's) preoccupation with the need to *"absorb and dilute* [the Aboriginal strain] *like a small dirty stream into a large and clear one"* (74; original italics indicating a quotation from A.O. Neville's eugenicist tome, *Australia's Coloured Minority*).

[10]In his Alfred Deakin Lecture in 2001 Scott drew attention to the irony of the settler desire to locate or inhabit the position of "first white man born." He noted: "In the archives I was also jostled by local historians elbowing one another to claim an ancestor as the 'first white man born in such and such an area.' To be descended from the first white man born. I thought their rivalry provided a curious parallel to Neville's photograph and plans. To claim the first white man born is to make a fresh start. To begin. To be noble pioneers creating a society."

[11]This practice appears to be unique to the experience of Australian Aborigines. Comparative studies of the treatment of Canadian, Aotearoan (New Zealand), and American Indigenous peoples has shown that the removal of children was carried out systematically, yet the names and origins of each child were rigorously recorded so that the structures existed for the possible tracing of families.

[12]My use of the term "rhizomatic" here was inspired in part by Gilles Deleuze and Felix Guattari's definition which opposes the rhizome to the tree: "unlike trees or their roots, the rhizome connects any point to any other point, and its traits are not necessarily linked to traits of the same nature" (21). However, the textual analysis that follows is in no other way recognisably "Deleuzean."

[13]See Larissa Behrendt's note on the subject in *Home* (43). This tradition is also central to Garimara's telling of her mother's story in that, Molly, Daisy and Gracie, the three sisters who make their daring escape are, in western terms, cousins.

References

Attwood, Bain. *Telling the Truth About Aboriginal History*. Crows Nest: Allen and Unwin, 2005.

Behrendt, Larissa. *Home*. St Lucia: University of Queensland Press, 2004.

Beresford, Quentin and Paul Omaji. *Our State of Mind: Racial Planning and the Stolen Generations*. Fremantle: Fremantle Arts Centre Press, 1998.

Brunton, Ron. "Betraying the Victims: The 'Stolen Generations' Report." *IPA Backgrounder* 10 (1) (1998): 1-24.

Cleven, Vivienne. *Her Sister's Eye*. St Lucia: University of Queensland Press, 2002.

Deleuze, Gilles and Felix Guattari. *A Thousand Plateaus: Capitalism and Schizophrenia*. Minneapolis: University of Minnesota Press, 1987.

Frow, John. "A Politics of Stolen Time." *Meanjin* 57 (1998): 351-367.

Garimara, Nugi. *Follow the Rabbit Proof Fence*. St Lucia: University of Queensland Press, 1996.

Haebich, Anna. *Broken Circles: Fragmenting Indigenous Families 1800-2000*. Fremantle: Fremantle Arts Centre Press, 2000.

Haebich, Anna. *For Their Own Good: Aborigines and Government in South West of Western Australia 1900-1940*. Nedlands: University of Western Australia Press, 1988.

Halbwachs, Maurice. *On Collective Memory*. Lewis A. Coser (trans.). Chicago: University of Chicago Press, 1992.

Human Rights and Equal Opportunity Commission (HREOC). *Bringing Them Home: Report of the National Inquiry into the Separation of Aboriginal and Torres Strait Islander Children from their Families*. Canberra: Commonwealth of Australia, 1997.

Lucashenko, Melissa. "More Migaloo Words? Three Responses to Robert Manne's *In Denial*." *Overland* 163 (2001): 16.

MacDonald, Rowena. *Between Two Worlds: The Commonwealth Government and the Removal of Aboriginal Children of Part Descent in the Northern Territory*. Alice Springs: IAD Press, 1995.

Macintyre, Stuart and Clark, Anna. *The History Wars*. Carlton: Melbourne University Press, 2003.

Moynihan, Daniel Patrick. "The Negro Family: The Case for National Action." Lee Rainwater and William L. Yancey. *The Moynihan Report and the Politics of Controversey*. Cambridge: MIT Press, 1967. 39-124.

Neville, A. O. *Australia's Coloured Minority: Its Place in the Community*. Sydney: Currawong Press, 1948.

Olubas, Brigitta and Lisa Greenwell. "Re-membering and Taking Up an Ethics of Listening: A Response to Loss and the Maternal in 'The Stolen Children.'" *Australian Humanities Review*. Online: http://www.lib.latrobe.edu.au/AHR/archive/Issue-July-1999/olubas.html. Accessed: September 19, 2006.

Parry, Suzanne. "Identifying the Process: The Removal of 'Half-Caste' Children from Aboriginal Mothers." *Aboriginal History* 19 (1995): 141-153.

Patterson, Orlando. *Slavery and Social Death. A Comparative Study*. Cambridge: Harvard University Press, 1982.

Scott, Kim. *Benang: From the Heart*. Fremantle: Fremantle Arts Centre Press, 1999.

Scott, Kim. "Australia's Continuing Neurosis: Identity, Race and History." Alfred Deakin Lecture, May 14, 2001. Online: http://www.abc.net.au/rn/deakin/